TWELVE CHANNELS OF
THE I CHING

TWELVE CHANNELS OF THE I CHING

Myles Seabrook

BLANDFORD

A BLANDFORD BOOK

First published in the UK by Blandford
A Cassell Imprint
Cassell Plc, Villiers House,
41/47 Strand, London WC2N 5JE

Distributed in the United States by Sterling Publishing Co., Inc.,
387 Park Avenue South, New York, NY 10016-8810

Distributed in Australia by Capricorn Link (Australia) Pty Ltd
2/13 Carrington Road, Castle Hill, NSW 2154

British Library Cataloguing-in-Publication Data
A catalogue entry for this title is available from the British Library

ISBN 0-7137-2452-8

Typeset by Litho Link Limited, Welshpool, Powys, Wales
Printed and bound in Finland by Werner Söderström Oy

for George Edward Seabrook

CONTENTS

INTRODUCTION

WELCOME TO THE I CHING, the most sophisticated system of divination ever devised. For 5,000 years it has proved successful as a tool for predicting future events, and it would come as no surprise to the sages who invented the original hexagrams that their ideas and observations are as relevant at the second millennium as they were in 3000BC. But it is important to remember that this is no static, unchangeable decree from the past; this is an evolving entity, and it evolves through being used. So every time the book is consulted, its scope is expanded and *your* understanding is added to its accumulated wisdom.

This is a version of the I Ching for today. It cuts through the confusing Chinese imagery, which has obscured its meaning for so long, and is relevant and accessible, while still retaining the wisdom of the ancient sages.

THE ART OF DIVINATION

Ancient Greek myth tells us that the gift of fire was stolen from the Gods and bestowed on an animal-like human race by Prometheus, who thereby gave man the tool that allowed the birth of civilization. Prometheus was cruelly punished by Zeus for his crime by being chained to a rock and tormented by an eagle, which pecked constantly at his liver. But as he writhed in agony, Prometheus cited some of the other gifts he had given to mankind — the wheel, agriculture, mathematics, writing, astronomy. In fact, according to Aeschylus: `All human skill and science was Prometheus' gift.'

It seems strange now that among these gifts, and considered equally important, was the art of *divination*. In our technological era divination sounds like something that belongs to the Dark Ages and that, like ducking witches, is something we have long grown out of. Yet in the classical world, so widely admired and imitated in our culture, it was regarded as having the same significance as the invention of agriculture. What a shame then, that what was once an art, has now been relegated to the status of mere superstition! Nevertheless, it lives on. Tarot, runes, numerology and many other methods of divination are the remnants of what was once considered an essential tool of civilization. It lives on instinctively as well, for who can resist a tantalizing glimpse into the future? And who, on hearing a prophecy of success, doesn't feel a little more confident? However, divination commits that most modern of sins – it defies logic.

It is hardly surprising that in our scientific age, which demands empirical proof before anything can be regarded as valid, the art of divination has all but disappeared. But the blame for its demise should not be laid at the door of technological advance alone; religious dogma has played an even greater part, mercilessly seeking out and eradicating anything that was seen as a threat, and labelling it blasphemy. This is a grave mistake, for divination and religion are two completely different subjects. Divination merely delves into the area just beyond our perception: religion deals with the infinitely broader area of creation and with the nature of God. Religious belief, or the lack of it, should not preclude a belief in the art of divination. It should be seen simply as a tool that can connect us with an as yet unexplained, but nonetheless fundamental, level of reality – possibly quantum reality, where two events, entirely separate in time and space, can be irrevocably connected through their meaning, where the laws of logic are suspended and where the human ego has no influence. This last point is important, for it seems to be a pre-condition that the needs and desires of the enquirer are excluded from the actual process of divination. Hence the need for a random element, such as the throwing of coins.

So, approach this book with an open mind, experiment with it and feel its power for yourself. Above all, believe in it, for it is belief that gives it its power.

THE I CHING

THE USUAL WAY TO APPROACH THE I CHING is by asking it questions: coins are thrown, the results noted and the corresponding material forms the answer to the enquiry. This is the way it has been used for thousand of years, and this is the use for which this book is intended.

It consists of 64 sections, each of which covers an archetypical situation. It can be said that these sections represent every possible situation we are likely to encounter in our lives. For each section the ancient Chinese sages added an oracle; this is either a description of a situation, advice on how best to act in that situation or a combination of both. To those hexagrams and lines where the likely outcome is not neutral is further added an indication of the likely outcome, defined in terms of success or failure, good or bad luck and so on. But where the I Ching exceeds the scope of any other form of divination is in its ability to take into account changes that are likely to occur in the original situation and to make a projection into the future. This gives a far more specific description of the likely outcome by describing an entirely new situation. Those of you who are familiar with its use will be aware of its astonishing degree of accuracy.

The wisdom of the I Ching is founded on a very basic premise. Every situation has an inherent tendency to change, and change can be observed to happen in cycles. From our perspective this is the only thing we can say with any certainty about reality, and this is the constant on which the I Ching, or *Book of Changes*, is based.

Much as the rules of musical harmony could be deduced from a study of Bach, so the ancient sages studied the changes in nature and their own very ordered society and were able to draw conclusions that could be represented symbolically.

The symbols used in the I Ching are the unbroken line, ——, and the broken line, – –. Change is represented by —— becoming – –, and – – becoming ——. These two symbols can represent any pair of polar opposites – light/dark, male/female, positive/negative, active/passive and so on. (This is also known as yin-yang theory, which is avoided here because these terms do not appear anywhere in the I Ching.) This can be applied to any situation, and the more lines that are used in combination, the more specific the situation that can be described.

The idea of combining lines is attributed to the legendary Chinese Emperor Fu Hsi, who is said to have lived some 5,000 years ago. Like Prometheus, he is credited with introducing the necessities of civilization to a barbaric people. The original symbols were composed of only three lines (*trigrams*) and therefore had only a limited scope in describing situations. There are eight possible combinations, and each of these combinations has certain attributes, according to the positions of the lines.

☰	*Ch'ien*	Heaven, sky, creative power, father.
☱	*Tui*	Lake, rain, joy, youngest daughter.
☲	*Li*	Fire, lightning, clarity, middle daughter.
☳	*Chen*	Thunder, arousing influence, eldest son.
☴	*Sun*	Wind, wood, gentle, penetration, eldest daughter.
☵	*K'an*	Water, danger, middle son.
☶	*Ken*	Mountain, stillness, permanence, youngest son.
☷	*K'un*	Earth, receptiveness, yielding, warm, mother.

It can be seen that this may have had a value in predicting events in a simple way, but the great stride forwards in the evolution of the I Ching is attributed to King Wen, c.1150BC. He had the idea of doubling the trigrams to form hexagrams, thereby allowing the description of 64 situations. From the attributes of the two trigrams that combine to form each hexagram, King Wen conceived the oracles that form the basis of this book. Shown below is hexagram 64, *Before Completion*.

Some of the lines in the hexagram are said to grow `old', and when this happens, they change into their opposites. As these lines change into their opposites, a new hexagram is formed. Shown below is the same hexagram, with two `old' lines.

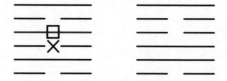

The second hexagram is 18, *Repair*, and this describes a new situation, which is a natural result of the changes that occurred in the first. King Wen's son, the Duke of Chou, is said to have added the oracles for each *moving* (`old') line, which also have to be taken into account when interpreting answers.

Another major influence was that of Confucius (55–479BC) and his followers. It is difficult to say what influence he might have had old King Wen`s original text, but to each hexagram he added his own commentary, known as the *Image*. To this was also added a treatise on the interpretation of the hexagrams, known as the *Ten Wings*.

While it is impossible to identify all the influences that have affected the I Ching, the very fact of its 5,000-year survival is a testament to the reverence with which it has always been regarded.

THE TWELVE CHANNELS*

THE PROBLEM FOR MOST WESTERNERS has always been the obscure nature of the oracles. Because they are cloaked in the imagery of an alien culture it can take much painstaking study to discover the meaning that lies behind them. It is, therefore, the intention of this book to unravel that mystery and to present the oracles in a straightforward way.

The original oracles are all analogies. For instance, one of them might describe an event that happened 3,000 years ago, which has to be seen in the light of your own situation. It is, therefore, very easy to misinterpret what the I Ching is trying to say to you. This problem has been overcome by taking the original analogies and interpreting them from twelve different perspectives, while still retaining the original meaning.

These twelve perspectives are called channels. Each channel covers a general area of life, and every oracle in the I Ching is interpreted in twelve different ways.

JUDGEMENT   This channel deals with making decisions and general questions of principle. A typical question might be: `How do I decide what to do for the best?'

INNOCENCE   When you do not understand what is happening to you or you feel out of your depth, this is the channel to use. A typical question might be: `What is happening to me?'

AWARENESS   This deals with questions of a spiritual or psychic nature. If you are interested in cultivating awareness, this is an area where the I Ching can be of real use. A typical question might be: `What is the higher significance of this event?'

EMOTION   Questions concerning love and emotional expression are dealt with here. A typical question might be: `How do I tell him/her how I feel?'

CREATIVITY   This deals with any questions involving a creative process, and its intention is to throw light on the best way to express ideas. A typical question might be: `How will this idea be received?'

COMMUNICATION   If you are wondering how to tell someone something or are anxious about a disagreement you may have had, this is the channel to use. A typical question might be: `How do I tell my best friend the truth?'

*The Twelve Channels are derived from a picture called `The Magic Circle of the Mind' by Tammo de Jongh, which forms the frontispiece to *The Purpose of Love* by Richard Gardner.

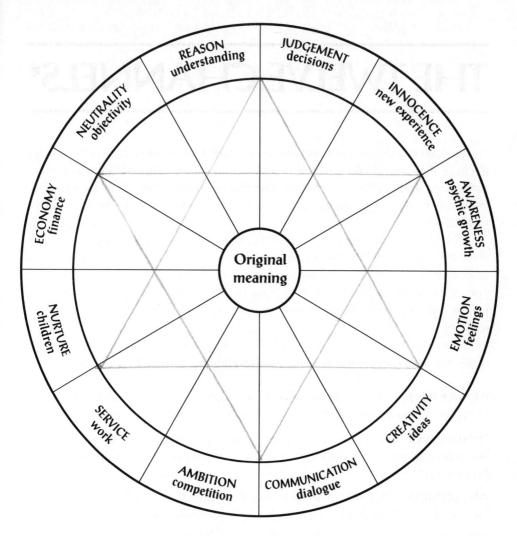

AMBITION   Questions about personal ambition or any area of activity of a competitive nature are answered here. A typical question might be: `How do I gain my promotion?'

SERVICE   Most of us serve a master in one way or another, and this channel deals with any questions where that relationship plays a part. A typical question might be: `How can I best get this job done?'

NURTURE   This channel deals with the relationship between parents and children from the point of view of a parent. The answers it gives typically refer to nurturing healthy growth in children. You might want to ask something like: `How can I help my child through this difficult period?'

ECONOMY   This won't tell you how to make a million, but at least it might keep you out of the bankruptcy courts! It deals with economic questions from the

---

standpoint of achieving financial stability as a goal. A typical question might be: `What is the best thing to do with my money?'

NEUTRALITY   This channel sees every situation from a totally objective point of view. It can throw light on any event at which you are merely a dispassionate observer. It can also help to clarify the information contained in other channels, as it describes the situation in its most basic terms. A typical question might be: `What are the consequences of this event?'

REASON   This deals with questions of logic or reason or any area where constructive or inventive thought is required. It answers questions such as: `How do I solve this problem?'

The advantage of this system is illustrated below. This is the original text for hexagram 64, **Before Completion:**

> *Before completion. Success.*
> *But if the little fox, after nearly completing the crossing,*
> *gets his tail in the water,*
> *there is nothing that would further.*

Now, for example, the text looks like this:

JUDGEMENT   A difficult decision is nearly made. Even at this stage a lack of deliberation can mean a mistake.

ECONOMY   Economic stability now seems feasible, but even at this stage a lack of prudence could lead to loss.

As can be seen, although the terms of reference are completely different, the intrinsic meaning remains the same.

THE METHOD

FRAME YOUR QUESTION, write it down and decide on the channel that is likely to give you the most relevant answer. Try to avoid questions that require a yes/no response. Take three coins, and give a value of three to the heads side and two to the tails side. The three coins are thrown, together, six times. After each throw the total obtained should be noted. For example:

throw 1 ➤ heads (3) + heads (3) + tails (2) = 8
throw 2 ➤ tails (2) + tails (2) + heads (3) = 7
throw 3 ➤ tails (2) + tails (2) + tails (2) = 6
throw 4 ➤ heads (3) + heads (3) + heads (3) = 9
throw 5 ➤ heads (3) + tails (2) + heads (3) = 8
throw 6 ➤ tails (2) + heads (3) + tails (2) = 7

To each value – 6,7,8 and 9 – is assigned a symbol:

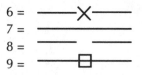

Totals and symbols are written from the bottom up, for example:

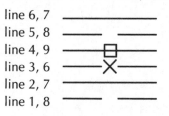

This is your first hexagram. The lines —◻— and — x — are said to be `moving' lines, and they have the property of turning into their opposites, so —◻— becomes — — and — x — becomes ——. In this way, a second hexagram can be constructed by changing the moving lines:

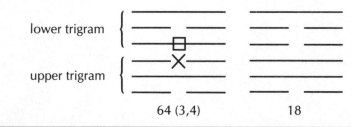

64 (3,4)   18

The next thing to do is to consult the key below. This is done by cross-referencing the upper trigram against the lower for both hexagrams. If there are no moving lines, there will be only one hexagram. The above example gives hexagram 64, *Before Completion*, with lines 3 and 4 moving, changing to hexagram 18, *Repair*. Look up hexagram 64 and read the text for the channel you have chosen. Do the same for each moving line or lines and also for the resultant second hexagram, 18. This forms the answer to your enquiry.

KEY

Upper / Lower	Chi'en	Chen	K'an	Ken	K'un	Sun	Li	Tui
Chi'en	1	34	5	26	11	9	14	43
Chen	25	51	3	27	24	42	21	17
K'an	6	40	29	4	7	59	64	57
Ken	33	62	39	52	15	53	56	31
K'un	12	16	8	23	2	20	35	45
Sun	44	32	48	18	46	57	50	28
Li	13	55	63	22	36	37	30	49
Tui	10	54	60	41	19	61	38	58

NOTES ON INTERPRETATION

THE I CHING IS A CLEVER BOOK, and if it has got something to say to you, it will find a way of saying it! So there are several ways of looking at the answers it gives.

1. For the most part, it is best to think of the first hexagram as representing the present situation and of the moving lines and second hexagram as being logical projections of that situation into the future. But it doesn't stop there.

2. It may be that the only thing the I Ching wants to tell you is contained in one of the moving lines, and in that case the other information is irrelevant. Only *you* can know this.

3. The answer it gives contains information that you understand deep down but do not want to admit to yourself. Again, only you can know this.

4. The answer refers to events that directly affect you but that cannot be seen from your present situation.

5. The answer refers to future events, the relevance of which will become clear only in retrospect.

6. You may think that the oracle refers to you, when in fact it is referring to someone else. (The perspective of the I Ching is universal, and for that reason the oracles contain no personal pronouns.)

7. If the answer seems contradictory, it may be illustrating a conflict in your own situation.

If the answer seems totally irrelevant, it is a good idea to scan the other channels. It may be that the answer to your question lies in a completely different area from the one you imagined. More often than not, this is the case, and you will find yourself saying, `Oh yes, of course, *that's* it!'

It is very tempting to go on asking questions until you get the answer you want. This is unwise because you will probably find that the answers become more and more confusing. This is usually the I Ching's way of telling you that it does not consider your subsequent questions worthy of an answer as it has already told you what it thinks.

The best way to approach the book is to ask your question once only and to repeat the same question only when the situation has changed.

Try not to think too much about how the I Ching works; this tends to weaken its effectiveness. Far more rewarding is to regard it as a wise old friend, who knows everything about you and wants only what is best for you. What it thinks and what you think might be two different things, but, as in any relationship, it is up to you to work it out. The problem is that the I Ching has only a limited vocabulary with which to communicate and what it wants to say is very important. So please, be patient with it, because it always knows best!

1
·ORIGINALITY·

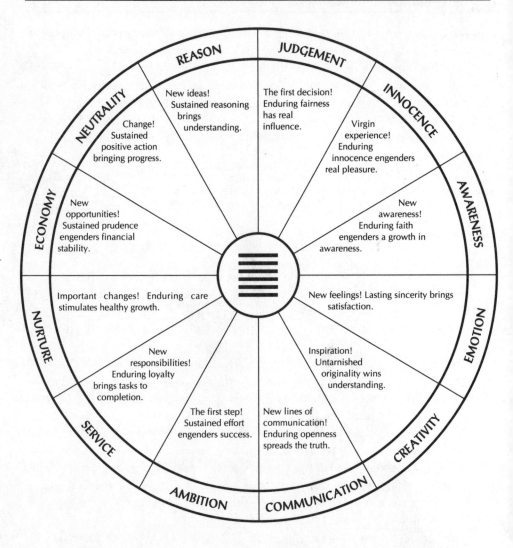

Perseverance permits great achievements

1 line 1

---□---

Do not act

JUDGEMENT   Not yet the time to make a decision.
INNOCENCE   Not yet the time for independent action.
AWARENESS   Not yet ready for higher awareness.
EMOTION   Not yet the time to bring feelings into the open.
CREATIVITY   Appreciation cannot yet be found.
COMMUNICATION   Not yet the time to speak.
AMBITION   Not yet the time for action.
SERVICE   Not yet ready to take on responsibility.
NURTURE   Not yet the time to allow independence.
ECONOMY   Not yet the time for speculation.
NEUTRALITY   Not yet ready for positive action.
REASON   A conclusion cannot be drawn yet.

1 line 2

---□---

Seek advice

JUDGEMENT   Principles are just, but there is not yet enough power.
INNOCENCE   Behaviour is correct, but this is not yet the time for independent action.
AWARENESS   Motives are sincere, but this is not yet the time for a growth in awareness.
EMOTION   Feelings are sincere, but not yet meaningful enough to express.
CREATIVITY   Ideas are good, but not yet strong enough.
COMMUNICATION   Words are sincere, but do not yet find agreement.
AMBITION   Ability cannot be denied, but ambitions cannot yet be achieved.
SERVICE   Devotion to duty is admirable, but this is not yet the time for responsibility.
NURTURE   Development is normal, but this is not yet the time to foster growth.
ECONOMY   Economic sense is commendable, but this is not yet the time for speculation.

NEUTRALITY   Progressing on course, but not yet the time for positive action.
REASON   A line of reasoning is correct, but this is not yet the time to draw a conclusion.

1 line 3

---□---

Blameless if temptation is resisted

JUDGEMENT   As others agree, there is a danger of the abuse of position.
INNOCENCE   As experience grows, there is a danger of over-confidence.
AWARENESS   As awareness deepens, there is a danger of moral superiority.
EMOTION   As feelings are satisfied, there is a danger of becoming numb to real emotion.
CREATIVITY   As appreciation is found, there is a danger of becoming pretentious.
COMMUNICATION   As more people listen, there is a danger of becoming a bore.
AMBITION   As success beckons, there is a danger of becoming over-ambitious.
SERVICE   As duties are successfully carried out, it is easy to become self-important.
NURTURE   As children grow more mature, there is a danger of over-reaction.
ECONOMY   As finances grow stronger, there is a danger of greed.
NEUTRALITY   Danger from being too positive.
REASON   As understanding grows, there is a danger from intellectual snobbery.

1 line 4

---□---

No blame either way

JUDGEMENT   Debating the best way to approach a decision.
INNOCENCE   Deciding the best way to go.
AWARENESS   Choosing the most suitable path to a growth in awareness.
EMOTION   Debating the best way to express a feeling.
CREATIVITY   Deciding on the best way to express an idea.
COMMUNICATION   Deciding on what to say for the best.
AMBITION   Questioning the best way to make progress.

SERVICE   Deciding the best way to be of use.

NURTURE   Debating what is best for a child.

ECONOMY   Deciding the most prudent method of financial growth.

NEUTRALITY   Choosing the best method.

REASON   Deciding the best way to tackle a problem.

1 line 5

─────▫─────

Seek advice

JUDGEMENT   Fairness is exemplified.

INNOCENCE   Learning proves pleasurable.

AWARENESS   Clarity through higher awareness.

EMOTION   A feeling shows the right way.

CREATIVITY   Inspiration finds expression.

COMMUNICATION   The truth finds the right words.

AMBITION   Abilities bring progress.

SERVICE   Abilities prove of value.

NURTURE   Natural behaviour proves beneficial.

ECONOMY   Financial planning proves worthwhile.

NEUTRALITY   Correct positive action.

REASON   Intuition proves logical.

1 line 6

─────▫─────

Reason for guilt

JUDGEMENT   Over-stepping the limits of power has unfortunate consequences.

INNOCENCE   Over-stepping the limits of propriety leads to sorrow.

AWARENESS   Unfortunate consequences come from over-stepping the limits of awareness.

EMOTION   Being over-emotional has unhappy consequences.

CREATIVITY   Taking an idea too far destroys creativity.

COMMUNICATION   Unfortunate consequences stem from saying too much.

AMBITION   Over-ambition has unfortunate repercussions.

SERVICE   Over-estimating abilities has unfortunate consequences.

NURTURE   Unhappy consequences stem from parental excesses.

ECONOMY   Over-stretching finances has unfortunate repercussions.

NEUTRALITY   Positive action taken too far, causing repercussions.

REASON   Over-estimating intellectual abilities has unfortunate consequences.

2
·FULFILLING DESTINY·

REASON

Obvious, methodical reasoning leads to answers. Inventiveness now would prove a mistake.

JUDGEMENT

An obvious decision is correct. It would be a mistake to take the lead.

INNOCENCE

It is correct simply to follow at this time. Independent action would prove to be a mistake.

NEUTRALITY

Events that are allowed to unfold for themselves prove positive. Interference is destructive.

AWARENESS

Following higher guidance while remaining morally correct allows awareness to become reality. Ego-led behaviour is wholly inappropriate.

ECONOMY

Following economic trends, while remaining prudent, permits financial growth. Independent action is a mistake.

NURTURE

Allowing instincts to lead, while remaining caring, permits real growth. Coercion is a mistake.

EMOTION

Letting events unfold for themselves, while remaining honest about feelings, leads to emotional satisfaction. Selfish feelings are wholly inappropriate.

SERVICE

Following orders to the best of abilities allows the completion of a task. Initiative would prove a mistake.

Allowing events to unfold, while continuing to do everything necessary, brings about success on its own. Pushing too hard would destroy it.

Allowing a dialogue to develop naturally, while playing a full and honest role, permits an accord to be reached. Taking the lead would destroy it.

Being an unwavering vehicle for inspiration leads to creative success. Forcing ideas does not work.

CREATIVITY

AMBITION

COMMUNICATION

Gentle perseverance brings luck

2 line 1

JUDGEMENT Minor errors of judgement now are symptomatic of incompetence in the future.
INNOCENCE Minor transgressions now can lead to big trouble in the future.
AWARENESS A lack of awareness now, though it may not seem important, makes later growth much more difficult.
EMOTION Minor indiscretions now are symptomatic of something more serious in the future.
CREATIVITY Laziness in developing ideas now leads to artistic failure in the future.
COMMUNICATION White lies now lead to big lies in the future.
AMBITION When laxity creeps in, failure can be predicted.
SERVICE Trivial lapses in duty lead to eventual failure.
NURTURE Minor irritations are symptomatic of an eventual rift.
ECONOMY Minor losses now add up to great loss in the future.
NEUTRALITY Minor laxity.
REASON Unimportant errors now add up to a big mistake in the future.

2 line 2

———×———

Achievements are easy

JUDGEMENT Decision-making is unchallenged, but this is how it should be.
INNOCENCE Life seems boring, but growth is occurring none the less.
AWARENESS There are no dramatic revelations, but awareness is growing none the less.
EMOTION Relationships are unexciting, but such is emotional stability.
CREATIVITY Ideas may appear mundane, but are valid none the less.
COMMUNICATION Conversation may seem boring but is, in fact, achieving something.
AMBITION Things may appear to be going nowhere, but everything is on course.
SERVICE Duties may be unrewarding but are part of a greater plan.

NURTURE Caring may be unappreciated but is necessary.
ECONOMY Great profits may not be forthcoming, but finances are gaining strength.
NEUTRALITY Unnoticed progress.
REASON Everything seems simple, but this is how it should be.

2 line 3

———×———

JUDGEMENT Do not make unnecessary decisions. Do only what is required.
INNOCENCE Do not act independently. Do only what is expected.
AWARENESS Do not force a growth in awareness. Allow it to occur in its own time.
EMOTION Do not make a show of feelings. Try to act calmly.
CREATIVITY Do not be outrageous. Express ideas in an acceptable way.
COMMUNICATION Do not attempt to become the centre of attention. Converse simply and no more.
AMBITION Do not be over-ambitious. Continue to work quietly.
SERVICE Do not seek extra responsibility. Quietly complete the job in hand.
NURTURE Do not seek to control. Let things develop naturally.
ECONOMY Do not give in to greed. Let finances build up slowly.
NEUTRALITY Not attempting to force positive action.
REASON Do not attempt to be clever. Work things out in traditional ways.

2 line 4

———×———

No appreciation, but no need for guilt

JUDGEMENT Power withheld.
INNOCENCE Anonymity.
AWARENESS Hidden awareness.
EMOTION Hidden emotion.
CREATIVITY Concealed creativity.
COMMUNICATION Withholding something.
AMBITION Concealed ambition.
SERVICE Concealed loyalties.
NURTURE Caring that does not express itself.

ECONOMY   Financial secrecy.
NEUTRALITY   Secrecy.
REASON   Hidden intelligence.

2 line 5

———×———

Very lucky

JUDGEMENT   Just decisions make the future easier.
INNOCENCE   Innocence invites protection.
AWARENESS   Humility opens the way for guidance.
EMOTION   Sincere feelings are more likely to be returned.
CREATIVITY   Unpretentious creativity is advantageous.
COMMUNICATION   Simple words lead to an honest dialogue.
AMBITION   Humility brings advantage.
SERVICE   Discretion is advantageous.
NURTURE   Unseen care nurtures maturity.
ECONOMY   A lack of ostentation is a financial advantage.
NEUTRALITY   Simple efficiency.
REASON   There is advantage in simple reasoning.

2 line 6

———×———

JUDGEMENT   Power for its own sake hurts everybody.
INNOCENCE   Self-indulgence is personally damaging and hurts those who care.
AWARENESS   Bringing the ego into the realm of higher awareness injures the self and decreases higher values.
EMOTION   Acting on false emotion is no good for anyone.
CREATIVITY   Ideas that are forced are of no value to anyone.
COMMUNICATION   Arguing is no help to anyone.
AMBITION   Unnecessary competition injures all.
SERVICE   Independent action is damaging both personally and to the greater cause.
NURTURE   Attempting to control another is damaging to both parties.
ECONOMY   Greed is personally damaging and also damages the broader economic situation.
NEUTRALITY   Negative action injuring all parties.
REASON   Intellectual competition hurts everyone.

3
DIFFICULT
·BEGINNINGS·

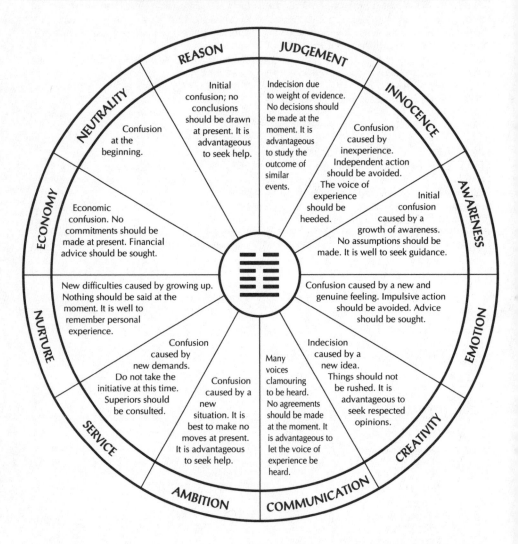

REASON — Initial confusion; no conclusions should be drawn at present. It is advantageous to seek help.

JUDGEMENT — Indecision due to weight of evidence. No decisions should be made at the moment. It is advantageous to study the outcome of similar events.

NEUTRALITY — Confusion at the beginning.

INNOCENCE — Confusion caused by inexperience. Independent action should be avoided. The voice of experience should be heeded.

AWARENESS — Initial confusion caused by a growth of awareness. No assumptions should be made. It is well to seek guidance.

ECONOMY — Economic confusion. No commitments should be made at present. Financial advice should be sought.

EMOTION — Confusion caused by a new and genuine feeling. Impulsive action should be avoided. Advice should be sought.

NURTURE — New difficulties caused by growing up. Nothing should be said at the moment. It is well to remember personal experience.

SERVICE — Confusion caused by new demands. Do not take the initiative at this time. Superiors should be consulted.

AMBITION — Confusion caused by a new situation. It is best to make no moves at present. It is advantageous to seek help.

COMMUNICATION — Many voices clamouring to be heard. No agreements should be made at the moment. It is advantageous to let the voice of experience be heard.

CREATIVITY — Indecision caused by a new idea. Things should not be rushed. It is advantageous to seek respected opinions.

Achievements are possible through perseverance

3 line 1

---□---

Persevere

JUDGEMENT Indecision can be overcome if advice is sought.
INNOCENCE Confusion can be eased with the help of those who are worthy of trust.
AWARENESS Confusion can be overcome by waiting for guidance.
EMOTION Emotional confusion can be eased with the help of friends.
CREATIVITY Uncertainty can be overcome if respected opinions are sought.
COMMUNICATION Disagreements can be smoothed over with help.
AMBITION Difficulties can be overcome with assistance.
SERVICE Difficulties can be overcome if the help of superiors is sought.
NURTURE Growing pains can be healed if personal experience is remembered.
ECONOMY Initial difficulties can be overcome if financial advice is sought.
NEUTRALITY Difficulties which necessitate aid.
REASON Problems can be overcome with help.

3 line 2

---□---

JUDGEMENT A decision seems obvious, but other avenues have not been explored. Only when this has been done is the obvious decision valid.
INNOCENCE It is easy to appear mature, but only when experience has been accumulated does this maturity mean anything.
AWARENESS A fleeting experience encourages claims of higher awareness; true growth would mean that no such claims would be made.
EMOTION A powerful feeling begs expression, but experience is lacking. Only with experience should such feelings be acted upon.
CREATIVITY One idea seems to be the best, but the others have not been explored. Only when this has been done is the original idea valid.
COMMUNICATION An agreement is possible but has not been fully discussed; only when this has been done is it acceptable.

AMBITION An easy way to succeed presents itself, but experience is lacking. Only when this experience has been gained is success deserved.
SERVICE An easy way to complete a task presents itself. Only when orders have been carried out to the letter can their importance be seen.
NURTURE Remedial action seems obvious, but compassion is lacking. Discipline has value only where there is empathy.
ECONOMY Easy profit is possible, but there is no solid financial base. Only when this is achieved is easy gain of any lasting worth.
NEUTRALITY An easy option.
REASON A solution presents itself, which is correct but not understood. Only when it is understood can it be accepted.

3 line 3

---×---

This course of action leads to regret

JUDGEMENT It is unwise to make a decision when not in full possession of the facts.
INNOCENCE It is unwise for the inexperienced to take a chance.
AWARENESS It is unwise for the selfish to claim moral superiority.
EMOTION It is unwise to be impulsive.
CREATIVITY Creativity without the necessary talent can only mean artistic failure.
COMMUNICATION It is unwise to speak for all without consultation.
AMBITION It is unwise to aim for an impractical goal.
SERVICE It is unwise to accept responsibility which is beyond capabilities.
NURTURE It is unwise to burden the young with expectations.
ECONOMY It is unwise to speculate without the necessary resources.
NEUTRALITY Over-estimation.
REASON It is unwise to tackle a problem without the relevant knowledge.

---

3 line 4

——×——

Lucky

JUDGEMENT Joint decisions are demanded.
INNOCENCE Mutual help is needed.
AWARENESS Esoteric matters require discussion.
EMOTION Emotional problems must be shared.
CREATIVITY Mutual criticism is required.
COMMUNICATION Problems need to be discussed.
AMBITION Difficulties demand mutual assistance.
SERVICE Problems must be shared with superiors.
NURTURE A child's pain has to be shared.
ECONOMY The advice of those with similar financial problems must be sought.
NEUTRALITY Difficulties demanding mutual help.
REASON A problem demands the attention of more than one mind.

3 line 5

——▢——

Luck, but only in small matters

JUDGEMENT It is better to make small decisions when they become obvious; big decisions would be resented.
INNOCENCE It is better to gain experience a step at a time; over-confidence would be seen as precociousness.
AWARENESS A growth in awareness can be achieved only in its own time; pushing too hard invites ridicule.
EMOTION Feelings should be treated with great care; impulsiveness would lead to suspicion.
CREATIVITY Ideas should be expressed subtly; spontaneity would draw criticism.
COMMUNICATION The truth should be introduced gradually; a blunt statement would be met with disbelief.
AMBITION Goals should be approached a step at a time; pushing too hard would fuel bad feeling.
SERVICE Duties should be carried out as and when ordered; initiative would annoy superiors.

NURTURE Growth should be gradual; thrusting children into situations for which they are not prepared would be damaging.
ECONOMY Economic growth should be gradual; greed would invite jealousy.
NEUTRALITY Moving a step at a time.
REASON It is better to tackle a problem a step at a time; delving too deep leads to being misunderstood.

3 line 6

——×——

JUDGEMENT Tough decisions prove too much.
INNOCENCE New experience proves too much.
AWARENESS New-found awareness proves too confusing.
EMOTION New-found emotion proves too powerful to deal with.
CREATIVITY The barriers to originality prove too great.
COMMUNICATION Initial disagreement is insurmountable.
AMBITION Initial difficulties mean giving up.
SERVICE New orders prove too difficult.
NURTURE Parents cannot understand.
ECONOMY Initial financial difficulties prove too much.
NEUTRALITY Initial difficulties proving insurmountable.
REASON Initial problems prove too great.

4

·INEXPERIENCE·

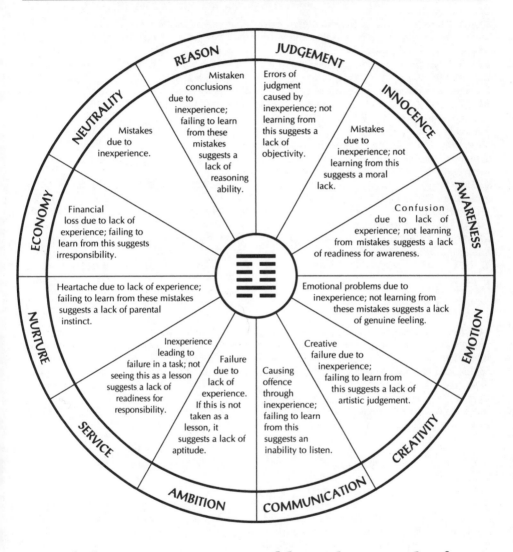

Achievements are possible with strength of character

4 line 1

———×———

Obstinacy leads to guilt

JUDGEMENT Better judgement requires objectivity, but this should not be allowed to become dogma.
INNOCENCE New experience requires self-discipline, but this should not be allowed to develop into inhibition.
AWARENESS Greater awareness requires moral discipline, but this should not be allowed to become self-righteousness.
EMOTION New feelings require a clear-headed response, but this should not be allowed to grow into coldness.
CREATIVITY Greater creativity requires artistic discipline, but this should not be allowed to degenerate into predictability.
COMMUNICATION Better dialogue requires self-discipline, but this should not be allowed to develop into secretiveness.
AMBITION New challenges necessitate self-discipline, but this should not be allowed to become competitiveness.
SERVICE New demands necessitate discipline, but this should not be allowed to become inflexibility.
NURTURE Better care requires discipline, but this should not be used for its own sake.
ECONOMY Economic growth necessitates prudence, but this should not become meanness.
NEUTRALITY Improvement requiring measured discipline.
REASON Better reasoning requires intellectual discipline, but this should not be allowed to become closed-mindedness.

4 line 2

———▫———

Lucky

JUDGEMENT Experience is required before just decisions can be made.
INNOCENCE Independence demands that lessons be learned from experience.
AWARENESS Higher awareness can be achieved only by experience.
EMOTION Emotional stability can come only with experience.
CREATIVITY Genuine creativity necessitates learning from experience.

COMMUNICATION Meaningful dialogue can occur only when diplomacy has been learned from experience.
AMBITION Any worthy success requires learning from experience.
SERVICE Responsibility necessitates experience.
NURTURE Genuine care is borne out of personal experience.
ECONOMY Prudence is borne out of experience.
NEUTRALITY Tolerance allowing experience to be gained.
REASON Reasoning ability can be learned only from practice.

4 line 3

———×———

Achievements are not possible

JUDGEMENT Imitating fairness is not enough.
INNOCENCE Following others achieves nothing.
AWARENESS Idolatry means nothing.
EMOTION Acting as others would expect is inadequate.
CREATIVITY Imitation is inadequate.
COMMUNICATION Trying to act like someone else means nothing.
AMBITION Merely imitating a role model is not enough.
SERVICE Pretended loyalty is inadequate.
NURTURE Imitating role models is inadequate.
ECONOMY Merely following an example of financial success is not enough.
NEUTRALITY Empty imitation.
REASON Merely following proven examples is inadequate.

4 line 4

———×———

Inevitable guilt

JUDGEMENT Inexperienced decisions cause respect to be lost.
INNOCENCE Inexperienced action leads to embarrassment.
AWARENESS Higher values in inexperienced hands lead to foolish actions.

EMOTION Acting on feelings without experience leads to a loss of self-respect.
CREATIVITY Inexperienced creativity invites criticism.
COMMUNICATION Inexperienced words are not believed.
AMBITION Mistakes due to inexperience mean a loss of prestige.
SERVICE Taking on too much because of inexperience means the confidence of superiors is lost.
NURTURE Mistakes due to inexperience lead to being perceived as uncaring.
ECONOMY Mistakes due to inexperience lead to a loss of financial standing.
NEUTRALITY Inexperienced action.
REASON Misunderstanding due to a lack of experience causes abilities to be doubted.

4 line 5

———×———

Lucky

JUDGEMENT Relinquishing preconceived ideas allows better decisions.
INNOCENCE Admitting ignorance permits greater learning.
AWARENESS Learning to still the mind permits higher awareness.
EMOTION Acting more naturally makes feelings more tangible.
CREATIVITY A lack of pretention permits greater creativity.
COMMUNICATION Careful listening allows more complete communication.
AMBITION Being open to advice permits greater progress.
SERVICE Flexibility allows greater responsibility to be shouldered.
NURTURE Rejecting preconceived ideas and learning from experience make a better parent.
ECONOMY Financial realism is the basis of economic growth.
NEUTRALITY Being realistic.
REASON Relinquishing pet theories permits better reasoning.

4 line 6

———▫———

Lucky if seen as a lesson, otherwise unfortunate

JUDGEMENT Errors of judgement due to inexperience should not be regarded negatively; they should be seen as preventing future mistakes.
INNOCENCE Mistakes due to inexperience should not mean a loss of self-belief; they should be seen as lessons in life.
AWARENESS A loss of awareness due to inexperience does not imply a loss of faith; it is more a lesson to be learned.
EMOTION Pain due to inexperience should not be regarded negatively; it should be seen as a growth in emotional strength.
CREATIVITY Artistic failure due to inexperience should not be seen as a lack of talent; it should be regarded in the light of creative development.
COMMUNICATION A misunderstanding caused by inexperience does not merit harsh words; it is a lesson in diplomacy.
AMBITION Failure due to inexperience should not be seen in a negative light; it should be a lesson for next time.
SERVICE Failure in a task due to inexperience is not ineptitude; it is experience gained.
NURTURE The mistakes of inexperience do not deserve punishment. Encouragement is preferable.
ECONOMY Financial loss due to inexperience does not deserve censure; it should be seen as a lesson in prudence.
NEUTRALITY Mistakes due to inexperience.
REASON Inexperience that causes wrong conclusions to be drawn should not be regarded as a lack of ability; these are lessons in reasoning.

5
·WAITING·

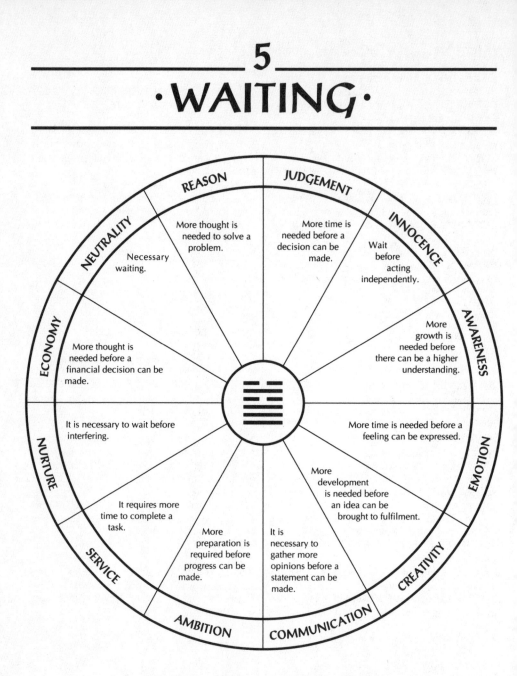

REASON

JUDGEMENT

INNOCENCE

NEUTRALITY

AWARENESS

ECONOMY

EMOTION

NURTURE

CREATIVITY

SERVICE

AMBITION

COMMUNICATION

More thought is needed to solve a problem.

More time is needed before a decision can be made.

Wait before acting independently.

Necessary waiting.

More growth is needed before there can be a higher understanding.

More thought is needed before a financial decision can be made.

It is necessary to wait before interfering.

More time is needed before a feeling can be expressed.

More development is needed before an idea can be brought to fulfilment.

It requires more time to complete a task.

More preparation is required before progress can be made.

It is necessary to gather more opinions before a statement can be made.

Lucky – plans can be made
Achievements are possible with perseverance

5 line 1

———□———

Patience avoids mistakes

JUDGEMENT For the time being, remain tolerant, thus avoiding wrong decisions.
INNOCENCE Do not ask questions for the time being; this avoids mistakes.
AWARENESS For the time being, carry on with everyday life; this avoids delusion.
EMOTION Carry on as if nothing had happened for the time being; this avoids getting hurt.
CREATIVITY Stick to conventional ideas at the moment; this avoids being misunderstood.
COMMUNICATION Say nothing for the time being; this avoids misunderstanding.
AMBITION Curb ambitions for the time being to avoid wasting energy.
SERVICE Remain dutiful for the time being; this avoids later recriminations.
NURTURE Be as understanding as possible at the moment; this avoids resentment.
ECONOMY For the time being, remain prudent; this avoids financial loss.
NEUTRALITY Carrying on as normal.
REASON In order to avoid mistakes, no conclusions should be drawn for the time being.

5 line 2

———□———

Lucky, but controversial

JUDGEMENT A reluctance to come to a decision may be seen as indecisiveness but is correct.
INNOCENCE A reluctance to trust may be misunderstood but is correct.
AWARENESS Not acting on an intuition may frustrate the ego but is correct.
EMOTION Reluctance to act on a feeling may be misconstrued but is justified.
CREATIVITY Not giving expression to an idea may seem uncreative but is ultimately justified.
COMMUNICATION Reticence may be misconstrued but is correct.
AMBITION Reluctance to grasp an opportunity may be seen as apathy but is correct.
SERVICE Reluctance to obey an order may be seen as failing in a duty but is ultimately shown to be right.

NURTURE A reluctance to reprimand may be seen as weak but is ultimately justified.
ECONOMY Financial reticence may be called mean but is correct.
NEUTRALITY Waiting being perceived as wrong.
REASON A reluctance to draw a conclusion may be seen as irrational but is correct.

5 line 3

———□———

JUDGEMENT Decisions made without due consideration bring challenges to authority.
INNOCENCE A step taken without understanding leads to inevitable insecurity.
AWARENESS Progress made prematurely leaves the way open for self-doubt.
EMOTION A commitment made prematurely leads to pain.
CREATIVITY Ill-thought out ideas can be seen as such by others.
COMMUNICATION Words spoken without due thought lead to argument.
AMBITION A step taken prematurely invites the enmity of others.
SERVICE Tackling a task that is too difficult means inadequacies can be seen.
NURTURE Action taken without consideration for feelings leads to resentment.
ECONOMY A commitment made without a solid financial base leads to problems.
NEUTRALITY Steps taken prematurely.
REASON Conclusions drawn without proper understanding are criticized.

5 line 4

———×———

JUDGEMENT A rashly made decision proves to be wrong; it is necessary to admit this.
INNOCENCE A situation that cannot be understood; trust, though difficult, is the only way out.
AWARENESS Ego-led behaviour masquerading as higher awareness; it is necessary to accept this as a fault.
EMOTION A commitment has been rashly made; honesty, though painful, is the only solution.
CREATIVITY The banal has been mistaken for inspiration; it is necessary to accept criticism.

COMMUNICATION The wrong thing has been said; it is best to remain silent.

AMBITION A wrong step has been taken; the only way out is to remain composed.

SERVICE A task is too difficult; the only way is to admit it.

NURTURE A lack of trust cannot be overcome by love; example is the only way.

ECONOMY Dire straits cannot be overcome by speculation; prudence is the only option.

NEUTRALITY Dangerous circumstances.

REASON A rashly drawn conclusion proves illogical; it is necessary to listen to alternative arguments.

5 line 5

———□———

Lucky if dedicated

JUDGEMENT Periods away from responsibility should be seen as fortification for difficult decisions in the future.

INNOCENCE There is nothing wrong with enjoying life between hard-learned lessons.

AWARENESS Occasional pleasure can renew faith.

EMOTION Occasional periods of separation can actually strengthen a relationship.

CREATIVITY Occasional enjoyment of the banal can be therapeutic.

COMMUNICATION Take pleasure from laughing and joking. Such moments are fortification for serious arguments ahead.

AMBITION Take pleasure in brief respites from the struggle. They are fortification for struggles ahead.

SERVICE Take full advantage of breaks from duty. They are necessary preparation for tasks ahead.

NURTURE Do not feel guilty about brief moments of self-indulgence. They fortify those who truly care.

ECONOMY Occasional treats make a financial struggle easier to bear.

NEUTRALITY Periods of relaxation, which are fortification for the future.

REASON Occasional flights of fancy should be seen as fortification in the struggle to make sense of things.

5 line 6

———×———

Lucky if seen as a lesson

JUDGEMENT A decision proves to be wrong, but there are vital lessons to be learned for future success.

INNOCENCE When all hope is lost, new friends appear.

AWARENESS A loss of awareness has to be endured, but this very loss leads to new insights.

EMOTION A relationship is over, but new and unexpected feelings are revealed.

CREATIVITY Creative ideas come to nothing, but there are new ideas hidden in this failure.

COMMUNICATION An argument is lost, but a new level of communication is established.

AMBITION Ambitions are thwarted, but new opportunities are there, if they can be seen.

SERVICE A task proves beyond capabilities, but other unrealized abilities will be of use.

NURTURE A clash is inevitable, but here are the seeds of a new understanding.

ECONOMY There is inevitable loss, but the means of recovery unexpectedly reveals itself.

NEUTRALITY Inevitable failure hiding the seeds of new beginnings.

REASON A wrong conclusion has been drawn, but the seeds of new understanding are hidden in this failure.

·CONFLICT·

REASON — A sensible theory meets with disagreement; compromise is preferable to not being understood.

JUDGEMENT — A just decision meets with disagreement; compromise is best. Forcing the issue causes resentment.

INNOCENCE — An innocent action results in conflict; compromise is preferable to bad feeling.

NEUTRALITY — Positive action leading to conflict.

ECONOMY — Speculative ideas cause a conflict of interests; compromise is preferable to financial risk.

AWARENESS — Higher values cause a conflict; compromise is preferable to alienation.

NURTURE — Caring engenders conflict; compromise is best.

EMOTION — Sincere feelings cause a disagreement; compromise is better than pig-headedness.

SERVICE — Loyalty engenders conflict; flexibility is preferable to rigidity.

AMBITION — Ambition causes a conflict; compromise is preferable to competition.

COMMUNICATION — Sincere words meet with disagreement; negotiation is the best way. Stubbornness causes arguments.

CREATIVITY — Artistic ideas meet with criticism; compromise is preferable to rejection.

With care, luck – take no chances – seek advice

6 line 1

——×——

Controversial, but ultimately lucky

JUDGEMENT Avoiding a disagreement may cause a loss of standing but is ultimately for the best.
INNOCENCE Avoiding a conflict causes lost pride but is for the best.
AWARENESS Avoiding a conflict of ideals may feel like a denial of faith but is the best way.
EMOTION Avoiding an argument causes frustration but is for the best in the end.
CREATIVITY Making ideas more acceptable may feel like compromise but is ultimately the best solution.
COMMUNICATION Avoiding an argument may cause gossip but is ultimately for the best.
AMBITION Avoiding a conflict may feel like a step in the wrong direction but is ultimately more successful.
SERVICE Avoiding a conflict may be seen as disloyalty but ultimately proves more sensible.
NURTURE Avoiding a clash of temperament may seem like a lack of parental control but is for the best in the end.
ECONOMY Avoiding financial competition may seem like throwing a chance away but ultimately proves more sensible.
NEUTRALITY Avoiding a conflict.
REASON Avoiding being misunderstood may seem like a lack of understanding but is ultimately for the best.

6 line 2

——□——

No need for guilt

JUDGEMENT It is best not to engage in unwinnable arguments.
INNOCENCE It is best to walk away from fights that cannot be won.
AWARENESS Intractable moral conflicts should be avoided.
EMOTION Hopeless arguments are best avoided.
CREATIVITY Artistic misunderstanding is best avoided.
COMMUNICATION It is best not to engage in hopeless argument.

AMBITION Unwinnable competition is best avoided.
SERVICE Conflict with superiors should be avoided.
NURTURE Situations in which a child would not back down should be avoided.
ECONOMY Avoid competition that is too strong.
NEUTRALITY Avoiding conflict to preserve resources.
REASON It is better not to look for a solution if it will not be understood.

6 line 3

——×——

Lucky, but dangerous

JUDGEMENT Holding on to principles invites misunderstanding but is ultimately for the best.
INNOCENCE Retaining an innocent attitude invites danger but is the best way.
AWARENESS Holding on to higher values may invite incredulity but is the best way.
EMOTION Being sincere is risky but ultimately for the best.
CREATIVITY Uncompromising originality means taking a chance but is ultimately the best way.
COMMUNICATION Diplomacy is risky but the best way. Do not try to broker agreements.
AMBITION Relying on ability is risky but the best way.
SERVICE Sticking to duty is risky but for the best. Do not seek more responsibility.
NURTURE Loving care, though difficult, is the best way.
ECONOMY Prudence may involve some risk but is the best way. Do not take responsibility for other people's money.
NEUTRALITY Positive values inviting danger but ultimately being the best way.
REASON Logicality invites disagreement but is the best way.

6 line 4

―――□―――

Lucky if dedicated

JUDGEMENT   It is best not to use power to force a decision but to let events take their own course.
INNOCENCE   It is best to walk away from fights and to watch what happens.
AWARENESS   It is best to avoid moral arguments and to trust in fate.
EMOTION   It is best to avoid an argument and to let fate take its course.
CREATIVITY   It is best not to answer criticism but to let creativity speak for itself.
COMMUNICATION   It is best to resist the temptation to win an argument and to let dialogue develop in its own way.
AMBITION   It is best to reject the chance of a cheap victory and to let events take their own course.
SERVICE   It is best to avoid conflict with superiors, even when correct. Events should be allowed to take their own course.
NURTURE   It is best to avoid conflict and simply to observe what happens.
ECONOMY   It is best to avoid risk and to let finances dictate their own course.
NEUTRALITY   Avoiding winnable arguments in order to let events take their own course.
REASON   It is best not to challenge a theory with logic but to let events follow their own course.

6 line 5

―――□―――

Very lucky

JUDGEMENT   Leaving a decision to a neutral party.
INNOCENCE   Letting someone in authority resolve an argument.
AWARENESS   Trusting a decision to fate.
EMOTION   Letting outside influences settle a quarrel.
CREATIVITY   Seeking an unbiased opinion to resolve a creative conflict.
COMMUNICATION   Letting an independent voice resolve an argument.
AMBITION   Competition before an unbiased referee.

SERVICE   Getting an independent opinion to resolve an argument with superiors.
NURTURE   Relying on outside influence to resolve a conflict.
ECONOMY   Letting a disinterested party resolve a financial conflict.
NEUTRALITY   Appointing an arbitrator to resolve a conflict.
REASON   Letting an independent mind resolve a logical argument.

6 line 6

―――□―――

JUDGEMENT   Winning an argument means decisions are challenged.
INNOCENCE   Winning a fight encourages those who would challenge.
AWARENESS   Forcing a moral issue to a conclusion invites moral criticism.
EMOTION   Winning a quarrel engenders resentment, which leads to more quarrels.
CREATIVITY   Creative success invites criticism.
COMMUNICATION   Winning an argument encourages more argument.
AMBITION   Winning encourages challengers.
SERVICE   Proving a superior wrong invites close observation and criticism.
NURTURE   Forcing a child to do something against its will invites rebellion.
ECONOMY   Financial success encourages jealous rivals.
NEUTRALITY   Victories encouraging challenges.
REASON   Proving a point invites criticism.

·7·
·DISCIPLINE·

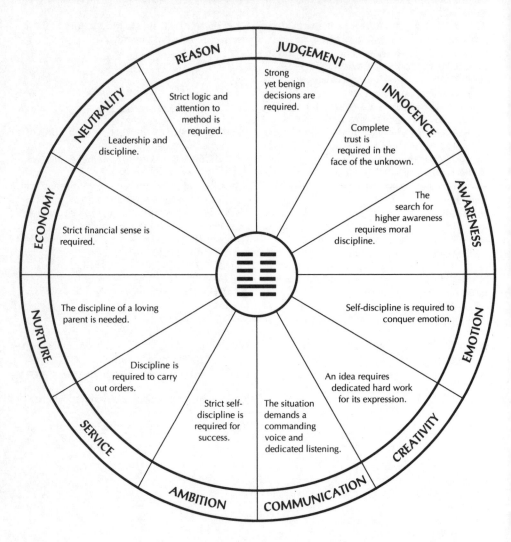

REASON — Strict logic and attention to method is required.

JUDGEMENT — Strong yet benign decisions are required.

INNOCENCE — Complete trust is required in the face of the unknown.

NEUTRALITY — Leadership and discipline.

AWARENESS — The search for higher awareness requires moral discipline.

ECONOMY — Strict financial sense is required.

EMOTION — Self-discipline is required to conquer emotion.

NURTURE — The discipline of a loving parent is needed.

CREATIVITY — An idea requires dedicated hard work for its expression.

SERVICE — Discipline is required to carry out orders.

AMBITION — Strict self-discipline is required for success.

COMMUNICATION — The situation demands a commanding voice and dedicated listening.

Lucky if discipline is maintained

7 line 1

——×——

Bad luck if discipline is not maintained

JUDGEMENT   Order must be maintained or failure threatens.
INNOCENCE   Anything less than total trust invites disaster.
AWARENESS   Anything less than total self-discipline would mean lost awareness.
EMOTION   Self-discipline must be total or old, unwanted emotions will rise again.
CREATIVITY   Anything less than total dedication risks an idea being wasted.
COMMUNICATION   Everyone must understand their significance in a discussion or dialogue will be wasted.
AMBITION   Self-discipline must be total or there is a real risk of failure.
SERVICE   Anything less than total dedication to duty invites failure.
NURTURE   Parents and children must know strictly where they stand or relationships will disintegrate.
ECONOMY   Finances must be set in proper order or there is a real risk of loss.
NEUTRALITY   Proper organization.
REASON   Method must be meticulous or wrong conclusions will be drawn.

7 line 2

——▫——

Lucky – correct

JUDGEMENT   Leading by example; in this way rewards are justified.
INNOCENCE   Being dedicated to learning brings justified rewards.
AWARENESS   Bringing higher awareness into everyday life brings justified rewards.
EMOTION   Demonstrating love through action brings justified rewards.
CREATIVITY   Creative ideas that can be appreciated by anyone bring justified rewards.
COMMUNICATION   Communicating ideas in terms that everyone can understand. Praise is justified.
AMBITION   Ambition dedicated to a common goal brings justified rewards.
SERVICE   Being an example of dedication brings justified rewards.

NURTURE   Being an example. The love that is returned is justified.
ECONOMY   Being an example of prudence brings justified rewards.
NEUTRALITY   Being an example.
REASON   Using inventiveness for a common goal. Any rewards are justified.

7 line 3

——×——

Unfortunate

JUDGEMENT   It is a mistake to allow power to be spread too widely.
INNOCENCE   Following too many examples serves only to confuse.
AWARENESS   Satisfying egotistical desire weakens the will to go higher.
EMOTION   Carrying too much unrequited emotion stifles the ability to love.
CREATIVITY   Working on too many ideas at the same time stifles creativity.
COMMUNICATION   Too many voices clamouring to be heard destroy effective dialogue.
AMBITION   Having too many goals weakens effectiveness.
SERVICE   Effectiveness is weakened by serving more than one master.
NURTURE   Allowing too much leeway destroys respect.
ECONOMY   Too many commitments weaken financial security.
NEUTRALITY   Leaders allowing subordinates too much say.
REASON   Looking for too many explanations only clouds the issue.

7 line 4

——×——

Blameless

JUDGEMENT   It is as well to admit that a decision cannot be made at the moment.
INNOCENCE   It is best to admit ignorance for now.
AWARENESS   It is as well to admit that awareness is unachievable at the present time.
EMOTION   Love is impossible at the moment; it is as well to walk away.

CREATIVITY When no ideas are forth-coming, it is as well to admit it, at least for the time being.

COMMUNICATION It is better to say nothing when others do not yet understand.

AMBITION In the face of overwhelming odds, it is as well to retreat, at least for the moment.

SERVICE A task proves too difficult; for the time being it is as well to admit it.

NURTURE It is as well to let children go their own way for the time being.

ECONOMY It is as well to admit that something is too expensive at the moment.

NEUTRALITY Retreating in the face of overwhelming odds.

REASON If there is no rational explanation at the moment, it is as well to admit it.

7 line 5

——×——

Obstinacy is unlucky

JUDGEMENT Vital decisions have to be made. Maturity is required. Carrying deci-siveness too far invites mistakes.

INNOCENCE There is something impor-tant to be learned, therefore the right attitude is required. Trying to experience too much could mask an important lesson.

AWARENESS The ego needs to be dealt with, but in a sympathetic way. Too much self-denial would only exacerbate the problem.

EMOTION Strong feelings need to be expressed, but a clear head is required. Being over-emotional could spoil a relationship.

CREATIVITY Difficult ideas beg expres-sion. Great subtlety is required. Outrageousness means artistic failure.

COMMUNICATION Something difficult needs to be said. Tact is essential. Saying too much leads to misunderstanding.

AMBITION There is a challenge to be faced; experience is needed. Over-ambition leads to failure.

SERVICE A difficult task needs to be tack-led. Strict obedience is required. Exceeding orders would prove costly.

NURTURE A painful situation needs to be corrected. Great understanding is required. Taking the matter too far could destroy trust.

ECONOMY A necessary expenditure has to be made. Prudence is essential. Extravagance could spell disaster.

NEUTRALITY Something needing to be done, but in a measured way.

REASON A problem has to be solved. Intelligence is required, but trying to be too clever would solve nothing.

7 line 6

——×——

JUDGEMENT Enlightened decisions are possible, but this process should not be allowed to degenerate into dogma.

INNOCENCE Incorporate newly learned knowledge into life but do not act in igno-rance.

AWARENESS Act in accordance with new-found clarity but avoid egotistical ten-dencies.

EMOTION Express what is truly felt but do not give way to those feelings that undermine emotional stability.

CREATIVITY Ideas can be successfully expressed but avoid those ideas that are less than worthy.

COMMUNICATION Say what has to be said but do not allow those who do not under-stand a voice.

AMBITION Do what has to be done but take care not to encourage those who would challenge.

SERVICE Take pride in being part of suc-cessful team but do not be tempted to allow that pride to become self-importance.

NURTURE Enjoy mutual trust and do not allow trivial irritations to spoil it.

ECONOMY Spend what needs to be spent but do not waste money on trivialities.

NEUTRALITY Doing what has to be done after a victory.

REASON Enjoy new-found understanding but do not allow it to degenerate into mere cleverness.

8
·COMMON INTEREST·

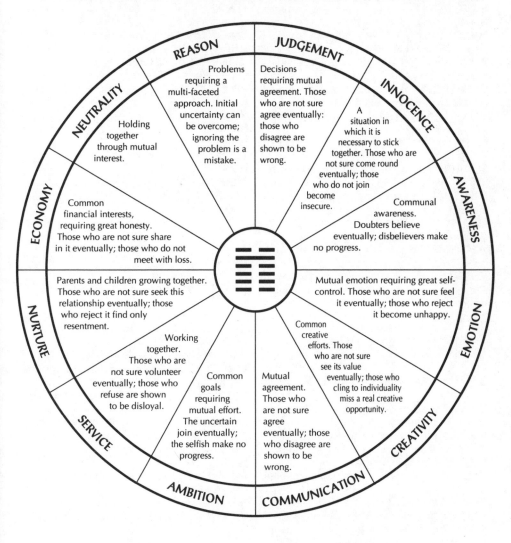

REASON — Problems requiring a multi-faceted approach. Initial uncertainty can be overcome; ignoring the problem is a mistake.

JUDGEMENT — Decisions requiring mutual agreement. Those who are not sure agree eventually: those who disagree are shown to be wrong.

NEUTRALITY — Holding together through mutual interest.

INNOCENCE — A situation in which it is necessary to stick together. Those who are not sure come round eventually; those who do not join become insecure.

ECONOMY — Common financial interests, requiring great honesty. Those who are not sure share in it eventually; those who do not meet with loss.

AWARENESS — Communal awareness. Doubters believe eventually; disbelievers make no progress.

Parents and children growing together. Those who are not sure seek this relationship eventually; those who reject it find only resentment.

EMOTION — Mutual emotion requiring great self-control. Those who are not sure feel it eventually; those who reject it become unhappy.

NURTURE — Working together. Those who are not sure volunteer eventually; those who refuse are shown to be disloyal.

Common creative efforts. Those who are not sure see its value eventually; those who cling to individuality miss a real creative opportunity.

Common goals requiring mutual effort. The uncertain join eventually; the selfish make no progress.

COMMUNICATION — Mutual agreement. Those who are not sure agree eventually; those who disagree are shown to be wrong.

SERVICE

AMBITION

CREATIVITY

Lucky with the right attitude

8 line 1

———×———

Correct – sincerity brings progress

JUDGEMENT Fairness, which finds general approval.
INNOCENCE Purity, which makes others feel protective.
AWARENESS Ego-less behaviour, which encourages mutual awareness.
EMOTION Selflessness, which engenders mutual emotion.
CREATIVITY A lack of pretension, which brings creative ideas together.
COMMUNICATION Honesty, encouraging dialogue.
AMBITION A lack of competitiveness, which inspires mutual help.
SERVICE Devotion to duty, inspiring loyalty in others.
NURTURE True caring, inspiring mutual affection.
ECONOMY Generosity for the sake of common financial interests.
NEUTRALITY Positive action, bringing unity.
REASON A lack of intellectual snobbery, allowing different strands of understanding to be brought together.

8 line 2

———×———

Perseverance brings luck

JUDGEMENT Relinquish the desire to control a situation.
INNOCENCE Just act innocently.
AWARENESS Live according to beliefs.
EMOTION Be unselfish.
CREATIVITY Allow true originality to pour forth.
COMMUNICATION Speak honestly.
AMBITION Relinquish competitiveness.
SERVICE Serve with dignity.
NURTURE Be truly caring.
ECONOMY Be generous when it is needed.
NEUTRALITY Honest values inspiring unity.
REASON Relinquish ideas of intellectual superiority and simply search for understanding.

8 line 3

———×———

JUDGEMENT Making decisions only to find approval.
INNOCENCE Following the wrong crowd.
AWARENESS Seeking awareness for the wrong reasons.
EMOTION Insincere feelings.
CREATIVITY Expressing an unworthy idea.
COMMUNICATION Agreeing with the wrong opinions.
AMBITION Aligning with the wrong people.
SERVICE Loyal to the wrong cause.
NURTURE Not in the cause of mutual growth.
ECONOMY Not in mutual financial interests.
NEUTRALITY Misplaced loyalty.
REASON Gathering ideas merely to gain intellectual superiority.

8 line 4

———×———

Perseverance brings luck

JUDGEMENT Open about opinions.
INNOCENCE Openly admitting reliance on others.
AWARENESS Openly admitting faith.
EMOTIONS Openly expressing mutual feeling.
CREATIVITY Uninhibited reaction to stimuli.
COMMUNICATION Open agreement.
AMBITION Unconcealed ability.
SERVICE Open loyalty.
NURTURE Caring openly.
ECONOMY Open about mutual financial interests.
NEUTRALITY Making union known.
REASON Openly asking for input.

8 line 5

———☐———

Lucky

JUDGEMENT Decisions that seem obvious to everyone.
INNOCENCE Mutual friendship.
AWARENESS Mutual awareness that proceeds naturally.
EMOTION Finding mutual feeling in a natural way.
CREATIVITY Reacting in a natural way to stimuli.
COMMUNICATION Conversation that leads naturally to agreement.
AMBITION Mutual goals achieved without competition.
SERVICE Loyalty that is instinctive.
NURTURE Bonds that are natural.
ECONOMY Mutual financial interests devoid of greed.
NEUTRALITY Mutual progress without special effort.
REASON Understanding that comes naturally.

8 line 6

———✕———

Unfortunate

JUDGEMENT Decisions that do not find mutual agreement are shown to be wrong.
INNOCENCE Those who do not make friends become insecure.
AWARENESS A refusal to believe denies any growth in awareness.
EMOTION Denying mutual feeling leads to unhappiness.
CREATIVITY Clinging to individuality for its own sake proves a mistake.
COMMUNICATION Not coming to an agreement proves to be wrong.
AMBITION The inability to discard competitiveness denies progress.
SERVICE Not working together shows disloyalty.
NURTURE A parent incapable of sharing gives nothing to a child.
ECONOMY Not seeing the need for mutual financial security leads to loss.
NEUTRALITY Inability to share.
REASON Being too superior to gather simple information leads to a mistake.

9
·MINOR RESTRAINT·

REASON

The answer is known, but cannot yet be proved. For the time being it must be treated as a supposition.

JUDGEMENT

A decision is made but cannot yet be implemented. It should not yet be made known.

NEUTRALITY

Restraint in small ways.

INNOCENCE

Experience has been gained but should not yet be acted upon.

ECONOMY

A chance of profit is seen, but it is not yet the right time for speculation.

AWARENESS

Higher awareness should be translated into everyday life in a restrained way.

NURTURE

A stage of growth has been achieved, but care is still required in small ways.

EMOTION

A feeling is real but should not yet be expressed.

SERVICE

Responsibility is held, but orders can only be carried out in a restrained way.

AMBITION

A worthy goal has been found, but progress should not yet be made in that direction.

COMMUNICATION

An agreement has been reached in principle but should not yet be made public.

CREATIVITY

An idea is good but is not yet ready for expression.

A small achievement is possible

9 line 1

---□---

Lucky

JUDGEMENT Let decisions become apparent in their own time.
INNOCENCE Do not rush into anything.
AWARENESS Allow awareness to return of its own accord.
EMOTION Let feelings become apparent in their own time.
CREATIVITY Let inspiration come in its own time.
COMMUNICATION Let dialogue proceed in its own way.
AMBITION Allow progress to be made naturally.
SERVICE Duties should be carried out in their own time.
NURTURE Allow growth to proceed in a natural way.
ECONOMY Let economic matters proceed at their own pace.
NEUTRALITY Allowing events to unfold for themselves.
REASON Let solutions appear for themselves.

9 line 2

---□---

Lucky

JUDGEMENT Avoid an impossible decision.
INNOCENCE Avoid a situation that is not understood.
AWARENESS Avoid a situation with no higher meaning.
EMOTION Avoid expressing a feeling that will not be understood.
CREATIVITY Avoid an idea that cannot be expressed.
COMMUNICATION Avoid an unwinnable argument.
AMBITION Avoid an insurmountable hurdle.
SERVICE Do not accept impossible tasks.
NURTURE Avoid a pointless clash of temperament.
ECONOMY Avoid a certain loss.
NEUTRALITY Avoiding the impossible.
REASON Let go of an insoluble problem.

9 line 3

---□---

JUDGEMENT Decisions are prevented by trivial evidence.
INNOCENCE Small worries prevent security.
AWARENESS Insignificant faults prevent awareness.
EMOTION Pettiness prevents real feeling.
CREATIVITY Trivial mistakes mar inspiration.
COMMUNICATION Petty arguments prevent agreement.
AMBITION Trivial obstacles prevent progress.
SERVICE Petty problems prevent the completion of a task.
NURTURE Childish traits prevent growth.
ECONOMY Profit is prevented by seemingly unimportant expenses.
NEUTRALITY Small problems denying positive progress.
REASON Small problems prevent a solution.

9 line 4

---×---

Correct

JUDGEMENT Fairness will eventually lead to an obvious answer.
INNOCENCE Holding on to innocence allows eventual security.
AWARENESS True faith permits eventual growth.
EMOTION Genuine feeling will eventually find expression.
CREATIVITY Genuine originality will be appreciated eventually.
COMMUNICATION Ultimately, the truth will be believed.
AMBITION Dedication to a worthy goal will allow eventual progress.
SERVICE Devotion to duty will win through in the end.
NURTURE True caring will be appreciated in the end.
ECONOMY Wise investments will see an eventual return.
NEUTRALITY Positive values allowing eventual progress.
REASON Logic will eventually lead to an answer.

9 line 5

—————◻—————

JUDGEMENT   Fairness wins respect.
INNOCENCE   The ability to feel genuine pleasure attracts others.
AWARENESS   True faith is enriching.
EMOTION   Sincere feelings are reciprocated.
CREATIVITY   Creativity is satisfying.
COMMUNICATION   Open dialogue is a reward in itself.
AMBITION   Abilities become a source of pleasure for their own sake.
SERVICE   Devotion to duty is appreciated.
NURTURE   Caring engenders mutual bonding.
ECONOMY   Prudence becomes a pleasure.
NEUTRALITY   Shared positive values.
REASON   Deep understanding attracts like minds.

9 line 6

—————◻—————

Further action is unlucky

JUDGEMENT   Do not go further than the obvious decision.
INNOCENCE   Be happy in the present situation. Adventures are risky.
AWARENESS   Be content with growth achieved so far. Looking for more could spoil what has been gained.
EMOTION   Be happy with a relationship as it stands. Being over-emotional could destroy it.
CREATIVITY   Be content with an idea as it stands. Further development could destroy it.
COMMUNICATION   Be happy with agreements reached so far. Further dialogue could lead to misunderstanding.
AMBITION   Be content with what has been achieved so far. Pushing ahead means danger.
SERVICE   Do not go further than the limits of an order.
NURTURE   Be content with the growth that has been achieved so far. Pushing could be dangerous.
ECONOMY   Be content with what has been gained so far. Further speculation is dangerous.

NEUTRALITY   Contentment with what has been achieved through restraint.
REASON   Be content with conclusions that have so far been drawn. Further deduction would be a mistake.

TWELVE CHANNELS OF THE I CHING

·TAKING A CHANCE·

REASON — Flouting logic in order to find a solution.

JUDGEMENT — Going against principles to make a decision.

NEUTRALITY — Taking a risk.

INNOCENCE — Tackling the unknown and remaining unscathed.

ECONOMY — Seemingly unwise speculation bringing return.

AWARENESS — Acting in opposition to higher values but suffering no loss of awareness.

NURTURE — Appearing uncaring in order to nurture growth.

EMOTION — Expressing a feeling at the wrong time but finding sympathy.

SERVICE — Not strictly obeying orders in order to complete a task.

CREATIVITY — An unusual idea proving successful.

AMBITION — Pushing too hard but making progress anyway.

COMMUNICATION — Saying the wrong thing but not causing offence.

A small achievement in the face of danger

10 line 1

———□———

Blameless

JUDGEMENT   Simple justice allows a correct decision.
INNOCENCE   Remaining uncorrupted allows a lesson to be learned.
AWARENESS   Simplicity allows a continued growth in awareness.
EMOTION   Remaining sincere allows a relationship to grow.
CREATIVITY   Remaining true to original ideas makes them more worthwhile.
COMMUNICATION   Continuing to listen allows dialogue to progress.
AMBITION   Abilities permit progress.
SERVICE   Continued loyalty is of great service.
NURTURE   Unnoticed care allowing growth.
ECONOMY   Continued prudence permits steady growth.
NEUTRALITY   Simple positive values permitting progress.
REASON   Remaining open-minded brings understanding.

10 line 2

———□———

Continuing in this way brings luck

JUDGEMENT   Simple justice allows danger to be avoided.
INNOCENCE   Innocent behaviour prevents the dangers of corruption.
AWARENESS   Simplicity allows the danger of moral superiority to be avoided.
EMOTION   Emotional balance avoids the extremes that lead to pain.
CREATIVITY   Expressing ideas simply avoids being misunderstood.
COMMUNICATION   Simple words prevent misunderstanding.
AMBITION   Simple progress allows pitfalls to be avoided.
SERVICE   Following orders in a straightforward way avoids the trap of self-importance.
NURTURE   Simplicity prevents care turning into discipline.
ECONOMY   Continued prudence allows dangerous speculation to be avoided.

NEUTRALITY   Simplicity in order to avoid danger.
REASON   Open-mindedness avoids the dead ends of logic.

10 line 3

———×———

Unfortunate

JUDGEMENT   Making a decision without enough evidence.
INNOCENCE   Independence without enough experience.
AWARENESS   Awareness without the necessary moral base.
EMOTION   Acting on a feeling that is not really sincere.
CREATIVITY   Expressing an idea that is unworthy.
COMMUNICATION   Arguing without enough relevant knowledge.
AMBITION   A challenge that is beyond abilities.
SERVICE   Accepting responsibility that is beyond capabilities. (This can be justified only in desperate circumstances.)
NURTURE   Loosening ties prematurely
ECONOMY   Taking a risk without adequate resources.
NEUTRALITY   Action without the necessary resources.
REASON   Drawing a conclusion that does not stand up to logical examination.

10 line 4

———□———

Eventual luck

JUDGEMENT   Careful deliberation allows a delicate decision to be made.
INNOCENCE   Danger, but caution allows eventual security.
AWARENESS   Great caution prevents a potentially dangerous loss of faith.
EMOTION   Caution allows a potentially painful feeling to be avoided.
CREATIVITY   Care allows a difficult idea to find expression.
COMMUNICATION   Careful words lead to the resolution of a potentially dangerous argument.

AMBITION Caution leads to success in a dangerous situation.

SERVICE Caution allows difficult tasks to be brought to completion.

NURTURE Great care can prevent a potentially damaging effect on a child.

ECONOMY A precarious situation, but caution can bring eventual profit.

NEUTRALITY A dangerous situation requiring caution.

REASON Attention to detail leads to the solution of a difficult problem.

10 line 5

─────□─────

A hazardous course

JUDGEMENT Hold on to ideals while remaining aware of the dangers of being dogmatic.

INNOCENCE Hold on to innocence, not forgetting the danger from outside.

AWARENESS Hold on to higher values while remaining aware of the dangers of moral superiority.

EMOTION Hold on to sincere feelings while remaining aware of their possible consequences.

CREATIVITY Express ideas sincerely while remaining aware of the dangers of pretentiousness.

COMMUNICATION Choose words carefully and remain aware of potential arguments.

AMBITION Make progress while remaining aware of danger.

SERVICE Remain dutiful while remaining aware of the dangers of self-importance.

NURTURE Remain caring while trying not to stifle.

ECONOMY Remain prudent while being aware of the dangers of meanness.

NEUTRALITY Continuing positively, but aware of danger.

REASON Hold on to logic while remaining aware of its pitfalls.

10 line 6

─────□─────

Very lucky if progress has been virtuous

JUDGEMENT A decision made with proper deliberation will surely be correct.

INNOCENCE Experiencing events in true innocence is real learning.

AWARENESS Moral correctness shows the certainty of a growth in awareness.

EMOTION Sincere conduct proves honest feeling.

CREATIVITY The expression of a truly original idea is surely art.

COMMUNICATION Honest words will surely find agreement.

AMBITION Honest effort will surely lead to a worthy goal.

SERVICE Devotion to duty shows a task will be completed.

NURTURE Unfaltering care will lead to real growth.

ECONOMY That which is acquired honestly is real wealth.

NEUTRALITY Positive action bringing positive results.

REASON A conclusion drawn with impeccable logic will surely be correct.

·HARMONY·

J

REASON — Logic and intuition used together to solve problems.

JUDGEMENT — Decisions are both firm and just.

NEUTRALITY — The decline of the negative in favour of the positive.

INNOCENCE — Both secure and receptive to learning.

ECONOMY — Economic stability permits generosity where it is needed.

AWARENESS — The goals of the ego and the higher self are the same.

NURTURE — Parents and children understand each other.

EMOTION — Feelings accord with practical considerations.

SERVICE — Happy to obey orders as part of a worthwhile cause.

CREATIVITY — Inspiration and talent are united.

AMBITION — Selfish goals are in accord with the general trend.

COMMUNICATION — True dialogue brings harmony.

Lucky – achievements are possible

11 line 1

———□———

Positive action is lucky

JUDGEMENT Fairness exemplified encourages others to be fair.
INNOCENCE Being willing to learn encourages others to do the same.
AWARENESS Personal growth encourages others to grow.
EMOTION Loving encourages other to love.
CREATIVITY Creative ideas inspire others.
COMMUNICATION Listening encourages others to listen.
AMBITION Enthusiasm is infectious.
SERVICE Pride in a job well done is an example to others.
NURTURE Children respond to a caring attitude by being caring themselves.
ECONOMY Others follow an example of prudent generosity.
NEUTRALITY Others follow positive examples.
REASON Reason inspires others to inventiveness.

11 line 2

———□———

JUDGEMENT Continued decisiveness requires empathy, firmness, attention to detail and a commitment not to abuse power.
INNOCENCE Continued security requires trust in superiors, an admission of ignorance, curiosity and the rejection of false ideals.
AWARENESS Continued growth requires discipline, constant self-examination, total acceptance and the surrender of the ego.
EMOTION Continued emotional balance requires empathy, self-restraint, openness and fidelity.
CREATIVITY Continued creativity requires self-belief, technical prowess, accessibility and acceptance of the mundane.
COMMUNICATION Continued dialogue requires a rejection of preconceived ideas, the ability to state the truth simply, diplomacy and a willingness to listen to anyone.
AMBITION Continued progress requires humility, endurance, preparedness and magnanimity in victory.

SERVICE Continued usefulness requires loyalty, hard work, meticulousness and genuine pride in being part of something worthwhile.
NURTURE Continued care requires tolerance, firmness, insight and mutual respect.
ECONOMY Continued economic stability requires prudence, planning, a lack of ostentation and generosity where is needed.
NEUTRALITY Sustained harmony requiring tolerance, resolve, foresight and unanimity.
REASON Continued inventiveness requires meticulous attention to method, the acceptance of simple ideas, practicality and a willingness to tackle what appears to be insoluble.

11 line 3

———□———

Continuing virtuously in this way is correct

JUDGEMENT Achieve as much as possible at this time, as its end is inevitable.
INNOCENCE Make the most of pleasurable experience because it will surely end.
AWARENESS Appreciate a period of higher awareness, as it will surely come to an end.
EMOTION Make the most of the time, because feelings are bound to change.
CREATIVITY Make the most of periods of creativity, as they are bound to come to an end.
COMMUNICATION Exchange as many ideas as possible at this time, as open dialogue will surely come to an end.
AMBITION Make as much progress as possible at this time, as it is bound to come to an end.
SERVICE Complete as many tasks as possible at this time, as circumstances must surely change.
NURTURE Make the most of mutual trust, as things will inevitably change.
ECONOMY Achieve as much as possible during a time of economic stability, as its end will surely come.
NEUTRALITY Making the most of the time.
REASON Achieve as much as possible at this time, as its end must surely come.

---

11 line 4

——×——

JUDGEMENT It is good to make no show of power in relationships with the powerless.
INNOCENCE It is best to make no show of purity in front of those who have been corrupted.
AWARENESS It is good to make no show of higher awareness in relationships with the materialistic.
EMOTION It is good to make no show of feelings in relationships with those who are emotionally cold.
CREATIVITY It is good to be modest about talent in honest relationships with those less talented.
COMMUNICATION It is good to forgo eloquence in important dialogues with those less eloquent.
AMBITION It is good to make no show of success in relationships with those less successful.
SERVICE It is good to make no show of loyalty in seeking the understanding of those who have no loyalties.
NURTURE It is good to come down to another's level in a caring relationship.
ECONOMY It is good to make no show of wealth in front of those who are less well-off.
NEUTRALITY Wanting better for those who are unaware of it.
REASON It is good to forgo cleverness in relationships with those are not likely to understand.

11 line 5

——×——

Contentment – very lucky

JUDGEMENT Accepting limits in the interest of fairness.
INNOCENCE Being more responsible.
AWARENESS Sacrifice for the growth of another.
EMOTION Suppressing feelings for the good of a relationship.
CREATIVITY Simplifying ideas for a wider appreciation.
COMMUNICATION Simplifying language for the sake of better communication.
AMBITION Sacrificing personal ambition for a greater goal.

SERVICE Accepting demotion for the common good.
NURTURE A loosening of protectiveness in order to stimulate growth.
ECONOMY Curbing greed for the common good.
NEUTRALITY Lowering standards for a common benefit.
REASON The acceptance of unproven facts for a wider understanding.

11 line 6

——×——

Unavoidable guilt

JUDGEMENT When a decision cannot be made, it is better to accept it than to use force.
INNOCENCE When innocence is lost, it is better to accept it as part of growth than to try to regain it.
AWARENESS When awareness is lost, acceptance is better than searching for it in vain.
EMOTION When emotion is dead, it is better to admit it than to pretend.
CREATIVITY When a period of creativity comes to an end, it is better to accept it than to search fruitlessly for ideas.
COMMUNICATION When open dialogue is no longer possible, it is better to retire gracefully than to argue.
AMBITION It is better to give in gracefully; fighting makes defeat worse.
SERVICE It is better to admit failure than to persist in a task that is beyond capabilities.
NURTURE When parental control is lost, it is better to let a child go its own way than to be over-protective.
ECONOMY When profitable times come to an end, it is better to face up to the situation than to waste resources trying to fight it.
NEUTRALITY At the end, surrender.
REASON When understanding is lost, it is better to accept it than to fight it with logic.

· GREED ·

REASON — Intelligence is used solely for gain.

JUDGEMENT — Sensible decision-making is ousted in favour of power for its own sake.

NEUTRALITY — The decline of the positive in favour of negativity.

INNOCENCE — Ignorance feeds on itself.

ECONOMY — Long-term security is abandoned in favour of quick profit.

AWARENESS — Higher awareness is abandoned in favour of ego-led behaviour.

NURTURE — Caring is wasted.

EMOTION — Emotional coldness means unhappiness.

SERVICE — Those who serve take no pride in their duties.

CREATIVITY — Creativity is ruled by commercialism.

AMBITION — Everyone is in competition.

COMMUNICATION — No one wants to listen to the truth.

Very difficult to remain virtuous

12 line 1

————×————

Luck – continuing in this way brings progress

JUDGEMENT Remaining fair-minded in the face of injustice is an example to others.
INNOCENCE Holding on to innocence in the face of temptation encourages others to do the same.
AWARENESS Holding on to higher values in difficult times is an inspiration to others.
EMOTION Emotional honesty in the face of selfishness is an example to others.
CREATIVITY Originality in mundane times is an example for others to follow.
COMMUNICATION Holding to the truth in the face of dishonesty shames others into doing the same.
AMBITION Resilience in times of difficulty is an example to others.
SERVICE Devotion to duty in times of difficulty is an example to others.
NURTURE Continuing to care in the face of heartache is an example the young will not forget.
ECONOMY Prudence amid a tide of opportunism is an example to others.
NEUTRALITY Remaining positive against a tide of negativity.
REASON Seeking understanding for its own sake is an example to others.

12 line 2

————×————

Luck in small matters

JUDGEMENT The self-defeating nature of power for its own sake stimulates the need for enlightened decisions.
INNOCENCE The lack of satisfaction derived from indulgence stimulates the need for recaptured innocence.
AWARENESS The empty nature of earthly satisfaction creates the need for higher awareness.
EMOTION The lack of satisfaction derived from selfish feelings stimulates the need for genuine emotion.
CREATIVITY The empty success of commercialism stimulates the need for genuine creativity.

COMMUNICATION Constant propaganda stimulates a yearning for the truth.
AMBITION The lack of satisfaction derived from selfish ambition stimulates a need for worthy endeavour.
SERVICE Neglect of duty creates a need for efficiency in those who loyally serve the greater cause.
NURTURE Letting the young have their head only brings them insecurity, thus stimulating a need for love.
ECONOMY The lack of security caused by opportunism creates a need for economic stability.
NEUTRALITY The self-destructive nature of negative goals stimulating the need for the positive.
REASON Logic that seeks simply to justify creates problems that stimulate the need for open-minded reasoning.

12 line 3

————×————

JUDGEMENT Those who make unfair decisions carry guilt inside.
INNOCENCE Those who are dishonest carry guilt inside.
AWARENESS Those who merely seek moral superiority are empty inside.
EMOTION Those who would deceive carry guilt inside.
CREATIVITY Those who achieve success through opportunism are aware of creative inadequacies.
COMMUNICATION Those who need to lie feel inadequate.
AMBITION Those who achieve success through unfair means feel inadequate inside.
SERVICE Those who are not up to a task know it inside.
NURTURE Inadequate parents know it inside.
ECONOMY Those who do not deserve wealth know it inside.
NEUTRALITY Those who are inadequate being secretly aware of it.
REASON Those who merely seek to appear clever are aware of their inadequacies inside.

12 line 4

———□———

No need for guilt

JUDGEMENT It is not wrong to make decisions for the highest motives. Those of like mind will understand.

INNOCENCE It is not wrong to admit ignorance. Others, who do not understand either, will be glad.

AWARENESS It is not wrong to act according to higher values. Those of like mind will understand.

EMOTION It is not wrong to be honest about feelings. Those who are sincere will understand.

CREATIVITY It is not wrong to act from purely artistic motives. Those of like mind will appreciate it.

COMMUNICATION It is not wrong to speak the truth. There are those who will agree.

AMBITION It is not wrong to harbour a worthy ambition. Those of like mind will understand.

SERVICE Devotion to duty for the sake of a greater cause is not wrong. Those who are loyal will understand.

NURTURE It is not wrong to act out of love for a child. They will eventually understand.

ECONOMY It is not wrong to make decisions in the light of long-term financial security. Those of like mind will see the sense in it.

NEUTRALITY Action for the highest motives.

REASON There is nothing wrong in seeking far-reaching conclusions. Those of like mind will understand.

12 line 5

———□———

Lucky for the virtuous

JUDGEMENT Those who merely seek power begin to destroy themselves. Only by being aware of danger can enlightened decisions be implemented.

INNOCENCE Acting in a headstrong way begins to lead to trouble. Remorse must be seen to be real.

AWARENESS Mere moral superiority begins to crumble in the face of true awareness. Ego-led behaviour must be constantly eradicated.

EMOTION Emotional coldness begins to crumble. New feelings must be handled with extreme care.

CREATIVITY The shallowness of commercialism begins to be seen, but the re-establishment of true originality must be handled with great care.

COMMUNICATION Liars begin to expose themselves with their own lies. In re-establishing the truth it is important to remain aware of dishonesty.

AMBITION Naked ambition begins to be seen for what it is. The introduction of more worthy goals must be handled with extreme caution.

SERVICE Dereliction of duty begins to become apparent. The re-establishment of discipline must be handled extremely carefully.

NURTURE Headstrong youngsters begin to feel insecure. Their return to the fold must be handled with great delicacy.

ECONOMY Greed begins to cause its own downfall. Economic recovery must be handled extremely carefully.

NEUTRALITY Negativity beginning to destroy itself.

REASON Unsound reasoning begins to crumble, but the re-establishment of open-mindedness must be handled with extreme care.

12 line 6

———□———

Eventual luck

JUDGEMENT The abuse of power comes to an end. The experience makes just decisions appreciated.

INNOCENCE A period of insecurity comes to an end. The experience makes security appreciated.

AWARENESS A period of darkness is over. The experience engenders appreciation of higher values.

EMOTION Emotional coldness gives way. This experience makes fresh new feelings appreciated.

CREATIVITY   A period of pure commercialism comes to an end. The experience makes originality appreciated.

COMMUNICATION   A period of suppression is over. This experience makes freedom of speech appreciated.

AMBITION   A period of struggle comes to an end. The experience makes mutual co-operation appreciated.

SERVICE   Dereliction of duty is exposed. This makes loyalty appreciated.

NURTURE   Remorseful offspring return to the fold. The experience engenders appreciation of care.

ECONOMY   A period of opportunism comes to an end. The experience makes financial stability appreciated.

NEUTRALITY   Negativity is over. The contrast makes positive values appreciated.

REASON   A period of ignorance comes to an end. The experience engenders appreciation of true understanding.

·SHARING·

REASON — Sharing ideas permits deep understanding.

JUDGEMENT — A communal sense of justice permits popular decisions.

INNOCENCE — Mutual trust permits shared pleasure.

NEUTRALITY — That which is in common permitting collective positive progress.

AWARENESS — Shared values permit a collective growth in awareness.

ECONOMY — Collective prudence permits widespread economic growth.

EMOTION — Shared feelings permit relationships to grow.

NURTURE — Mutual affection permits the growth of a child.

CREATIVITY — Ideas in common permit collective creativity.

SERVICE — Shared responsibility makes duties easy.

AMBITION — Mutual respect permits collective achievement.

COMMUNICATION — Interests in common permit mutual agreement.

Continuing in this way can lead to achievements – chances can be taken

13 line 1

———□———

Blameless

JUDGEMENT   There are basic principles in common.
INNOCENCE   The basis of friendship.
AWARENESS   Higher values find shared agreement.
EMOTION   The basis of a relationship.
CREATIVITY   Creative ideas find popular appreciation.
COMMUNICATION   Basic truth finds mutual agreement.
AMBITION   Shared goals bring unity.
SERVICE   Loyal to a common cause.
NURTURE   A natural bond between parent and child.
ECONOMY   Common economic interest
NEUTRALITY   Common values.
REASON   Shared understanding.

13 line 2

———×———

Eventual regret

JUDGEMENT   Adherence to dogma splits opinion.
INNOCENCE   Friends splitting into groups.
AWARENESS   Adherence to dogma that splits collective awareness.
EMOTION   Mutual feeling, interpreted differently.
CREATIVITY   Creativity that divides opinion.
COMMUNICATION   Splitting into factions.
AMBITION   Selfish aims that fuel competition.
SERVICE   A cause seen differently by followers and leaders.
NURTURE   Resentment caused by clinging to a role.
ECONOMY   Prudence that becomes selfishness.
NEUTRALITY   Division into factions.
REASON   Intellectual elitism.

13 line 3

———□———

JUDGEMENT   Differing opinions, which are kept hidden in the meantime.
INNOCENCE   Dishonesty, which is not uncovered until later.
AWARENESS   Hidden moral superiority; not perceived until later.
EMOTION   Selfishness, which is not apparent until later.
CREATIVITY   Pretentiousness, which is apparent only in retrospect.
COMMUNICATION   Dishonesty, the reasons for which are not discovered until later.
AMBITION   Naked ambition biding its time.
SERVICE   Disloyalty, which is not apparent until later.
NURTURE   Resentment, which does not surface until later.
ECONOMY   Hidden greed, discovered only at a later date.
NEUTRALITY   Hidden motives.
REASON   Lack of understanding, which is not apparent until later.

13 line 4

———□———

Lucky

JUDGEMENT   Differences of opinion expressed openly pave the way for future decisions.
INNOCENCE   Open antagonism; at least it is obvious what has to be done.
AWARENESS   It is easier to come to terms with an open rejection of higher values than it is to deal with moral superiority.
EMOTION   Open quarrels clear the air.
CREATIVITY   Originality that meets with a hostile reception.
COMMUNICATION   Argument in the open brings agreement closer.
AMBITION   Open competition means knowing what must be done.
SERVICE   Grievances that are expressed openly make them easier to deal with.
NURTURE   Open defiance shows what must be done.
ECONOMY   Greed that is obvious is easy to deal with.
NEUTRALITY   Open disagreement.

REASON Disagreement with theories, expressed openly, paves the way for future discoveries.

13 line 5

---□---

JUDGEMENT Mutual respect for justice permits the acceptance of decisions.
INNOCENCE Friendship that is not broken by disagreement.
AWARENESS Shared values permitting differences in belief to be overcome.
EMOTION Mutual feeling allowing petty differences to be overcome.
CREATIVITY Mutual respect that is not destroyed by criticism.
COMMUNICATION Shared principles allowing differences in opinion to be overcome.
AMBITION Mutual respect that belies competitive attitudes.
SERVICE Differences in rank that do not affect shared loyalty.
NURTURE The bond between parent and child permitting problems to be overcome.
ECONOMY Shared economic interests that override personal greed.
NEUTRALITY What is in common, allowing difficulties to be overcome.
REASON Intellectual equals who can overcome theoretical differences.

13 line 6

---□---

No need for guilt

JUDGEMENT Alliances for convenience rather than principle.
INNOCENCE Shallow friendships.
AWARENESS Shared values rather than shared beliefs.
EMOTION A relationship based on convenience more than emotion.
CREATIVITY Similarities in expression rather than ideas.
COMMUNICATION Merely getting on together.
AMBITION Comradeship among competitors.
SERVICE Comradeship for reasons of common rank.
NURTURE Acting for the sake of a relationship rather than for another's growth.
ECONOMY Friendship due to shared economic standing.
NEUTRALITY Gathering together for convenience.
REASON Shared knowledge rather than shared understanding.

_14_
·SUCCESS·

REASON — Intelligence used modestly, allowing great conclusions to be drawn.

JUDGEMENT — Just decisions engendering respect.

INNOCENCE — Purity inviting protection.

NEUTRALITY — Great power used properly.

ECONOMY — Prudence encouraging wealth.

AWARENESS — Power encouraging belief in others.

NURTURE — A great capacity for caring engendering mutual trust.

EMOTION — Openness inspiring real emotion.

SERVICE — Being happy in a position and therefore gaining the respect of those above and below and.

Unselfish ambitions breeding success.

CREATIVITY — A receptive attitude inviting great ideas.

COMMUNICATION — Modest words engendering sympathetic understanding.

AMBITION

Major achievements

14 line 1

———□———

With care, blame can be avoided

JUDGEMENT   Fair decisions now mean no recriminations later.
INNOCENCE   Innocence maintained now means no cause for regret in the future.
AWARENESS   Dealing with the ego now means no cause for regret in the future.
EMOTION   Being honest about feelings now, means no regrets later.
CREATIVITY   Maintaining artistic integrity now means no cause for regret in retrospect.
COMMUNICATION   Honest discussion now means no recriminations in the future.
AMBITION   Real effort now means no cause for regret in the future.
SERVICE   Devotion to duty now means no criticism later.
NURTURE   Unselfish care avoids resentment in the future.
ECONOMY   Prudence now avoids financial problems in the future.
NEUTRALITY   Attention to proper methods now avoiding problems in the future.
REASON   Faultless reasoning now means no cause for regret in the future.

14 line 2

———□———

Positive action is correct

JUDGEMENT   Objectivity allows important decisions to be made.
INNOCENCE   Admitting ignorance allows great learning.
AWARENESS   Honest self-examination permits growth.
EMOTION   Honesty allows feelings to be expressed.
CREATIVITY   Depth of talent allows great ideas to be expressed.
COMMUNICATION   Honest discussion allows words of wisdom to be spoken.
AMBITION   Reserves of strength allow great achievements.
SERVICE   Devotion to duty allows great tasks to be completed.
NURTURE   Genuine care permits substantial growth.
ECONOMY   Wealth allows investment.

NEUTRALITY   Resources are available for an undertaking.
REASON   Deep understanding allows profound conclusions to be drawn.

14 line 3

———□———

JUDGEMENT   Decisions made for the common good; those who merely seek power cannot do this.
INNOCENCE   Security; indulgent behaviour precludes this.
AWARENESS   A profound understanding of life; this is not possible when the ego is allowed to rule.
EMOTION   Shared emotion; this is not possible for selfish people.
CREATIVITY   Art that can be appreciated by all; mere self-indulgence cannot accomplish this.
COMMUNICATION   A real exchange of ideas; those who do not listen cannot participate in this.
AMBITION   Making progress for the common good; selfish ambition does not permit this.
SERVICE   To feel part of something worthwhile; this is not possible for those who are not loyal.
NURTURE   Mutual respect; this is not possible for those who will not let go.
ECONOMY   General wealth; greed does not permit such a situation.
NEUTRALITY   Using resources for the common good.
REASON   Deep understanding, which benefits all; mere cleverness cannot accomplish this.

14 line 4

———□———

Free of blame

JUDGEMENT   It is better to stand back from power struggles.
INNOCENCE   A reluctance to compete is not wrong.
AWARENESS   It is not wrong to withdraw from the competitiveness of life.
EMOTION   Any rivalry between partners should be avoided.

CREATIVITY Art is not an area for competition.
COMMUNICATION It is better not to try to shout the loudest.
AMBITION It is better to avoid rivalry.
SERVICE Competition is inappropriate in loyal service.
NURTURE Rivalry between parent and child should be avoided.
ECONOMY It is better not to compete financially.
NEUTRALITY Refusing to be competitive.
REASON It is better to avoid intellectual rivalry.

14 line 5

———×———

Lucky if motives are virtuous

JUDGEMENT Explaining decisions wins the respect of others.
INNOCENCE Simple honesty wins friends.
AWARENESS Sincere and unpretentious belief wins disciples.
EMOTION Explaining feelings wins sympathy.
CREATIVITY A lack of pretension wins admirers.
COMMUNICATION The truth expressed in a simple way wins sympathetic listeners.
AMBITION Dignified ambition wins respect.
SERVICE Simple devotion to duty wins respect.
NURTURE Empathy earns trust.
ECONOMY A lack of ostentation averts envy.
NEUTRALITY Accessibility and dignity winning respect.
REASON Simplifying difficult concepts wins the understanding of others.

14 line 6

———□———

Luck – growth

JUDGEMENT Enlightened decisions win support.
INNOCENCE Others feel the need to protect the innocent.
AWARENESS Under the protection of a higher power.
EMOTION Genuine feeling is protection in itself.
CREATIVITY Genuine ideas find their own expression.
COMMUNICATION Others want to hear the truth spoken.
AMBITION Success is willed by others.
SERVICE Superiors encourage abilities.
NURTURE Deep bonds nurture growth.
ECONOMY Outside influences protect economic interests.
NEUTRALITY Positive action with no opposition.
REASON Others encourage intellectual advances.

15
·MODESTY·

REASON — An unpretentious willingness to learn permits the gathering of great knowledge.

JUDGEMENT — Modesty engenders real respect and permits difficult decisions.

INNOCENCE — A modest attitude attracts friends.

NEUTRALITY — Simplicity that permits positive achievements.

ECONOMY — Modesty about economic success engenders admiration.

AWARENESS — Modesty permits a growth in awareness.

NURTURE — A trustful attitude in a parent makes it easier for a child to express itself.

EMOTION — Modesty is very attractive.

SERVICE — A modest attitude encourages trust and enables responsibility to be shouldered.

CREATIVITY — Unpretentious talent finds easier appreciation.

AMBITION — Being modest about abilities engenders respect and permits progress.

COMMUNICATION — Modest words encourage agreement.

Achievements are possible

15 line 1

――――×――――

Lucky – chances can be taken

JUDGEMENT Modesty and fair-mindedness permit difficult decisions to be made.
INNOCENCE Innocence, combined with modesty, permits new experience.
AWARENESS Faith expressed modestly permits higher awareness.
EMOTION The modest expression of honest feelings can engender mutual emotion.
CREATIVITY A lack of pretension, combined with modesty, permits great creativity.
COMMUNICATION Honesty and modesty together permit new depths of mutual understanding.
AMBITION Simple ability together with a worthwhile ambition permit chances to be taken.
SERVICE Modest devotion to duty permits the shouldering of responsibility.
NURTURING Trust and care creating a nurturing environment.
ECONOMY Modesty and prudence together permit speculation.
NEUTRALITY Modest simplicity permitting positive action.
REASON Modesty where intellectual abilities are concerned allows difficult problems to be tackled.

15 line 2

――――×――――

Following a virtuous course is lucky

JUDGEMENT Humility wins respect.
INNOCENCE Modesty is very appealing.
AWARENESS Simplicity brings awareness.
EMOTION Expressing feelings in a simple way shows depth of emotion.
CREATIVITY Unpretentious originality shows depth of talent.
COMMUNICATION Modest words win listeners.
AMBITION Being modest about abilities wins the support of others.
SERVICE Simple efficiency wins trust.
NURTURE Simple trust encourages a child's love.
ECONOMY A lack of ostentation prevents jealousy.

NEUTRALITY Modesty expressed in actions.
REASON Modesty makes original thought attractive to others.

15 line 3

――――▱――――

Lucky – achievements are possible

JUDGEMENT Fair-mindedness, combined with an attitude of humility, allows a difficult decision to be made.
INNOCENCE Innocence and modesty together permit new learning.
AWARENESS Faith and modesty together permit greater awareness.
EMOTION Honest feelings expressed modestly draw a commitment.
CREATIVITY Talent and a lack of pretension result in creative success.
COMMUNICATION Honesty, combined with modesty, allows agreement to be reached.
AMBITION Simple ability and a worthwhile goal result in success.
SERVICE Modesty, combined with devotion to duty, permits the completion of tasks.
NURTURE Care and trust permit real growth.
ECONOMY Prudence, combined with modesty, permits financial growth.
NEUTRALITY Modest simplicity permitting successful action.
REASON Intellectual modesty allows conclusions to be drawn.

15 line 4

――――×――――

Progress

JUDGEMENT Modesty in power permits far-reaching decisions.
INNOCENCE An attitude of humility opens up new avenues of experience.
AWARENESS Modesty opens up new areas of awareness.
EMOTION Modesty allows new feelings.
CREATIVITY Simplicity allows inspiration.
COMMUNICATION Modest words invoke new dialogue.
AMBITION Simple ability shows the way to a new goal.

SERVICE   Modesty opens up new areas of responsibility.
NURTURE   Trust permits new areas of growth.
ECONOMY   A lack of materialism opens up new areas of financial growth.
NEUTRALITY   Modesty opening up new areas.
REASON   Modesty about intellectual abilities opens up new areas of understanding.

15 line 5

———×———

Necessary action

JUDGEMENT   Regardless of modesty, decisions must be made.
INNOCENCE   Independent action is demanded, regardless of humility.
AWARENESS   Regardless of humility, it is necessary to act according to higher values.
EMOTION   A strong feeling requires expression, regardless of humility.
CREATIVITY   An idea requires expression, regardless of creative modesty.
COMMUNICATION   Regardless of modesty, it is necessary to tell the truth.
AMBITION   Progress must be made, regardless of humility.
SERVICE   Regardless of modesty, duties must be carried out.
NURTURE   Regardless of loving care, strong action is required.
ECONOMY   Regardless of modesty, financial muscle needs to be used.
NEUTRALITY   Positive action required in spite of modesty.
REASON   Reasoning abilities must be used, regardless of intellectual modesty.

15 line 6

———×———

JUDGEMENT   Humility expressed by adherence to principles.
INNOCENCE   Modesty expressed by being worthy of trust.
AWARENESS   Humility expressed in self-discipline.
EMOTION   Modesty expressed in emotional balance.
CREATIVITY   Modesty expressed in simple originality.
COMMUNICATION   Modesty expressed by the use of simple words.
AMBITION   Modesty expressed through self-discipline.
SERVICE   Modesty expressed in devotion to duty.
NURTURE   Humility expressed through true caring.
ECONOMY   Modesty expressed as prudence.
NEUTRALITY   Modesty expressing itself as discipline.
REASON   Modesty that expresses itself as intellectual discipline.

16
·ENTHUSIASM·

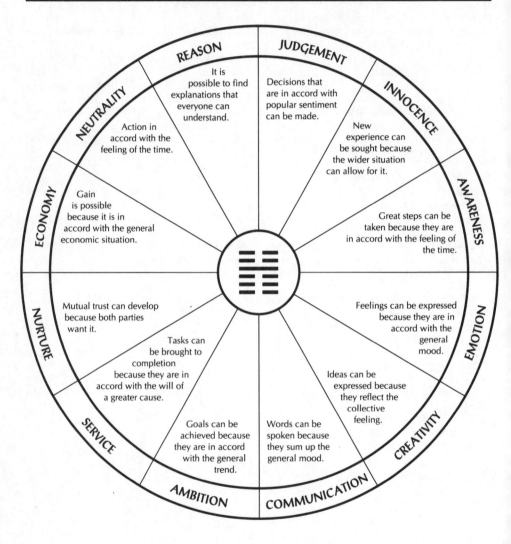

REASON

It is possible to find explanations that everyone can understand.

JUDGEMENT

Decisions that are in accord with popular sentiment can be made.

NEUTRALITY

Action in accord with the feeling of the time.

INNOCENCE

New experience can be sought because the wider situation can allow for it.

ECONOMY

Gain is possible because it is in accord with the general economic situation.

AWARENESS

Great steps can be taken because they are in accord with the feeling of the time.

NURTURE

Mutual trust can develop because both parties want it.

EMOTION

Feelings can be expressed because they are in accord with the general mood.

Tasks can be brought to completion because they are in accord with the will of a greater cause.

Ideas can be expressed because they reflect the collective feeling.

SERVICE

Goals can be achieved because they are in accord with the general trend.

Words can be spoken because they sum up the general mood.

CREATIVITY

AMBITION

COMMUNICATION

Put plans into action

16 line 1

———×———

Unfortunate

JUDGEMENT   Enjoying power for its own sake leads to errors of judgement.
INNOCENCE   Selfishness leads to loneliness.
AWARENESS   Egotistical enthusiasm leads to a loss of awareness.
EMOTION   One-sided emotion leads to pain.
CREATIVITY   Deliberate self-indulgence means artistic failure.
COMMUNICATION   Expressing a selfish point of view ends a meaningful dialogue.
AMBITION   Naked ambition leads to failure.
SERVICE   Allowing selfish motives to intrude means failure in a task.
NURTURE   Selfish motives destroy trust.
ECONOMY   Personal greed leads to loss.
NEUTRALITY   Over-enthusiasm inviting failure.
REASON   Simply demonstrating cleverness leads to mistakes.

16 line 2

———×———

Perseverance brings luck

JUDGEMENT   Not relying on dogma allows the seeds of change to be seen.
INNOCENCE   Not being carried away by enthusiasm allows the first signs of danger to be seen.
AWARENESS   Honest self-examination allows the first signs of egotism to be seen.
EMOTION   Genuine openness allows the first sign of changing feelings to be seen.
CREATIVITY   Open-mindedness allows the first sign of changing trends to be seen.
COMMUNICATION   Unopinionated listening allows the first signs of a change in mood to be seen.
AMBITION   Being honest about motives allows the first seeds of failure to be spotted.
SERVICE   Genuine pride in a job allows the first signs of laxity to be seen.
NURTURE   Genuine care allows the first sign of a problem to be seen.
ECONOMY   Genuine prudence allows the first signs of economic change to be seen.

NEUTRALITY   Resistance to general trends allowing changes to be observed.
REASON   Keeping a clear head allows minute errors to be spotted.

16 line 3

———×———

Hesitancy leads to guilt

JUDGEMENT   Waiting for a decision to become obvious leads to regret.
INNOCENCE   Waiting to be led means a lost opportunity.
AWARENESS   Waiting for guidance means lost growth.
EMOTION   Not acting on a feeling at the right time leads to regret.
CREATIVITY   Waiting for the right idea to come along means a lost creative opportunity.
COMMUNICATION   Waiting for the right moment to speak means a lost opportunity.
AMBITION   Hesitancy means an opportunity lost.
SERVICE   Not acting on initiative leads to regret.
NURTURE   Waiting for a child to do something for themselves leads to regret.
ECONOMY   Waiting for finances to right themselves leads to a lost opportunity.
NEUTRALITY   An opportunity lost through waiting for the right time.
REASON   Waiting for an obvious explanation means a lost opportunity.

16 line 4

———□———

Great achievements

JUDGEMENT   A positive attitude makes decisions easy and wins the respect of others.
INNOCENCE   A positive attitude induces happiness and makes others want to help.
AWARENESS   Being positive opens up the way to higher awareness, and engenders the support of others.
EMOTION   A positive attitude brings feelings into the open and encourages others to do the same.

CREATIVITY Positive thoughts lead to original ideas, which are appreciated by others.

COMMUNICATION Positive words lead to agreement and encourage others to be open.

AMBITION Positive action leads to achievements and makes others want to help.

SERVICE A positive attitude means that tasks can be completed and that others will want to help.

NURTURE A positive attitude means that trust will be reciprocated.

ECONOMY A positive attitude brings financial success and encourages others to be generous.

NEUTRALITY Enthusiasm making things happen.

REASON A positive attitude leads to correct conclusions, which others understand.

16 line 5

——×——

JUDGEMENT Decisions are not wanted and would be pointless anyway.

INNOCENCE A willingness to learn is ignored, but there is nothing of value to be learned anyway.

AWARENESS Awareness is stifled but would have been wasted anyway.

EMOTION Feelings are suppressed but would not have been appreciated anyway.

CREATIVITY Positive ideas are stifled, but it stops creative energies being wasted.

COMMUNICATION Positive words are ignored but would have been wasted anyway.

AMBITION Positive action is stifled, but it stops energy being wasted.

SERVICE Talents go unused, but at least they are not wasted.

NURTURE Growth is not possible, but at least care is not wasted.

ECONOMY Investment is not possible, but it stops money being wasted.

NEUTRALITY Stifled enthusiasm, but energy is not wasted.

REASON Reason is ignored but would not be understood anyway.

16 line 6

——×——

Correct, if not left too late

JUDGEMENT Decisions are wrong, but mistakes can be rectified before damage is done.

INNOCENCE Ideas are based on ignorance but can be rectified when the mistake is seen.

AWARENESS The ego is intruding, but this can be rectified before it is too late.

EMOTION Feelings are misdirected, but this can be changed before it results in pain.

CREATIVITY Ideas are not as good as they seem, but this can be corrected.

COMMUNICATION Words are misdirected, but it is possible to withdraw them before they cause misunderstanding.

AMBITION Actions are directed towards the wrong goal, but it is possible to correct the situation before problems arise.

SERVICE Abilities are being misused, but bringing attention to the fact can correct it.

NURTURE A caring attitude is misdirected, but this can be changed if it is spotted in time.

ECONOMY Investment in the wrong area; this can be corrected before loss is incurred.

NEUTRALITY Misdirected enthusiasm.

REASON A search for understanding is misdirected, but this can be changed before a wrong conclusion is drawn.

17
·FOLLOWING·

REASON — Following a line of reasoning is correct.

JUDGEMENT — Following principles is correct.

INNOCENCE — It is right to follow those who can be trusted.

NEUTRALITY — Following positive values.

AWARENESS — Following deeply held convictions is correct.

ECONOMY — It is correct to follow good sense.

EMOTION — It is right to follow an honest feeling.

NURTURE — Following natural instinct is correct.

CREATIVITY — It is right to follow where inspiration leads.

SERVICE — Following orders is correct.

AMBITION — It is right to follow.

COMMUNICATION — Following the line of conversation is correct.

Great achievements are possible

17 line 1

———□———

Perseverance brings luck

JUDGEMENT Listening to differing opinions while holding on to principles permits fair decisions.

INNOCENCE Going along with others while remaining sensible permits innocent pleasure.

AWARENESS Examining different beliefs permits higher awareness.

EMOTION Genuine empathy brings satisfaction.

CREATIVITY Swapping ideas without losing originality leads to creativity.

COMMUNICATION Listening to others while holding on to the truth allows agreements to be reached.

AMBITION Sharing problems without losing sight of a goal permits progress.

SERVICE Being flexible while retaining a sense of duty enables tasks to be completed.

NURTURE Empathy while remaining responsible allows growth to occur.

ECONOMY Examining new ideas while remaining prudent leads to a financial opportunity.

NEUTRALITY Being open to new input.

REASON Being open to new ideas while retaining a logical standpoint permits conclusions to be drawn.

17 line 2

———×———

JUDGEMENT A short-sighted perspective can prevent a wise decision.

INNOCENCE Clinging to old ways can deny maturity.

AWARENESS Ego-led behaviour can prevent higher awareness.

EMOTION Self-centred behaviour can deny real emotion.

CREATIVITY Refusing to take chances can deny creative potential.

COMMUNICATION Merely wishing to be heard can prevent meaningful dialogue.

AMBITION Merely being competitive can prevent real progress.

SERVICE Self-importance can obscure real worth.

NURTURE Discipline for its own sake can prevent real growth.

ECONOMY Meanness can deny real opportunities for financial growth.

NEUTRALITY A narrow perspective denying a greater purpose.

REASON Sticking to what is known can close the mind to great ideas.

17 line 3

———×———

Persevere

JUDGEMENT A short-sighted attitude should be abandoned. Following principles eases a decision.

INNOCENCE An old attitude must be left behind. Following trustfully brings security.

AWARENESS Ego-led behaviour must be denied. Following guidance brings a growth in awareness.

EMOTION Self-centred attitudes must be abandoned. Following real feelings brings satisfaction.

CREATIVITY An inhibiting attitude must be abandoned. Following inspiration beings artistic success.

COMMUNICATION Merely wanting to be heard is an attitude that must be abandoned. Following the flow of a conversation brings agreement.

AMBITION Competitiveness should be abandoned. Following allows a goal to be achieved.

SERVICE Self-importance should be left behind. Following orders gets a job done.

NURTURE Discipline for its own sake should be abandoned. Natural instincts nurture growth best.

ECONOMY Greed should be rejected. Following economic sense brings gain.

NEUTRALITY Discarding a narrow perspective.

REASON A blinkered attitude should be abandoned. Following a line of reasoning brings a solution.

17 line 4

———□———

Pretence is unlucky – genuine behaviour is not wrong

JUDGEMENT Following false values in order to gain control. Following real principles allows wiser decisions.

INNOCENCE Pretending in order to find approval; honesty brings real understanding of the situation.

AWARENESS Going through the motions; genuine awareness brings real clarity.

EMOTION Saying the right things to avoid pain; honesty brings out real emotion.

CREATIVITY Following trends to gain acceptance, but only originality is of real value.

COMMUNICATION Pretending to be open to gain acceptance, but real honesty brings deep understanding.

AMBITION Showing off ability to gain the respect of others, but real ability is enjoyed for its own sake.

SERVICE Being servile to find approval, but real devotion to duty brings an understanding of what must be done.

NURTURE Doing what is right for appearances, but real caring means empathy.

ECONOMY Generosity in order to gain acceptance; real generosity stems from financial wisdom.

NEUTRALITY Following positive values for ulterior motives.

REASON Following intellectual values only to gain acceptance; sincerity brings real insight.

17 line 5

———□———

Lucky

JUDGEMENT Just values that are worthy of dedication.

INNOCENCE Worthy of trust.

AWARENESS Higher values that should be followed.

EMOTION Feelings that are worth following.

CREATIVITY Artistic values that are worth following.

COMMUNICATION A dialogue worth following.

AMBITION Standards that are worth following.

SERVICE Orders that are worth obeying.

NURTURE It is good to follow instincts.

ECONOMY Economic standards that are worth following.

NEUTRALITY Positive values worthy of dedication.

REASON A line of reasoning that is worth following.

17 line 6

———×———

JUDGEMENT A decision made leads to more decisions.

INNOCENCE A new level of maturity means more to learn.

AWARENESS A new level of awareness demands even more self-discipline.

EMOTION As one feeling is satisfied, more appear.

CREATIVITY As one idea is completed, more appear, demanding expression.

COMMUNICATION An agreement made leads to more negotiation.

AMBITION A goal is achieved, but new goals appear.

SERVICE A task completed demands further loyalty.

NURTURE As one stage of growth is completed, even more care is required.

ECONOMY Economic success leading to further speculation.

NEUTRALITY Success leading to further effort.

REASON A problem solved brings more problems.

18
·REPAIR·

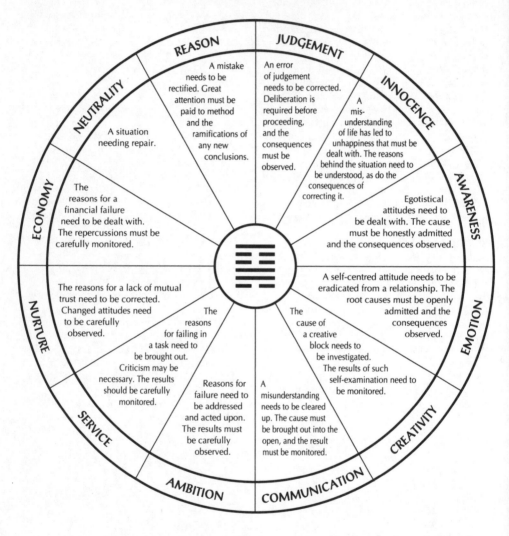

REASON — A mistake needs to be rectified. Great attention must be paid to method and the ramifications of any new conclusions.

JUDGEMENT — An error of judgement needs to be corrected. Deliberation is required before proceeding, and the consequences must be observed.

NEUTRALITY — A situation needing repair.

INNOCENCE — A misunderstanding of life has led to unhappiness that must be dealt with. The reasons behind the situation need to be understood, as do the consequences of correcting it.

ECONOMY — The reasons for a financial failure need to be dealt with. The repercussions must be carefully monitored.

AWARENESS — Egotistical attitudes need to be dealt with. The cause must be honestly admitted and the consequences observed.

NURTURE — The reasons for a lack of mutual trust need to be corrected. Changed attitudes need to be carefully observed.

SERVICE — The reasons for failing in a task need to be brought out. Criticism may be necessary. The results should be carefully monitored.

AMBITION — Reasons for failure need to be addressed and acted upon. The results must be carefully observed.

COMMUNICATION — A misunderstanding needs to be cleared up. The cause must be brought out into the open, and the result must be monitored.

CREATIVITY — The cause of a creative block needs to be investigated. The results of such self-examination need to be monitored.

EMOTION — A self-centred attitude needs to be eradicated from a relationship. The root causes must be openly admitted and the consequences observed.

Perseverance allows achievements

18 line 1

———×———

Danger, but eventual luck

JUDGEMENT   Received dogma has been allowed to taint decisions. Though dangerous, it is not too late to rectify the situation.
INNOCENCE   Following the example of others has been a corrupting influence. Though awkward, it is not too late to change the situation.
AWARENESS   Misguided   awareness; although it may be difficult to let go of old beliefs, it is still possible to change.
EMOTION   Residual bad feeling has been allowed to taint a relationship. Though difficult, it is possible to let go of these feelings.
CREATIVITY   Old ideas have led to a creative rut. Though difficult, it is possible to let go of them.
COMMUNICATION   Words from the past are marring an honest dialogue. Though difficult, the feelings that these words arouse must be dealt with.
AMBITION   Past failures are weakening the will to succeed. Though difficult, the reasons must be addressed.
SERVICE   Old ways are inadequate for a task. Though difficult, new methods can be learned.
NURTURE   Past misunderstandings are spoiling a relationship. Though painful, the situation can be resolved.
ECONOMY   Old debts are inhibiting financial growth. Though difficult, the situation can be turned around.
NEUTRALITY   Mistakes of the past affecting the present.
REASON   Old thinking is restricting understanding. Though difficult, the old ways can be eradicated.

18 line 2

———◻———

Be sensible

JUDGEMENT   Rectifying decisions that were made in moments of weakness requires tact.
INNOCENCE   Mistakes made through ignorance need to be dealt with sympathetically.
AWARENESS   Human weakness must be dealt with gently.
EMOTION   Emotional problems caused through human weakness must be dealt with very gently.
CREATIVITY   A lack of creativity caused by laziness needs to be dealt with carefully.
COMMUNICATION   A lack of communication caused through misunderstanding must be dealt with tactfully.
AMBITION   Weakness, as a reason for failure, needs to be examined sympathetically.
SERVICE   Personal reasons for a neglect of duty need to be dealt with carefully.
NURTURE   Human weakness must be dealt with sympathetically.
ECONOMY   Commitments made in moments of weakness must be handled with prudence.
NEUTRALITY   What has been damaged through weakness.
REASON   Rectifying mistakes due to human error requires delicacy.

18 line 3

A little at fault – no real need for guilt

JUDGEMENT   It is right to correct the mistakes of the past, though it should not be taken to extremes.
INNOCENCE   Making up for past mistakes should not be taken too far, though it is not wrong.
AWARENESS   Making up for a lack of faith in the past is correct, but should not be taken to extremes.
EMOTION   Making up for hurt caused in the past is correct, but should not be taken too far.
CREATIVITY   Trying to make up for a lack of creativity in the past is correct, but should not be taken to extremes.
COMMUNICATION   Trying to make up for what has been said in the past is correct, but should not be taken too far.
AMBITION   It is right to make up for past failures, but best not to take it too far.
SERVICE   It is right to make up for past neglect of duty but best not to go to extremes.
NURTURE   It is right to try to make up for past mistakes, though this should not be taken too far.

ECONOMY   It is right to want to make up for past financial mistakes, though this should not be taken to extremes.
NEUTRALITY   Rectifying past mistakes.
REASON   It is right to correct past mistakes, though this should not be taken too far.

18 line 4

―――×―――

Carrying on as before leads to regret

JUDGEMENT   It is foolish not to correct wrong decisions made in the past.
INNOCENCE   It is foolish not to correct past mistakes.
AWARENESS   It is foolish not to correct weaknesses that have their roots in the past.
EMOTION   It is foolish not to make up for pain caused in the past.
CREATIVITY   It is foolish to want to develop unworthy ideas from the past.
COMMUNICATION   It is foolish not to retract incorrect statements made in the past.
AMBITION   It is foolish not to examine the reasons for past failures.
SERVICE   It is foolish to ignore past neglect of duty.
NURTURE   It is foolish not to deal with behaviour that has its roots in the past.
ECONOMY   It is foolish not to pay off old debts.
NEUTRALITY   Not dealing with the problems of the past.
REASON   It is foolish to base calculations on incorrect conclusions drawn in the past.

18 line 5

―――×―――

Worthy of praise

JUDGEMENT   Correcting wrong decisions from the past meets with approval.
INNOCENCE   Admitting the mistakes of the past wins friends.
AWARENESS   Admitting past mistakes brings improved awareness.
EMOTION   Making up for the pain of the past wins love.
CREATIVITY   Eradicating worn-out ideas brings new creativity.
COMMUNICATION   Apologies for the past bring new listeners.

AMBITION   Learning from past failures encourages success.
SERVICE   Making up for past disloyalty meets with approval.
NURTURE   Making up for the mistakes of the past engenders a new trust.
ECONOMY   Paying off old debts encourages economic confidence.
NEUTRALITY   Making up for past mistakes.
REASON   Correcting past mistakes meets with general approval.

18 line 6

―――▢―――

JUDGEMENT   Forsaking power in order to make a far-reaching decision.
INNOCENCE   Taking a more mature view.
AWARENESS   Withdrawing from the world for the sake of a growth in awareness.
EMOTION   Forsaking a casual relationship for the sake of deeper feeling.
CREATIVITY   Leaving behind the mundane in favour of expressing bigger ideas.
COMMUNICATION   Shunning small talk in favour of saying something more important.
AMBITION   Withdrawing from petty competition in order to achieve higher goals.
SERVICE   Using experience in an advisory capacity.
NURTURE   Taking a broader view of a child's development.
ECONOMY   Withdrawing from a financial commitment because of bigger opportunities.
NEUTRALITY   Withdrawing to take a broader view of the situation.
REASON   Forsaking mere cleverness for a deeper understanding.

·THE RISE TO POWER·

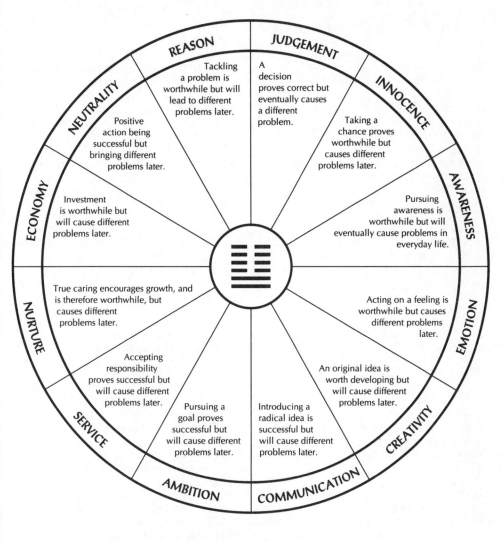

Reading clockwise from top, the wheel segments contain:

REASON — Tackling a problem is worthwhile but will lead to different problems later.

JUDGEMENT — A decision proves correct but eventually causes a different problem.

INNOCENCE — Taking a chance proves worthwhile but causes different problems later.

AWARENESS — Pursuing awareness is worthwhile but will eventually cause problems in everyday life.

EMOTION — Acting on a feeling is worthwhile but causes different problems later.

CREATIVITY — An original idea is worth developing but will cause different problems later.

COMMUNICATION — Introducing a radical idea is successful but will cause different problems later.

AMBITION — Pursuing a goal proves successful but will cause different problems later.

SERVICE — Accepting responsibility proves successful but will cause different problems later.

NURTURE — True caring encourages growth, and is therefore worthwhile, but causes different problems later.

ECONOMY — Investment is worthwhile but will cause different problems later.

NEUTRALITY — Positive action being successful but bringing different problems later.

Achievements through perseverance –
unlucky later

---

19 line 1

———□———

Continuing in this way brings luck

JUDGEMENT Decisions find general agreement.
INNOCENCE Pleasure and learning are the same thing.
AWARENESS Higher values and practical considerations are in accord.
EMOTION Feelings are leading in the same direction as events.
CREATIVITY Original ideas are in accord with trends.
COMMUNICATION Words are in accord with general feeling.
AMBITION Personal ambitions are in accord with general trends.
SERVICE The goals of followers and leaders are the same.
NURTURE Parents and children want the same thing.
ECONOMY Personal finances are in accord with the general economic trend.
NEUTRALITY Positive action in accord with the time
REASON Logic and intuition point in the same direction.

19 line 2

———□———

Lucky – inevitable progress

JUDGEMENT Decisions are fair, even if others do not agree.
INNOCENCE Innocence is worth hanging on to, even if others do not understand.
AWARENESS Awareness is worth pursuing, even when practical considerations make it difficult.
EMOTION It is worth being honest about feelings, even when the situation is difficult.
CREATIVITY Original ideas are worthwhile, even if they are not appreciated.
COMMUNICATION The truth is worthwhile, even if no one wants to listen.
AMBITION Ambitions are worthwhile, even if they go against the general trend.
SERVICE Devotion to duty is worthwhile, even if others do not understand.
NURTURE True caring is worthwhile, even if children do not understand.

ECONOMY Sensible investment is worthwhile, even against the general economic trend.
NEUTRALITY Positive action in adverse circumstances.
REASON Inventiveness is worthwhile, even when it is not understood.

19 line 3

———×———

Addressing a fault is correct – doing nothing is a mistake

JUDGEMENT Power for its own sake achieves nothing but if this fault is addressed, it is forgivable.
INNOCENCE Self-indulgence achieves nothing, but it is forgivable if the fault is addressed.
AWARENESS Moral superiority achieves nothing, but if this fault is addressed, it is forgivable.
EMOTION Impulsiveness achieves nothing, but if this fault is addressed, it is forgivable.
CREATIVITY Pretentiousness achieves nothing, but it is forgivable if the fault is addressed.
COMMUNICATION Nothing is achieved by talking for its own sake, but it is forgivable if addressed as a fault.
AMBITION Competitiveness for its own sake achieves nothing, but if this fault is addressed, it is forgivable.
SERVICE Neglect of duty achieves nothing, but it is forgivable if the fault is addressed.
NURTURE An inflexible attitude distorts growth, but if this fault is addressed, it is forgivable.
ECONOMY Nothing is achieved by extravagance, but if this fault is addressed, it is forgivable.
NEUTRALITY Unchecked positive action achieving nothing.
REASON Mere cleverness achieves nothing but is forgivable if seen as a fault.

19 line 4

————×————

Blameless

JUDGEMENT It is worth listening to any advice.
INNOCENCE Something of value can be learned from anyone.
AWARENESS There is nothing wrong in simple faith.
EMOTION There is nothing wrong with simple emotion.
CREATIVITY There is nothing wrong with a simple idea.
COMMUNICATION It is worth listening to anyone.
AMBITION It is not wrong to take even the smallest steps.
SERVICE It is not wrong to accept any help.
NURTURE It is not wrong to listen to a child.
ECONOMY It is not wrong to make small economies.
NEUTRALITY Positive help obtained from any source.
REASON It is not wrong to be open-minded.

19 line 5

————×————

Lucky – blameless

JUDGEMENT Advice should be accepted or rejected according to its merits.
INNOCENCE Others should be judged on their sincerity.
AWARENESS Guidance should be judged on its worth.
EMOTION Feelings should be judged on their sincerity.
CREATIVITY Ideas should be judged according to their worth.
COMMUNICATION Words should be judged on the meaning behind them.
AMBITION Help should be accepted only when and where it is needed.
SERVICE Help should be sought when necessary.
NURTURE Outside influences should be judged on their appropriateness.
ECONOMY Financial advice should be judged on its record.

NEUTRALITY Knowing how much outside influence to allow.
REASON Received knowledge should be judged on its merit.

19 line 6

————×————

Lucky – correct

JUDGEMENT The approval of the wise.
INNOCENCE The approval of protectors.
AWARENESS The approval of a sage.
EMOTION The approval of the emotionally experienced.
CREATIVITY The approval of a master.
COMMUNICATION The approval of the diplomat.
AMBITION The approval of previous winners.
SERVICE The approval of the old soldier.
NURTURE The approval of experienced parents.
ECONOMY The approval of the prudent.
NEUTRALITY The approval of experience.
REASON The approval of the intelligent.

·CONCENTRATION·

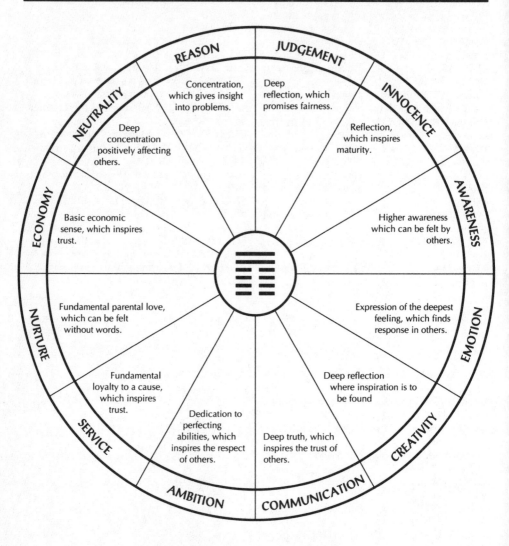

Continue with dignity

20 line 1

———×———

Excusable in those who do not know better

JUDGEMENT Bias is not necessarily wrong, but if acting on enlightened principles, it is.

INNOCENCE It is not wrong to look at things selfishly, but it is wrong if maturity is what is desired.

AWARENESS Moral superiority is not necessarily wrong; it becomes wrong only when a growth in awareness is the goal.

EMOTION Selfish feelings are not really wrong, they become so only when mutual emotion is what is sought.

CREATIVITY A lack of originality does not really matter but is a real flaw if looking for true creativity.

COMMUNICATION Occasional white lies are unimportant, but they become critical if honest agreement is what is sought.

AMBITION Selfish ambition is forgivable but becomes wrong if aiming for a truly worthy goal.

SERVICE Self-importance does not always matter, but it is wrong if truly devoted to a cause.

NURTURE Expecting due respect is not wrong, but it becomes wrong if real nurture is the goal.

ECONOMY Wanting profit for its own sake is not necessarily wrong, but it is wrong if widespread financial stability is the goal.

NEUTRALITY A short-sighted view.

REASON It is not necessarily wrong to want to prove intellectual superiority, but it is wrong if real understanding is the goal.

20 line 2

———×———

Persevere in small matters

JUDGEMENT A narrow perspective is adequate for obvious decisions.

INNOCENCE An immature attitude does not matter in childish situations.

AWARENESS Ego-led attitudes are adequate for materialistic situations.

EMOTION Selfish feelings are excusable where they do not affect others.

CREATIVITY A lack of originality does not matter if that is all that is required.

COMMUNICATION Talking for its own sake is excusable where there is no great agreement to be sought.

AMBITION Ambition is understandable in a strictly competitive situation.

SERVICE Self-importance does not matter where it is not a question of loyalty to a cause.

NURTURE Discipline for its own sake is excusable where it is not a question of nurturing growth.

ECONOMY Greed is understandable in the short term.

NEUTRALITY A narrow perspective adequate for small matters.

REASON A narrow understanding is adequate for small problems.

20 line 3

———×———

JUDGEMENT A decision requires honesty about personal values.

INNOCENCE A situation requires a more mature view.

AWARENESS Inner truth decides which way to go.

EMOTION The way to make a decision is to be entirely honest about feelings.

CREATIVITY An idea should be judged entirely on personal artistic values.

COMMUNICATION Honesty should decide the course of an argument.

AMBITION An honest assessment of abilities should determine goals.

SERVICE Real loyalties should be examined before accepting responsibility.

NURTURE The true nature of a relationship should be examined before a decision is made.

ECONOMY Personal finances should be examined minutely before deciding upon a speculation.

NEUTRALITY Self-examination before a decision.

REASON Complete objectivity should decide the way to tackle a problem.

20 line 4

—————×—————

JUDGEMENT A wider perspective makes opinions welcome.
INNOCENCE True innocence is valued by others.
AWARENESS Higher values are contemplated by others.
EMOTION Looking at feelings from a higher perspective is of value to a relationship.
CREATIVITY A wider perspective brings influential ideas.
COMMUNICATION Words from a higher perspective find a respectful audience.
AMBITION The ability to see higher goals makes abilities respected.
SERVICE Acting out of loyalty to a greater cause inspires respect.
NURTURE Being able to see growth from a higher perspective shows where care is needed.
ECONOMY Seeing a broader economic trend shows where speculation should be concentrated.
NEUTRALITY A greater perspective allowing influence.
REASON Deep understanding of a problem gives a right to suggest solutions.

20 line 5

—————□—————

Blameless

JUDGEMENT There is nothing wrong in making decisions based on the highest personal values.
INNOCENCE It is not wrong to enjoy innocence.
AWARENESS There is nothing wrong in acting from inner truth.
EMOTION It is not wrong to express honest feelings.
CREATIVITY It is not wrong to base creativity on personal artistic values.
COMMUNICATION It is not wrong to express a personal truth.
AMBITION It is not wrong to cultivate personal abilities.
SERVICE It is not wrong to contemplate where loyalties truly lie.

NURTURE It is not wrong to try to understand.
ECONOMY It is not wrong to want personal financial growth.
NEUTRALITY Contemplation of personal values.
REASON It is not wrong to want a deeper understanding.

20 line 6

—————□—————

Correct

JUDGEMENT There is nothing wrong in making enlightened decisions.
INNOCENCE It is not wrong to resist corruption.
AWARENESS There is nothing wrong in acting on higher values.
EMOTION It is not wrong to respond to honest emotion.
CREATIVITY It is not wrong to base creativity on the highest artistic values.
COMMUNICATION It is not wrong to engage in honest dialogue.
AMBITION It is not wrong to seek worthy goals.
SERVICE It is not wrong to be loyal to a worthy cause.
NURTURE It is not wrong to want the best for children.
ECONOMY It is not wrong to want general financial growth.
NEUTRALITY Contemplation of general values.
REASON It is not wrong to want to find deep understanding.

21
·DECISIVENESS·

- REASON — It is a good time to draw logical conclusions.
- JUDGEMENT — It is a good time to draw the threads of an argument together and to make a decision.
- INNOCENCE — It is a good time to decide which way to go.
- NEUTRALITY — Administering justice.
- AWARENESS — It is a good time to act on the higher truth of a situation.
- ECONOMY — It is a good time to make financial decisions.
- EMOTION — it is a good time to draw feelings out into the open.
- NURTURE — It is a good time to administer discipline.
- CREATIVITY — It is a good time to bring ideas together into a creative whole.
- SERVICE — It is a good time to decide where loyalties lie.
- COMMUNICATION — It is a good time to bring opposing ideas into agreement.
- AMBITION — It is a good time to choose a goal worth pursuing.

Achievements are possible through administering justice

21 line 1

———□———

Avoiding blame

JUDGEMENT Small errors of judgement that can be corrected.
INNOCENCE Forgivable mistakes.
AWARENESS Trivial, ego-led behaviour that can be corrected.
EMOTION Self-centred feelings that can be eradicated.
CREATIVITY Slight pretentiousness that can be corrected.
COMMUNICATION Trivial dishonesty that can be rectified.
AMBITION Over-ambition that can be curbed.
SERVICE Self-importance that can be corrected.
NURTURE It is possible to make up for a lack of care.
ECONOMY Financial errors of judgement that can be rectified.
NEUTRALITY Errors that can be corrected.
REASON Small mistakes that can be rectified.

21 line 2

———×———

Correct

JUDGEMENT Changing a decision, even though it may not meet with complete agreement.
INNOCENCE Experiencing justifiable punishment, even though it may feel too severe.
AWARENESS Correcting ego-led behaviour, even if it is taken too far.
EMOTION Curbing selfish feelings, even though it may seem out of character.
CREATIVITY Eradicating pretentiousness, even though it may mean spoiling an idea.
COMMUNICATION Apologizing, even though it may seem unnecessary.
AMBITION Eradicating selfish ambition, even at the expense of progress.
SERVICE Punishment for neglect of duty, even though it may seem too severe.
NURTURE Disciplining bad habits, even though it may seem too severe.
ECONOMY Pulling out of a venture, even though it may mean a loss.

NEUTRALITY Correction, even at the expense of going too far.
REASON Correcting a mistake, even at the expense of a loss of understanding.

21 line 3

———×———

A little regret, but still correct

JUDGEMENT A necessary decision, inspiring some resentment.
INNOCENCE Resentment at a punishment.
AWARENESS Awareness exposing a fundamental character flaw.
EMOTION Honesty exposing bad feeling underneath.
CREATIVITY Re-examination of an idea, showing it to be flawed.
COMMUNICATION Decisive conversation, throwing up resentment.
AMBITION Finding underlying competitiveness.
SERVICE Orders exposing deep-rooted disloyalty.
NURTURE Discipline causing resentment.
ECONOMY Necessarily pulling out of a financial commitment and causing loss all round.
NEUTRALITY Justice causing resentment.
REASON Correcting a mistake that exposes fundamental problems.

21 line 4

———□———

Luck, with perseverance

JUDGEMENT A very difficult decision requiring firm adherence to principles.
INNOCENCE A very difficult situation requiring great resistance to temptation.
AWARENESS A problematic situation requiring firm adherence to higher values.
EMOTION A confrontation with hardened feelings requiring great emotional courage.
CREATIVITY The correction of a flawed idea requiring great artistic integrity.
COMMUNICATION A bitter argument requiring firm adherence to the truth.
AMBITION A very competitive situation requiring great ability.

TWELVE CHANNELS OF THE I CHING

SERVICE   A very demanding task requiring great loyalty.
NURTURE   Deep-rooted problems that require very firm discipline.
ECONOMY   Encountering deep-rooted economic problems that require great prudence.
NEUTRALITY   Justice requiring great firmness.
REASON   A difficult problem requiring unfaltering reasoning.

21 line 5

———×———

Dangerous, but perseverance is correct

JUDGEMENT   Decisions are obvious but difficult to implement. Impartiality is required.
INNOCENCE   A situation is simple to understand, but hard to live with. Great restraint is required.
AWARENESS   A higher significance is obvious but difficult to come to terms with. Great faith is required.
EMOTION   Feelings are basic but hard to express. Great care is required.
CREATIVITY   Ideas are simple but difficult to express. Careful artistic judgement is required.
COMMUNICATION   Arguments are simple but hard to put across. Great tact is required.
AMBITION   The way to progress is obvious, but hard to achieve. Great perseverance is required.
SERVICE   Orders are simple but difficult to carry out. Devotion to duty is required.
NURTURE   Problems are straightforward but hard to deal with. Great care is required.
ECONOMY   Profit is simple in theory but harder in practice.
NEUTRALITY   Problems requiring strict impartiality.
REASON   Problems are easy to solve in theory but hard in practice. A deep understanding is necessary.

21 line 6

———□———

Unfortunate

JUDGEMENT   Repeated wrong decisions.
INNOCENCE   Repeated foolish behaviour.
AWARENESS   Repeated ego-led behaviour.
EMOTION   Persistent selfishness.
CREATIVITY   Repeated pretentiousness.
COMMUNICATION   Repeated dishonesty.
AMBITION   Consistent naked ambition.
SERVICE   Repeated disloyalty.
NURTURE   Consistent lack of care.
ECONOMY   Repeated wastes of money.
NEUTRALITY   Incorrigible faults.
REASON   Repeated mistakes.

22
·FORM·

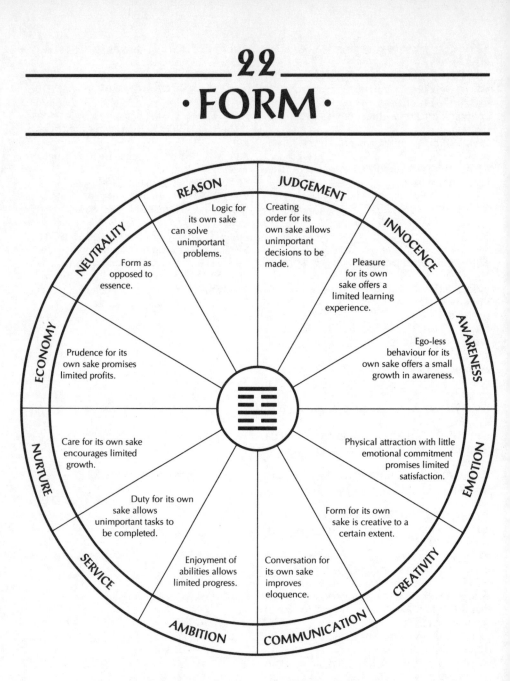

REASON — Logic for its own sake can solve unimportant problems.

JUDGEMENT — Creating order for its own sake allows unimportant decisions to be made.

NEUTRALITY — Form as opposed to essence.

INNOCENCE — Pleasure for its own sake offers a limited learning experience.

AWARENESS — Ego-less behaviour for its own sake offers a small growth in awareness.

ECONOMY — Prudence for its own sake promises limited profits.

EMOTION — Physical attraction with little emotional commitment promises limited satisfaction.

NURTURE — Care for its own sake encourages limited growth.

CREATIVITY — Form for its own sake is creative to a certain extent.

SERVICE — Duty for its own sake allows unimportant tasks to be completed.

AMBITION — Enjoyment of abilities allows limited progress.

COMMUNICATION — Conversation for its own sake improves eloquence.

Persevere in small matters

22 line 1

—▫—

JUDGEMENT Electing not to make an uninformed decision.
INNOCENCE Choosing to learn through experience.
AWARENESS Choosing to grow through simplicity.
EMOTION Choosing to be emotionally honest.
CREATIVITY Starting an idea from scratch.
COMMUNICATION Choosing to make a point through logical argument.
AMBITION Choosing to make progress through practical abilities.
SERVICE Electing to tackle a task methodically.
NURTURE Deciding to try to understand a child.
ECONOMY Deciding not to be ostentatious.
NEUTRALITY Rejecting easy options.
REASON Choosing to look for solutions through deep understanding.

22 line 2

——✕——

JUDGEMENT Cultivating the trappings of power.
INNOCENCE Showing off.
AWARENESS Cultivating grace for its own sake.
EMOTION Exaggerating feelings.
CREATIVITY Beauty on the surface.
COMMUNICATION Trying to appear eloquent.
AMBITION The trappings of success.
SERVICE Self-importance.
NURTURE Trying to appear caring.
ECONOMY Being ostentatious.
NEUTRALITY Attention to what is on the surface.
REASON Enjoying being clever.

22 line 3

——▫——

Perseverance brings luck

JUDGEMENT Fairness exemplified but requiring constant perseverance.

INNOCENCE Feelings of pure pleasure, but they cannot last forever.
AWARENESS The beauty of unfolding awareness, but this should not be sought for its own sake.
EMOTION A beautiful feeling, but these feelings should not be chased.
CREATIVITY A beautiful idea, but beauty should not be cultivated for its own sake.
COMMUNICATION Eloquent speech, but do not allow it to develop for its own sake.
AMBITION Confidence; not to be sought for its own sake.
SERVICE Rightfully proud but requiring constant devotion to duty.
NURTURE The rewards of caring; these feelings should not be sought for their own sake.
ECONOMY An easy profit, but it cannot be like this all the time.
NEUTRALITY Perfection on the surface.
REASON Beautifully logical, but logic should not be applied for that reason alone.

22 line 4

——✕——

JUDGEMENT A choice between power and fairness; the answer will become obvious.
INNOCENCE A choice between pleasure and learning; what to do will become obvious.
AWARENESS Moral superiority or true awareness? The way will become clear.
EMOTION Short-term satisfaction or real commitment? The right way will show itself.
CREATIVITY A choice between form and true originality; ideas will present themselves.
COMMUNICATION Pleasant conversation or meaningful dialogue? The direction will become apparent.
AMBITION Personal ambition or concentration on improving abilities? The way to progress will become clear.
SERVICE Self-importance or real service? The choice will become obvious.
NURTURE The rewards of parenthood or real nurture? There will be only one way.
ECONOMY Easy profit or steady financial growth? The choice should be obvious.
NEUTRALITY Form or substance
REASON A choice between applied logic and true understanding. The answer will become clear.

JUDGEMENT Dedication to principles may be seen as powerlessness but is ultimately shown to be right.

INNOCENCE Resisting temptation may be ridiculed but ultimately wins respect.

AWARENESS Higher values may be derided but prove correct in the end.

EMOTION Being honest about a feeling may cause problems but is for the best in the end.

CREATIVITY Originality may be scorned but its value is seen in the end.

COMMUNICATION The truth may be derided but its validity is proved in the end.

AMBITION Strength may cause resentment but is ultimately respected.

SERVICE Loyalty to a cause may be derided but ultimately proves correct.

NURTURE True caring may not be appreciated but its value is seen in the end.

ECONOMY Prudence may be seen as meanness but is ultimately shown to be the right way.

NEUTRALITY Clinging to positive values.

REASON Holding a position may seem impractical but ultimately proves correct.

JUDGEMENT It is not wrong to follow simple principles.

INNOCENCE There is nothing wrong in innocence.

AWARENESS There is nothing wrong in simplicity.

EMOTION There is nothing wrong in honest feeling.

CREATIVITY There is nothing wrong in simplicity.

COMMUNICATION It is not wrong to state something simply.

AMBITION There is nothing wrong in simply being strong.

SERVICE There is nothing wrong in simple devotion to duty.

NURTURE There is nothing wrong in simple caring.

ECONOMY It is not wrong to be prudent.

NEUTRALITY The beauty of simplicity.

REASON There is nothing wrong in simple logic.

23
· DISINTEGRATION ·

REASON — Deep understanding will receive no attention at this time.

JUDGEMENT — Enlightened decisions will not be understood at this time.

INNOCENCE — Purity will be ridiculed at this time.

NEUTRALITY — A time of overwhelming negativity.

ECONOMY — Prudence will not be understood at this time.

AWARENESS — Higher awareness will be scorned at this time.

NURTURE — True caring will not be appreciated at this time.

EMOTION — Honest emotion will not be reciprocated at this time.

SERVICE — Loyalty will not be appreciated at this time.

CREATIVITY — Creative ideas will not be appreciated at this time.

AMBITION — Worthy goals are not achievable at this time.

COMMUNICATION — Open dialogue is not possible at this time.

Do not act

23 line 1

———×———

Unlucky – perseverance brings a downfall

JUDGEMENT Principles are being secretly undermined; nothing can be done.
INNOCENCE Others secretly ridicule innocence, and nothing can be done.
AWARENESS Others secretly see higher awareness as threatening; nothing can be done.
EMOTION Genuine emotion is a pretence; nothing can be done to change the situation.
CREATIVITY Creative ideas are secretly scorned; nothing can be done.
COMMUNICATION A breakdown of communication due to dishonesty; nothing can be done about it.
AMBITION Failure due to the underhand methods of others; nothing can be done about it.
SERVICE Loyalty is being gradually undermined; nothing can be done.
NURTURE A caring attitude is unappreciated; nothing can be done to change it.
ECONOMY Economic stability is being gradually undermined; nothing can be done about it.
NEUTRALITY Foundations being undermined.
REASON Deep understanding is secretly scorned; nothing can be done.

23 line 2

———×———

Unlucky – perseverance leads to a downfall

JUDGEMENT Decisions are openly challenged; holding to this position means a loss of power.
INNOCENCE Innocence is openly ridiculed; fighting leads to insecurity.
AWARENESS Higher values are directly challenged; perseverance means a loss of awareness.
EMOTION Honest emotion is openly rejected; great pain results from perseverance.
CREATIVITY Genuine creativity is openly criticized, holding to this position leads to a loss of credibility.
COMMUNICATION Hostility greets the truth; holding to this position leads to a breakdown of communication.
AMBITION Rivals are in the open; continued rivalry means inevitable loss.
SERVICE Superiors are in opposition; perseverance means duties cannot be carried out.
NURTURE Care is openly rejected; continuing in this way leads to permanent resentment.
ECONOMY Debts can no longer be ignored; great loss threatens if they are not settled.
NEUTRALITY Threats showing themselves openly.
REASON Reason is openly challenged; logical arguments will be lost.

23 line 3

———×———

Avoiding blame

JUDGEMENT Openly criticizing incorrect decisions is not wrong.
INNOCENCE Open defiance is not wrong.
AWARENESS Speaking up from a higher perspective is not wrong.
EMOTION Expressing an opposing feeling is not wrong.
CREATIVITY Flouting convention is not wrong.
COMMUNICATION It is not wrong to disagree openly.
AMBITION An open challenge is not wrong.
SERVICE Openly criticizing superiors is not wrong.
NURTURE Openly questioning behaviour is not wrong.
ECONOMY It is not wrong to go against an economic trend.
NEUTRALITY Open opposition.
REASON Open opposition to ignorance is not wrong.

TWELVE CHANNELS OF THE I CHING

23 line 4

——×——

Unlucky

JUDGEMENT   A loss of control cannot be avoided.
INNOCENCE   Insecurity cannot be avoided.
AWARENESS   Realities cannot be avoided.
EMOTION   There is no escape from emotional pain.
CREATIVITY   The mundane cannot be avoided.
COMMUNICATION   A breakdown of communication cannot be avoided.
AMBITION   Failure cannot be avoided.
SERVICE   Clashes with superiors cannot be avoided.
NURTURE   Hostility is inevitable.
ECONOMY   Loss cannot be avoided.
NEUTRALITY   Inevitable loss.
REASON   Ignorance cannot be avoided.

23 line 5

——×——

All-round progress

JUDGEMENT   Control is regained. This is beneficial for all.
INNOCENCE   Persecutors turn protectors. This benefits all.
AWARENESS   Higher awareness finds acceptance. This is good for all.
EMOTION   Genuine feeling is no longer rejected. Everyone is happy.
CREATIVITY   Creative ideas no longer meet with opposition. This benefits all.
COMMUNICATION   The opposition starts to listen. This is good for everyone.
AMBITION   Rivals yield. This is of benefit to everyone.
SERVICE   The opposition of superiors gives way. This helps everyone.
NURTURE   Care is now appreciated. This brings parent and child together.
ECONOMY   Creditors relax the pressure. This benefits all.
NEUTRALITY   Inferior elements voluntarily giving up.
REASON   The ignorant yield to reason. This is good for everyone.

23 line 6

——□——

Virtue brings rewards

JUDGEMENT   Enlightened decisions receive support. The opposition destroys itself.
INNOCENCE   Innocence is protected. Those who would seek to destroy it, destroy themselves.
AWARENESS   Higher awareness is given a voice. Non-believers are destroyed by their own arguments.
EMOTION   Honest emotion is reciprocated. Self-centred feelings are shown for what they are.
CREATIVITY   Creative ideas are appreciated. The mundane is exposed in its shallowness.
COMMUNICATION   The truth is believed. Liars destroy their own creditability.
AMBITION   Worthy ambition is successful. Unprincipled rivals destroy themselves.
SERVICE   Devotion to duty is appreciated. Those less loyal are seen for what they are.
NURTURE   A bond is repaired. Lesser feelings fade away.
ECONOMY   Economic balance is restored. The dishonest ruin themselves.
NEUTRALITY   The positive asserting itself while the negative destroys itself.
REASON   The power of reason is restored. The ignorant destroy their own arguments.

24

·RETURN·

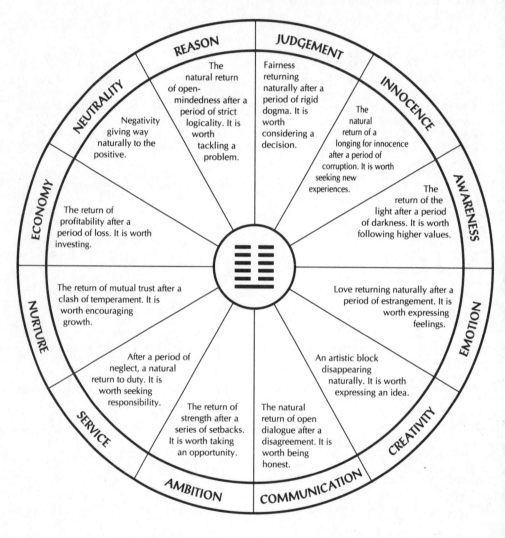

REASON — The natural return of open-mindedness after a period of strict logicality. It is worth tackling a problem.

JUDGEMENT — Fairness returning naturally after a period of rigid dogma. It is worth considering a decision.

NEUTRALITY — Negativity giving way naturally to the positive.

INNOCENCE — The natural return of a longing for innocence after a period of corruption. It is worth seeking new experiences.

ECONOMY — The return of profitability after a period of loss. It is worth investing.

AWARENESS — The return of the light after a period of darkness. It is worth following higher values.

NURTURE — The return of mutual trust after a clash of temperament. It is worth encouraging growth.

EMOTION — Love returning naturally after a period of estrangement. It is worth expressing feelings.

SERVICE — After a period of neglect, a natural return to duty. It is worth seeking responsibility.

CREATIVITY — An artistic block disappearing naturally. It is worth expressing an idea.

AMBITION — The return of strength after a series of setbacks. It is worth taking an opportunity.

COMMUNICATION — The natural return of open dialogue after a disagreement. It is worth being honest.

Correct – all-round progress

24 line 1

───□───

Lucky – no need for guilt

JUDGEMENT Rejecting bias before it is able to corrupt.

INNOCENCE Admitting a lack of experience before it leads to insecurity.

AWARENESS Exposing ego-led behaviour before it corrupts awareness.

EMOTION Being honest about feelings before becoming committed.

CREATIVITY Seeing the lack of worth in an idea before bringing it to expression.

COMMUNICATION Admitting dishonesty before it becomes a fully fledged lie.

AMBITION Admitting selfish motives before they corrupt ability.

SERVICE Admitting self-interest before it corrupts a greater cause.

NURTURE Correcting an uncaring attitude before it causes damage.

ECONOMY Pulling out of a risky speculation before loss is incurred.

NEUTRALITY Correcting errors in time.

REASON Dealing with intellectual superiority before it corrupts understanding.

24 line 2

───×───

Lucky

JUDGEMENT Easily resisting the lure of bias.

INNOCENCE A change of mind made easy.

AWARENESS Easily resisting the urgings of the ego.

EMOTION Resisting selfish feelings with ease.

CREATIVITY Happily rejecting unworthy ideas.

COMMUNICATION Easily resisting the temptation to be dishonest.

AMBITION Happily rejecting an unethical chance.

SERVICE Rejecting the temptation of disloyalty with ease.

NURTURE Easily resisting the temptation to stifle.

ECONOMY Happily resisting less than scrupulous dealings.

NEUTRALITY Easily turning away from negativity.

REASON Easily resisting the temptation to be clever.

24 line 3

───×───

No need for guilt, but beware

JUDGEMENT Fluctuating between principles and the lure of power is dangerous but not entirely wrong.

INNOCENCE It is dangerous to fluctuate between innocence and corruption but not wholly wrong.

AWARENESS It is not entirely wrong to vacillate between ego-led behaviour and higher awareness, but it is dangerous.

EMOTION Vacillating between selfish and unselfish emotions can lead to problems but is not all bad.

CREATIVITY It is not entirely wrong to fluctuate between originality and the mundane, but it can lead to creative confusion.

COMMUNICATION Fluctuating between eloquence and honesty causes confusion but is not entirely wrong.

AMBITION It is dangerous to vacillate between nurturing abilities and naked ambition but not wholly wrong.

SERVICE It is not entirely wrong to fluctuate between self-importance and devotion to duty, but it is dangerous.

NURTURE Inconsistency in parental attitude, while not being entirely wrong, is very confusing for a child.

ECONOMY Fluctuating between prudence and irresponsibility is dangerous but not wholly wrong.

NEUTRALITY Fluctuation between positive and negative.

REASON Vacillating between open-mindedness and strict logic is dangerous but not entirely wrong.

24 line 4

——×——

JUDGEMENT Returning to principles alone.
INNOCENCE Resisting temptation alone.
AWARENESS Alone in returning to higher values.
EMOTION Alone in admitting true feelings.
CREATIVITY Going back to originality alone.
COMMUNICATION Alone in renouncing dishonesty.
AMBITION Alone in resisting competitiveness.
SERVICE Returning to duty alone.
NURTURE Alone in wanting a caring relationship.
ECONOMY Alone in rejecting greed.
NEUTRALITY Isolated in rejecting negativity.
REASON Alone in wanting to be open-minded.

24 line 5

——×——

No need for guilt

JUDGEMENT Correcting a wrong decision for the sake of a principle.
INNOCENCE Admitting ignorance for the sake of greater learning.
AWARENESS Correcting ego-led behaviour for the sake of a growth in awareness.
EMOTION Expressing a painful feeling for the good of a relationship.
CREATIVITY Weeding out unworthy ideas for the sake of artistic integrity.
COMMUNICATION Being painfully honest for the sake of agreement.
AMBITION Admitting motives for the sake of fair competition.
SERVICE Accepting the limitations of position for the sake of a greater cause.
NURTURE Relinquishing control for the sake of growth.
ECONOMY Rejecting greed for the common good.
NEUTRALITY Rejecting negativity for more important reasons.
REASON Admitting a mistake for the sake of greater understanding.

24 line 6

——×——

Very unfortunate

JUDGEMENT Stubbornness in not taking the opportunity to correct a mistake leads to a loss of respect.
INNOCENCE Stubbornly refusing to admit a mistake leads to inevitable insecurity.
AWARENESS Not admitting ego-led behaviour, even when it is obvious, leads to an inevitable loss of awareness.
EMOTION Not giving in, when obviously wrong, leads to inevitable unhappiness.
CREATIVITY Stubbornly clinging to an unworthy idea leads to a loss of artistic respect.
COMMUNICATION Not apologizing when the opportunity presents itself leads to a loss of credibility.
AMBITION Stubbornly refusing to admit defeat leads to complete failure.
SERVICE Refusing to admit obvious unsuitability for a task leads to a complete loss of trust.
NURTURE Refusing to understand drives a wedge between parent and child.
ECONOMY Refusing the opportunity to back out of a risky speculation leads to crippling loss.
NEUTRALITY The refusal to admit an error.
REASON Refusing the opportunity to correct a mistake leads to a loss of understanding.

·SIMPLICITY·

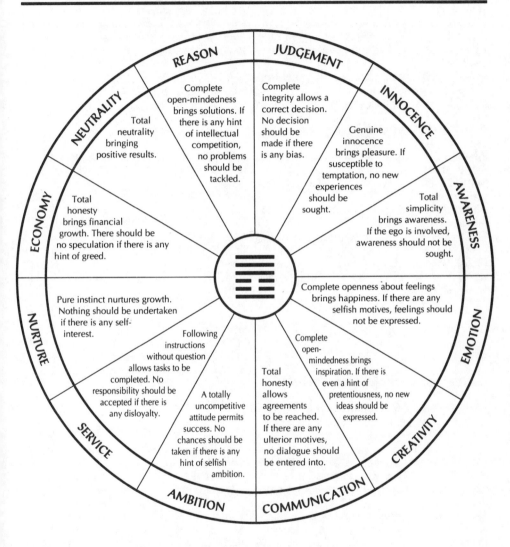

REASON
Complete open-mindedness brings solutions. If there is any hint of intellectual competition, no problems should be tackled.

JUDGEMENT
Complete integrity allows a correct decision. No decision should be made if there is any bias.

NEUTRALITY
Total neutrality bringing positive results.

INNOCENCE
Genuine innocence brings pleasure. If susceptible to temptation, no new experiences should be sought.

ECONOMY
Total honesty brings financial growth. There should be no speculation if there is any hint of greed.

AWARENESS
Total simplicity brings awareness. If the ego is involved, awareness should not be sought.

NURTURE
Pure instinct nurtures growth. Nothing should be undertaken if there is any self-interest.

Complete openness about feelings brings happiness. If there are any selfish motives, feelings should not be expressed.

EMOTION

Following instructions without question allows tasks to be completed. No responsibility should be accepted if there is any disloyalty.

A totally uncompetitive attitude permits success. No chances should be taken if there is any hint of selfish ambition.

SERVICE

Total honesty allows agreements to be reached. If there are any ulterior motives, no dialogue should be entered into.

Complete open-mindedness brings inspiration. If there is even a hint of pretentiousness, no new ideas should be expressed.

CREATIVITY

AMBITION

COMMUNICATION

Achievements are possible –
ulterior motives are out of the question

25 line 1

———□———

Positive action is lucky

JUDGEMENT Instinctive fairness allows correct decisions.
INNOCENCE Following innocently allows a secure footing to be found.
AWARENESS Following the simple impulses of the heart engenders higher awareness.
EMOTION Being honest about feelings brings happiness.
CREATIVITY An unpretentious attitude permits inspiration.
COMMUNICATION Instinctive words lead the way to an agreement.
AMBITION Untainted natural ability permits progress to be made.
SERVICE Instinctive loyalty means duties are carried out correctly.
NURTURE Following instincts permits nurture.
ECONOMY Instinctive honesty permits financial growth.
NEUTRALITY Natural aptitude.
REASON Instinctive reasoning shows the way to solutions.

25 line 2

———×———

It is worth taking positive action

JUDGEMENT It is worth making a decision for the sake of fairness rather than for the sake of the consequences.
INNOCENCE It is worth acting instinctively without thinking of the consequences.
AWARENESS It is worth following higher values for their own sake without looking for the rewards.
EMOTION It is worth expressing an honest feeling without worrying about the consequences.
CREATIVITY It is worth expressing an original idea for its own sake rather than looking for appreciation.
COMMUNICATION It is worth being honest without worrying about the consequences.
AMBITION It is worth using abilities without thought of ultimate goals.

SERVICE It is worth being dutiful without thought of reward.
NURTURE It is worth being caring for its own sake.
ECONOMY It is worth making an investment without considering eventual profit.
NEUTRALITY Positive action without regard to consequences.
REASON It is worth tackling a problem for the sake of understanding rather than simply to find a solution.

25 line 3

———×———

Undeserved bad luck

JUDGEMENT Fairness is abused.
INNOCENCE Taking advantage of innocence.
AWARENESS Undeserved abuse of higher values.
EMOTION Honest feelings are abused.
CREATIVITY Original ideas are stolen.
COMMUNICATION Honest words are twisted.
AMBITION An uncompetitive attitude is abused.
SERVICE Taking advantage of loyalty.
NURTURE Taking advantage of a caring attitude.
ECONOMY Financial integrity is abused.
NEUTRALITY Abused integrity.
REASON Intellectual integrity is abused.

25 line 4

———□———

Continuing in this way proves correct

JUDGEMENT Holding to just principles is not wrong.
INNOCENCE Resisting temptation is not wrong.
AWARENESS It is not wrong to hold on to higher values.
EMOTION It is not wrong to hold on to a feeling.
CREATIVITY It is not wrong to believe in original ideas.
COMMUNICATION It is not wrong to cling to the truth.
AMBITION It is not wrong to remain confident in abilities.

SERVICE It is not wrong to remain loyal.
NURTURE It is not wrong to continue to care.
ECONOMY It is not wrong to keep financial integrity.
NEUTRALITY Holding to positive values.
REASON Remaining loyal to a theory is not wrong.

25 line 5

————◻————

JUDGEMENT An undeserved abuse of fairness will correct itself.
INNOCENCE The undeserved pain of corrupted innocence will pass of its own accord.
AWARENESS An undeserved abuse of awareness will find its own resolution.
EMOTION Undeserved emotional pain will heal itself.
CREATIVITY Stolen ideas will be exposed.
COMMUNICATION It will become apparent that words have been undeservedly twisted.
AMBITION Cheats will eventually be exposed.
SERVICE When loyalty is abused, the situation will correct itself.
NURTURE The pain of unappreciated care will heal itself.
ECONOMY When financial integrity is undeservedly abused, the situation will eventually right itself.
NEUTRALITY An abuse of integrity, correcting itself.
REASON It will become apparent that intellectual integrity has been undeservedly abused.

25 line 6

————◻————

Unfortunate – no progress

JUDGEMENT Fairness would be abused.
INNOCENCE Innocence would be abused.
AWARENESS Acting from higher awareness would be a waste of time.
EMOTION Being honest about feelings would lead to unhappiness.
CREATIVITY Instinctive originality would be misunderstood.
COMMUNICATION Honest words would be misunderstood.
AMBITION Others would take advantage of a lack of competitiveness.
SERVICE Instinctive loyalty would be wasted.
NURTURE Care would not be appreciated.
ECONOMY Economic integrity would be abused.
NEUTRALITY Instinctive positive action being abused.
REASON Ideas would not be understood.

26
·GREAT RESTRAINT·

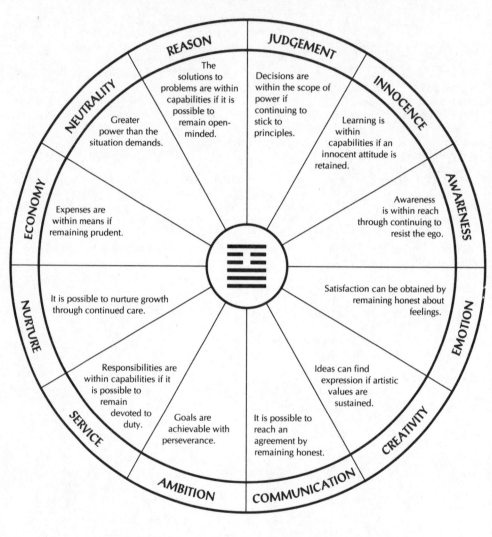

REASON

JUDGEMENT

NEUTRALITY

INNOCENCE

AWARENESS

ECONOMY

EMOTION

NURTURE

CREATIVITY

SERVICE

AMBITION

COMMUNICATION

The solutions to problems are within capabilities if it is possible to remain open-minded.

Decisions are within the scope of power if continuing to stick to principles.

Greater power than the situation demands.

Learning is within capabilities if an innocent attitude is retained.

Expenses are within means if remaining prudent.

Awareness is within reach through continuing to resist the ego.

It is possible to nurture growth through continued care.

Satisfaction can be obtained by remaining honest about feelings.

Responsibilities are within capabilities if it is possible to remain devoted to duty.

Ideas can find expression if artistic values are sustained.

Goals are achievable with perseverance.

It is possible to reach an agreement by remaining honest.

Persevere – chances can be taken

26 line 1

─────────☐─────────

Danger – stop

JUDGEMENT Pull back from a difficult decision to preserve powers.
INNOCENCE Avoid a new experience in order to resist temptation.
AWARENESS Avoid a situation in order to retain awareness.
EMOTION Unhappiness threatens; it is best to pull back.
CREATIVITY Let go of an idea in order to forestall a loss of credibility.
COMMUNICATION Say nothing to avoid being misunderstood.
AMBITION Avoid a challenge in order to retain strength.
SERVICE Resist taking on more responsibility in order to safeguard efficiency.
NURTURE Danger threatens; it is wise to keep a tight hold.
ECONOMY Loss threatens; it is best to avoid speculation.
NEUTRALITY Avoiding danger to preserve energy.
REASON Let go of a problem in order to safeguard intellectual powers.

26 line 2

─────────☐─────────

Accept the situation

JUDGEMENT Decisions are impossible.
INNOCENCE Insecurity is inevitable.
AWARENESS A growth in awareness is not possible.
EMOTION Emotional satisfaction is not possible.
CREATIVITY Ideas are not appreciated.
COMMUNICATION Agreement is not possible.
AMBITION Progress is not possible.
SERVICE Orders cannot be carried out.
NURTURE Growing pains are inevitable.
ECONOMY Losses are inevitable.
NEUTRALITY Negative forces are overwhelming.
REASON Problems are insurmountable.

26 line 3

─────────☐─────────

Demanding, but progress is possible

JUDGEMENT Carrying on according to principles while remaining aware of danger. It is worth considering a decision.
INNOCENCE Acting naturally while being aware of temptations. It is worth seeking new experience.
AWARENESS Following higher values while remaining aware of the danger from the ego. It is worth trying to be more moral.
EMOTION Letting the heart lead while remaining aware of the dangers. It is worth following a feeling.
CREATIVITY Following artistic values while remaining aware of the dangers of pretentiousness. It is worth expressing an idea.
COMMUNICATION Talking openly while remaining aware of the dangers of being honest. It is worth trying to seek agreement.
AMBITION Continued progress with awareness of the pitfalls. It is worth having a goal.
SERVICE Loyal service with an awareness of the dangers of self-importance. It is worth accepting more responsibility.
NURTURE Continuing to care while remaining aware of the danger of stifling a child. It is worth encouraging growth.
ECONOMY Speculating while remaining prudent. It is worth considering an investment.
NEUTRALITY Following positive values with awareness of danger.
REASON Progressing logically with an awareness of the danger of not being open-minded. It is worth tackling a problem.

26 line 4

———×———

Very lucky

JUDGEMENT Resisting the temptation of bias before it compromises fairness.
INNOCENCE Resisting temptation before it corrupts.
AWARENESS Dealing with ego-led behaviour before it becomes a problem.
EMOTION Dealing with selfish feelings before they become problems.
CREATIVITY Rejecting second-rate ideas at the beginning.
COMMUNICATION Snuffing out arguments before they start.
AMBITION Addressing problems before they become dangers.
SERVICE Addressing neglect of duty before it becomes disloyalty.
NURTURE Dealing with bad habits before they become part of character.
ECONOMY Settling accounts before they become problems.
NEUTRALITY Dealing with problems before they start.
REASON Correcting mistakes before they obscure understanding.

26 line 5

———×———

Lucky

JUDGEMENT removing the roots of corruption.
INNOCENCE Rejecting temptation.
AWARENESS Eradicating the roots of ego-led behaviour.
EMOTION Eradicating the roots of selfishness.
CREATIVITY Discarding sub-standard ideas at the moment of conception.
COMMUNICATION Exposing and dealing with the root causes of arguments.
AMBITION Getting to the root causes of failure.
SERVICE Eradicating basic disloyalty.
NURTURE Getting to the roots of bad habits.
ECONOMY Paying off debts completely.
NEUTRALITY Removing the root causes of a problem.
REASON Getting to the roots of a problem.

26 line 6

———□———

Achievement is possible

JUDGEMENT It is possible to act according to principles.
INNOCENCE Being able to act without fear.
AWARENESS Higher values can be put into practice.
EMOTION Feelings can be expressed and understood.
CREATIVITY It is possible to express original ideas.
COMMUNICATION The way is open to reach an agreement.
AMBITION it is possible to make progress.
SERVICE Having the capability to tackle a task.
NURTURE The opportunity to stimulate growth.
ECONOMY Financial growth is possible.
NEUTRALITY The ability to act positively.
REASON Finding the right way to approach a problem.

TWELVE CHANNELS OF THE I CHING

27

·STIMULATION·

REASON
Examine intellectual stimuli.

JUDGEMENT
Look at the reality of personal opinions.

NEUTRALITY
Examining motivations.

INNOCENCE
Examine what is found pleasurable.

ECONOMY
Take a look at motives for gain.

AWARENESS
Examine personal motives for a growth in awareness.

NURTURE
Observe what is stimulating growth.

EMOTION
Examine the causes of feelings.

Examine fundamental loyalties.

Examine the influences that stimulate creativity.

SERVICE

CREATIVITY

AMBITION
Examine basic motivations.

COMMUNICATION
Observe what is said casually.

If lessons are learned, continuing in this way brings luck

27 line 1

———□———

Unfortunate

JUDGEMENT   Letting go of principles in favour of control over a situation.
INNOCENCE   Sacrificing innocence to succumb to temptation.
AWARENESS   Losing real awareness in favour of moral superiority.
EMOTION   Selfishness overcoming real feelings.
CREATIVITY   Sacrificing originality for the sake of acceptance.
COMMUNICATION   Forgoing total honesty in order to win an argument.
AMBITION   Surrendering talent for the sake of personal ambition.
SERVICE   Turning away from real loyalties for the sake of self-importance.
NURTURE   Forgoing natural care for the sake of a quiet life.
ECONOMY   Sacrificing prudence for the sake of greed.
NEUTRALITY   Sacrificing positive values.
REASON   Sacrificing real understanding for the sake of appearing clever.

27 line 2

———×———

Continuing in this way brings bad luck

JUDGEMENT   Adhering to wrong principles.
INNOCENCE   Turning away from natural growth.
AWARENESS   Motivated by the wrong ideals.
EMOTION   Not being honest about feelings.
CREATIVITY   Not being original.
COMMUNICATION   Arguing the wrong case.
AMBITION   Seeking the wrong goal.
SERVICE   Being loyal to the wrong cause.
NURTURE   Encouraging growth in the wrong way.
ECONOMY   Speculating in the wrong area.
NEUTRALITY   The wrong path.
REASON   Motivated by the wrong ideas.

27 line 3

———×———

Unlucky – do not act

JUDGEMENT   Wanting control and achieving nothing of real value.
INNOCENCE   Merely looking for gratification and learning nothing.
AWARENESS   Seeking moral superiority and achieving no growth in awareness.
EMOTION   Not honest about feelings and therefore finding no satisfaction.
CREATIVITY   Merely seeking appreciation and consequently being uninspired.
COMMUNICATION   Losing sympathy through seeking to win an argument.
AMBITION   Aiming for the wrong goal and failing.
SERVICE   Being disloyal and sacrificing respect.
NURTURE   Not caring in the right way and growing apart.
ECONOMY   Speculating in the wrong area and making a loss.
NEUTRALITY   Taking the wrong path.
REASON   Seeking intellectual superiority and as a consequence finding no understanding.

27 line 4

———×———

Lucky – blameless

JUDGEMENT   Seeking out advice with good results.
INNOCENCE   Trusting someone and learning something positive.
AWARENESS   Seeking guidance with a resultant increase in awareness.
EMOTION   Being open to love and finding happiness.
CREATIVITY   Looking at other ideas and finding inspiration.
COMMUNICATION   Asking questions and getting honest answers.
AMBITION   Different goals permitting progress.
SERVICE   A changed attitude allowing tasks to be tackled successfully.
NURTURE   Outside stimulation engendering health growth.
ECONOMY   Looking for help and stimulating financial growth.

NEUTRALITY A different path bringing progress.
REASON Being hungry for new knowledge with good results.

27 line 5

———×———

Continuing in this way brings luck, but take no chances

JUDGEMENT A necessary acceptance of dogma. No decisions should be made.
INNOCENCE It is necessary to trust others while remaining uncorrupted. No new experience should be sought.
AWARENESS A necessary acceptance of events. Higher awareness should not be sought.
EMOTION Having to deal with unwanted emotions. Feelings should not be expressed.
CREATIVITY Turning away from originality through necessity. No original ideas should be expressed.
COMMUNICATION Having to agree with something for the sake of peace. New agreements should not be sought.
AMBITION Having to deviate from a goal. No chances should be taken.
SERVICE A necessary deviation from duty. No responsibility should be sought.
NURTURE Not able to be as caring as necessary because of circumstances. Nothing new should be tried.
ECONOMY Finances having to adjust to unforeseen circumstances. Prudence makes this possible. No new speculation should be considered.
NEUTRALITY Necessary deviation from a path.
REASON Necessary dependence on what is not wholly understood. No new problems should be tackled.

27 line 6

———▭———

Lucky, but dangerous – necessary chances can be taken

JUDGEMENT Fundamentally sound principles. It is good to be aware of criticism. Decisions can be made.
INNOCENCE A good nature. Be aware of the dangers of corruption. New experiences can be sought.
AWARENESS The source of higher values. Be aware of the ego. Greater awareness can be sought.
EMOTION Fundamental emotions. Be aware of selfishness. Feelings can be expressed.
CREATIVITY Fundamental artistic values. Remain aware of the dangers of pretentiousness. It is worth expressing an idea.
COMMUNICATION Basic honesty. Keep listening to others. It is worth trying to find agreement.
AMBITION Fundamental ability. Beware of ambition for its own sake. Opportunities can be taken.
SERVICE Basic loyalty. Be aware of self-importance. Responsibilities can be shouldered.
NURTURE The natural bond between parent and child. Beware of the inclination to stifle. Healthy growth can be stimulated.
ECONOMY Basic economic sense. Beware of greed. Investment can be made.
NEUTRALITY The source of fundamental principles.
REASON Intellectually sound ideas. An open mind makes it possible to tackle new problems.

28
·STRESS·

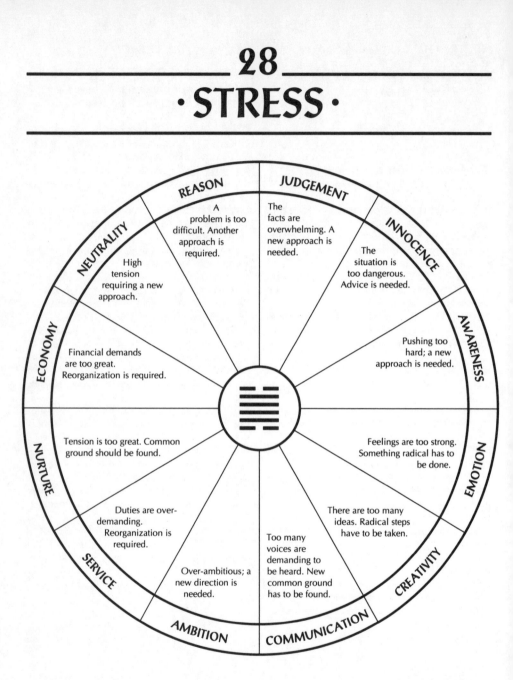

REASON

A problem is too difficult. Another approach is required.

JUDGEMENT

The facts are overwhelming. A new approach is needed.

NEUTRALITY

High tension requiring a new approach.

INNOCENCE

The situation is too dangerous. Advice is needed.

ECONOMY

Financial demands are too great. Reorganization is required.

AWARENESS

Pushing too hard; a new approach is needed.

NURTURE

Tension is too great. Common ground should be found.

EMOTION

Feelings are too strong. Something radical has to be done.

Duties are over-demanding. Reorganization is required.

There are too many ideas. Radical steps have to be taken.

SERVICE

Over-ambitious; a new direction is needed.

Too many voices are demanding to be heard. New common ground has to be found.

CREATIVITY

AMBITION

COMMUNICATION

A goal is needed, then achievements are possible

TWELVE CHANNELS OF THE I CHING

28 line 1

———×———

Blameless

JUDGEMENT Facts must be weighed very carefully.
INNOCENCE Great patience is required.
AWARENESS Great faith is required.
EMOTION Much sensitivity is needed.
CREATIVITY Great discernment is required.
COMMUNICATION Great tact is required.
AMBITION Much skill is required.
SERVICE Much attention to detail is needed.
NURTURE Great sensitivity is required.
ECONOMY Great prudence is required.
NEUTRALITY Taking great care.
REASON Much thought is required.

28 line 2

———□———

Progress

JUDGEMENT Examining basic facts throws new light on a decision.
INNOCENCE Eradicating immature behaviour permits real learning.
AWARENESS Isolating a basic character flaw renews a growth in awareness.
EMOTION Rediscovering a fundamental attraction breathes new life into a relationship.
CREATIVITY Going back to basics brings new inspiration.
COMMUNICATION Basic communication inspires a new understanding.
AMBITION Dealing with fundamental flaws renews strength.
SERVICE Solving a basic problem renews enthusiasm.
NURTURE Dealing with a problem that stems from childhood renews growth.
ECONOMY Fundamental reforms inspire economic growth.
NEUTRALITY Renewal through dealing with fundamental problems.
REASON Examining fundamentals inspires new understanding.

28 line 3

———□———

Unfortunate

JUDGEMENT Being dogmatic leads to a wrong decision.
INNOCENCE Continuing in ignorance leads to insecurity.
AWARENESS Obstinacy precludes awareness.
EMOTION Obstinacy leads to a split.
CREATIVITY Clinging to unworthy ideas leads to artistic failure.
COMMUNICATION Obstinacy leads to complete misunderstanding.
AMBITION Trying to achieve too many goals leads to failure.
SERVICE Taking on too much responsibility leads to failure.
NURTURE Failure to find common ground leads to a rift.
ECONOMY Failure to deal with financial pressure leads to loss.
NEUTRALITY Failure to deal with tension.
REASON Obstinacy in the face of a problem precludes any chance of finding a solution.

28 line 4

———□———

Luck, but a lack of virtue leads to regret

JUDGEMENT A difficult decision is made, but even now the slightest bias would be unfortunate.
INNOCENCE Insecurity is avoided, but any arrogance now would be unfortunate.
AWARENESS The ego has been overcome, but even minor selfish behaviour could prevent awareness.
EMOTION Pain is avoided, but any hidden feelings could have unfortunate consequences.
CREATIVITY Artistic failure is avoided, but even the slightest pretension could be unfortunate.
COMMUNICATION Misunderstanding is avoided, but even the smallest lie could be unfortunate.

AMBITION Failure is avoided, but even the slightest laxity could lead to unfortunate consequences.

SERVICE Failure in a task is avoided, but even the slightest inattention to duty could be unfortunate.

NURTURE Heartache is avoided, but even a slight misunderstanding could have unfortunate consequences.

ECONOMY Financial pressure is eased, but even the smallest extravagance now would be unfortunate.

NEUTRALITY Narrowly avoiding danger.

REASON Understanding is achieved, but even the slightest error would be unfortunate.

28 line 5

—————□—————

Pointless

JUDGEMENT Dogmatic leadership achieves nothing.

INNOCENCE Repeating immature behaviour achieves nothing.

AWARENESS The correction of trivial faults alone does not lead to awareness.

EMOTION Trying to recapture old feelings achieves nothing.

CREATIVITY Regurgitating old ideas is meaningless.

COMMUNICATION Going over the same ground achieves nothing.

AMBITION Repeating the same success is meaningless.

SERVICE Loyalty to a lost cause is pointless.

NURTURE Trying to go back to the way it was achieves nothing.

ECONOMY Investment at this late stage is profitless.

NEUTRALITY Repeating old ways.

REASON Old methods are ineffectual.

28 line 6

—————×—————

Unfortunate, but not to blame

JUDGEMENT A decision made in good faith is wrong.

INNOCENCE An unavoidable loss of innocence.

AWARENESS A sacrifice for what is right.

EMOTION Genuine emotion is not reciprocated.

CREATIVITY A genuinely creative idea is not appreciated.

COMMUNICATION The truth is not believed.

AMBITION An unavoidable failure.

SERVICE Circumstances prevent the completion of a task.

NURTURE The young do not understand.

ECONOMY A loss due to unavoidable circumstances.

NEUTRALITY An unavoidable loss.

REASON Logic fails to find an answer.

29
· PROBLEMS ·

The wheel contains the following sections:

REASON — Many problems, which cannot be overcome by using logic. Trial and error is the only way.

JUDGEMENT — Many difficult decisions, all requiring minute examination.

INNOCENCE — A very confusing situation, which appears to have no end. Only time can resolve it.

NEUTRALITY — Danger everywhere.

AWARENESS — Great danger caused by the ego. Awareness can be found only by eradicating all selfish motives.

ECONOMY — Hard times; every expense must be taken into account.

EMOTION — It is unwise to express feelings at this time, and the pain of suppression may be great, but that which is sincere finds its expression in the end.

NURTURE — Repeated heartache must be endured before the young learn.

SERVICE — Every task must be completed meticulously. There is danger in not doing so.

AMBITION — Danger lies in not starting afresh after repeated losses. This is the only way of assuring eventual success.

COMMUNICATION — Lies and deceit abound. They must run their course before the truth can be spoken.

CREATIVITY — The mundane is everywhere. There is danger in mistaking a banal idea of inspiration.

Danger – repeated difficulties
Great perseverance can lead to eventual achievement

29 line 1

———×———

Unfortunate

JUDGEMENT   A detail overlooked leads to a wrong decision.
INNOCENCE   Making a move in ignorance leads to total insecurity.
AWARENESS   A selfish motive leads to loss of awareness.
EMOTION   A feeling expressed at the wrong time leads to unhappiness.
CREATIVITY   A banal idea is mistaken for inspiration.
COMMUNICATION   Truth spoken at the wrong time means it will never be believed.
AMBITION   The inability to learn from failure leads to total defeat.
SERVICE   A task not meticulously completed leads to the failure of the greater plan of which it is a part.
NURTURE   A lack of care leads to permanent resentment.
ECONOMY   A small expense overlooked leads to indebtedness.
NEUTRALITY   No escaping from danger.
REASON   A lack of thoroughness leads to an error.

29 line 2

———□———

Danger – minor progress

JUDGEMENT   Only small decisions should be made.
INNOCENCE   Only small chances can be taken in a situation that is not understood.
AWARENESS   The ego lurks, so only small steps can be taken towards awareness.
EMOTION   Feelings should only be intimated.
CREATIVITY   It is necessary to be content with the mundane.
COMMUNICATION   The truth can only be implied.
AMBITION   It is necessary to be content with only small gains.
SERVICE   Difficult tasks should be tackled only one step at a time.
NURTURE   Trust can only be built up slowly.
ECONOMY   In hard times it is necessary to hedge bets.

NEUTRALITY   Extreme care in the face of danger.
REASON   Understanding can be found only a step at a time.

29 line 3

———×———

Take great care

JUDGEMENT   The evidence is full of contradictions. If it is not weighed minutely, a wrong decision will be made.
INNOCENCE   There is confusion everywhere. It is necessary to wait, as a wrong move would lead to being permanently lost.
AWARENESS   The ego lurks everywhere. This must be borne in mind or delusion will result.
EMOTION   Emotions are dangerously confused. Wait! Acting impulsively leads to lasting pain.
CREATIVITY   Surrounded by the mundane; examine any creative idea for its worth or talent will be wasted.
COMMUNICATION   No one is listening. Wait for the right time or the truth will never be believed.
AMBITION   Wait before trying to force progress. A wrong move now will lead to inevitable failure.
SERVICE   The difficulties of a task are not understood by those above or below. Mark time, as any move now would be deemed a failure.
NURTURE   Be patient with loved-ones. Anything else would lead to an irrevocable loss of trust.
ECONOMY   Dire straits; exercise great caution in expenditure or ruin beckons.
NEUTRALITY   Danger in every direction.
REASON   Every rational explanation has pitfalls. Each option has to be investigated or a wrong conclusion will be drawn.

29 line 4

———×———

Correct eventually

JUDGEMENT   Some decisions hinge on very basic facts.
INNOCENCE   Sometimes simple trust, without asking why, is enough.

AWARENESS Sometimes simple acceptance is necessary.

EMOTION No blame can be attached to the simple expression of honest emotion.

CREATIVITY In uninspiring times, there is no shame in unpretentious ideas.

COMMUNICATION There is nothing wrong in expressing the truth in its simplest terms, if motives are correct.

AMBITION Using honest means to make progress means no recriminations.

SERVICE No one can complain about essential tasks carried out without ceremony.

NURTURE Empathy expressed in the simplest terms may be all that is needed.

ECONOMY There is nothing wrong in making economies.

NEUTRALITY No niceties in the time of danger.

REASON Insoluble problems may benefit from a very basic approach.

29 line 5

———————— □ ————————

Correct

JUDGEMENT Consider only the pertinent evidence.

INNOCENCE Place only as much trust in something as is necessary.

AWARENESS There is no benefit in self-denial taken to extremes.

EMOTION There is nothing to be gained from over-dramatizing feelings.

CREATIVITY Ideas should be practical.

COMMUNICATION It is necessary to say only what is needed and no more.

AMBITION There is no point in being over-ambitious.

SERVICE It is not necessary to exceed orders.

NURTURE Be only as protective as is necessary.

ECONOMY Economies taken too far are pointless.

NEUTRALITY Following the line of least resistance in a time of danger.

REASON Draw conclusions only from what is known.

29 line 6

———————— × ————————

Unfortunate

JUDGEMENT because of an ill-considered decision, it will be a long time before others trust again.

INNOCENCE Acting in ignorance causes long-term insecurity.

AWARENESS The ego has been allowed to take control. It will take much self-denial to overcome its influence now.

EMOTION A feeling having been expressed, it will be a long time before a relationship can return to normal.

CREATIVITY A pretentious idea; nothing will be taken seriously for a long time.

COMMUNICATION Words are not believed. It will be a long time before others listen again.

AMBITION Over-ambition has caused a situation in which it will be very hard to start again.

SERVICE The confidence of superiors is lost and cannot be regained for a long time.

NURTURE Over-protectiveness; it will be a long time before the wound heals.

ECONOMY Over-spending causes long-term debts.

NEUTRALITY Imprisoned by danger.

REASON A wrong conclusion has been drawn. It will be a long time before the solution shows itself.

30
·CLARITY·

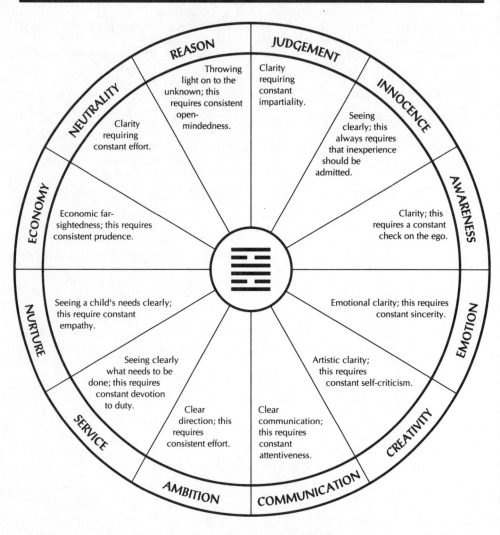

REASON

Throwing light on to the unknown; this requires consistent open-mindedness.

JUDGEMENT

Clarity requiring constant impartiality.

NEUTRALITY

Clarity requiring constant effort.

INNOCENCE

Seeing clearly; this always requires that inexperience should be admitted.

ECONOMY

Economic far-sightedness; this requires consistent prudence.

AWARENESS

Clarity; this requires a constant check on the ego.

NURTURE

Seeing a child's needs clearly; this require constant empathy.

EMOTION

Emotional clarity; this requires constant sincerity.

Seeing clearly what needs to be done; this requires constant devotion to duty.

Artistic clarity; this requires constant self-criticism.

CREATIVITY

Clear direction; this requires consistent effort.

Clear communication; this requires constant attentiveness.

SERVICE

AMBITION

COMMUNICATION

Achievements are possible through perseverance – humility brings luck

---□---

Blameless

JUDGEMENT Initial indecision can be overcome if a genuinely fair decision is the goal.
INNOCENCE Initial difficulty can be overcome if genuine learning is the goal.
AWARENESS Initial problems with the ego can be overcome if a growth in awareness is the goal.
EMOTION Initial difficulties can be overcome if a feeling is genuine.
CREATIVITY Initial problems can be overcome if an idea is worth expressing.
COMMUNICATION Initial misunderstandings can be overcome if a real exchange of ideas is the goal.
AMBITION Initial difficulties can be overcome if an ambition is worthy.
SERVICE It is possible to overcome initial difficulties where dedicated service is the goal.
NURTURE Initial heartache can be overcome if the growth of another is the goal.
ECONOMY It is possible to overcome initial problems if broad-based economic growth is the goal.
NEUTRALITY Initial problems.
REASON Initial confusion can be overcome if deep understanding is the goal.

30 line 2

---×---

Very lucky

JUDGEMENT Weighing evidence properly encourages fair decisions.
INNOCENCE Acting naturally brings genuine learning.
AWARENESS Being natural encourages awareness.
EMOTION Acting naturally encourages real emotion.
CREATIVITY Allowing ideas to flow naturally is truly creative.
COMMUNICATION Natural conversation is truly constructive.
AMBITION Sensibly applied effort encourages success.
SERVICE Acting within sensible limits encourages the completion of a task.

NURTURE Acting according to natural instincts encourages the welfare of a child.
ECONOMY Natural prudence encourages economic growth.
NEUTRALITY Natural action that does not go to extremes.
REASON Open-minded thought encourages understanding.

30 line 3

---□---

Unfortunate

JUDGEMENT External circumstances are allowed to cloud judgement.
INNOCENCE External circumstances are allowed to prevent maturity.
AWARENESS External circumstances are used as an excuse for a lack of real awareness.
EMOTION Circumstances are allowed to prevent the expression of true feeling.
CREATIVITY External circumstances are allowed to stifle creativity.
COMMUNICATION The physical situation is allowed to stifle an exchange of ideas.
AMBITION External circumstances are allowed to stifle ambitions.
SERVICE Duty is used as an excuse for a lack of initiative.
NURTURE Convention is allowed to control what should be a natural process.
ECONOMY Outside pressures are allowed to control personal finances.
NEUTRALITY Outside influences stifling natural abilities.
REASON External circumstances are allowed to stifle intelligence.

30 line 4

---□---

JUDGEMENT Instant decisions are often wrong.
INNOCENCE Acting without thinking usually proves to be an error.
AWARENESS Sudden faith usually proves insubstantial.
EMOTION Emotions that are quick to appear usually die just as quickly.
CREATIVITY Instant ideas often prove of no value.
COMMUNICATION Speaking without thinking usually leads to misunderstanding.

AMBITION Ill-thought out goals are usually abandoned quickly.
SERVICE Spontaneous initiative is usually a mistake.
NURTURE Reacting without thought usually proves to be a mistake.
ECONOMY Spontaneous speculation usually proves to be foolish.
NEUTRALITY What appears quickly, disappearing just as quickly.
REASON Quickly drawn conclusions are often shown to be incorrect.

30 line 5

———×———

Lucky

JUDGEMENT A crisis point demands a fundamental decision.
INNOCENCE A moment of truth demands immediate growth.
AWARENESS A crisis point demands real awareness.
EMOTION An emotional crisis demands great honesty.
CREATIVITY Creative abilities are put on the spot.
COMMUNICATION A serious disagreement requires total honesty.
AMBITION A serious situation requires real strength.
SERVICE An emergency forces devotion to duty.
NURTURE A crisis shows the true depths of a bond.
ECONOMY A desperate situation forces serious economic measures.
NEUTRALITY A desperate situation.
REASON A desperate problem forces a radical solution.

30 line 6

———□———

Correct

JUDGEMENT In re-evaluating a decision it is better to examine the reasons rather than the consequences.
INNOCENCE When a mistake has been made, it is best to face up to the real reasons rather than to make excuses.
AWARENESS In regaining awareness it is the core reasons for bad habits that have to be dealt with. The habits themselves may be harmless.
EMOTION In working out an emotional problem it is better to look at the fundamental reasons rather than at the problems it has caused.
CREATIVITY In improving a work it is better to look at the fundamental idea rather than at its expression.
COMMUNICATION In admonishment it is better to say the important things and forget the trivialities.
AMBITION It is best to deal with the reasons for failure rather than with the consequences.
SERVICE Superiors must take the blame rather than those who merely followed orders.
NURTURE In re-establishing a bond it is better to deal with fundamental feelings rather than with what has happened.
ECONOMY For economic recovery it is best to deal with the root causes for failure.
NEUTRALITY The cause rather than its consequences.
REASON In reconsidering a problem it is better to examine the deeper reasons for an error rather than the method used.

31
· ATTRACTION ·

REASON — Lessening intellectual standards in order to assimilate new ideas.

JUDGEMENT — Relinquishing some control for the sake of fairness.

NEUTRALITY — Deferring to a weaker power for more positive results.

INNOCENCE — An attractive influence.

ECONOMY — An attractive speculation.

AWARENESS — Voluntarily deferring to a higher power.

NURTURE — Showing trust for the sake of a deeper bond.

EMOTION — Mutual attraction.

SERVICE — Finding more suitable duties.

CREATIVITY — Simpler ideas for a greater artistic whole.

AMBITION — Lowering sights in order to progress towards a more suitable goal.

COMMUNICATION — Communicating in a simpler way for the sake of mutual agreement.

Achievements are possible with perseverance – yielding brings luck

31 line 1

————×————

JUDGEMENT Merely contemplating a decision.
INNOCENCE Thinking about the future.
AWARENESS Contemplating a new belief.
EMOTION Mutual attraction in thought only.
CREATIVITY Merely ideas to contemplate.
COMMUNICATION Hinting at something.
AMBITION Merely contemplating a new goal.
SERVICE An inkling of more suitable duties.
NURTURE A hint of future character.
ECONOMY Merely contemplating a speculation.
NEUTRALITY A hint of what is to come.
REASON Toying with an idea.

31 line 2

————×————

Acting now would be unfortunate – waiting brings luck

JUDGEMENT No real need for a decision yet; it is better to wait for the right time.
INNOCENCE Pretending; it is better to wait for the real thing.
AWARENESS Forcing awareness; it is better to let it happen naturally.
EMOTION No genuine mutual attraction; it is better to wait for the real thing.
CREATIVITY Not really an original idea; it is better to wait for inspiration.
COMMUNICATION Not genuine agreement; it is better to wait.
AMBITION Not really a worthy goal; it is better to wait for the right opportunity.
SERVICE Not really of use; it is better to wait until better use can be made of abilities.
NURTURE Forcing growth; it is better to let it happen naturally.
ECONOMY Speculation for its own sake; a better opportunity will come in time.
NEUTRALITY Not a genuine influence.
REASON Not a real conclusion; it is better to wait until one presents itself.

31 line 3

————□————

Regret

JUDGEMENT It is not good to make judgements automatically.
INNOCENCE An automatic reaction; it is not good to continue in this way.
AWARENESS It is not good to follow blindly.
EMOTION Acting without thinking can lead to humiliation.
CREATIVITY Expressing every idea in an automatic way is not good.
COMMUNICATION Speaking just for the sake of conversation is not good.
AMBITION It is not good to chase every goal for the sake of it.
SERVICE It is not good to respond to every whim of a superior.
NURTURE Beware of responding without thinking.
ECONOMY Speculation for its own sake is not good.
NEUTRALITY Reacting automatically.
REASON Making automatic assumptions can lead to mistakes.

31 line 4

————□————

Continuing in this way brings luck – no need for guilt

JUDGEMENT True fairness has great effect, but power for its own sake has limited results.
INNOCENCE True innocence engenders protective feelings in others, but showing off has only a limited effect.
AWARENESS Higher values are appreciated, but moral superiority finds little sympathy.
EMOTION Real feeling finds reciprocation, but empty words are seen for what they are.
CREATIVITY True originality finds appreciation, while pretentious ideas find none.
COMMUNICATION The truth has a great effect, while empty words are ignored.

TWELVE CHANNELS OF THE I CHING

AMBITION   Real ability means progress, but naked ambition achieves little.
SERVICE   True devotion to duty is appreciated, while merely going through the motions has little effect.
NURTURE   Real care is good for a child, while little is achieved by merely going through the motions.
ECONOMY   Prudence achieves financial growth, while greed shows only short-term profits.
NEUTRALITY   Positive values getting results; negative values achieving little.
REASON   Genuine reasoning finds valid solutions, while little is achieved by mere cleverness.

31 line 5

———□———

No need for guilt

JUDGEMENT   Strong-willed fairness has great effect.
INNOCENCE   Strength of character is needed.
AWARENESS   A strong faith brings a growth in awareness.
EMOTION   Strong feelings find expression.
CREATIVITY   Strong ideas are worth expressing.
COMMUNICATION   Truthful dialogue is constructive.
AMBITION   A strong will makes progress.
SERVICE   Unwavering devotion to duty gets things done.
NURTURE   A strong will is respected.
ECONOMY   A big speculation requiring prudence.
NEUTRALITY   Strong influence.
REASON   Genuine reasoning leads to solutions.

31 line 6

———×———

JUDGEMENT   Influenced by power.
INNOCENCE   Influenced by superficial ideas.
AWARENESS   Influenced by empty beliefs.
EMOTION   Influenced by false emotion.
CREATIVITY   Influenced by superficiality.
COMMUNICATION   Influenced by empty words.
AMBITION   Influenced by selfish ambition.
SERVICE   Influenced by self-importance.
NURTURE   Using parental influence.
ECONOMY   Influenced by greed.
NEUTRALITY   Influence in superficial ways.
REASON   Influenced by mere cleverness.

32
· PERMANENCE ·

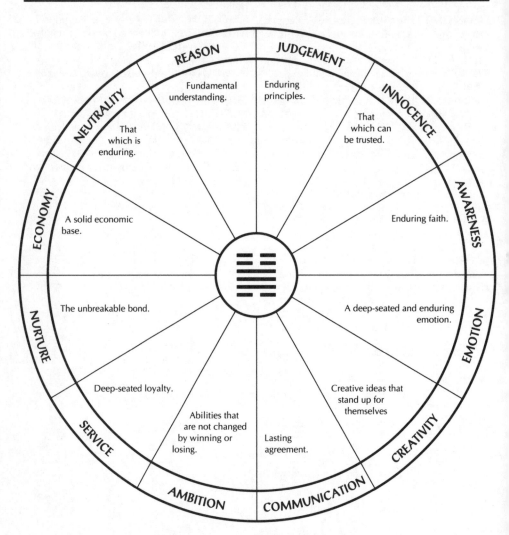

REASON — Fundamental understanding.

JUDGEMENT — Enduring principles.

INNOCENCE — That which can be trusted.

NEUTRALITY — That which is enduring.

AWARENESS — Enduring faith.

ECONOMY — A solid economic base.

EMOTION — A deep-seated and enduring emotion.

NURTURE — The unbreakable bond.

SERVICE — Deep-seated loyalty.

AMBITION — Abilities that are not changed by winning or losing.

COMMUNICATION — Lasting agreement.

CREATIVITY — Creative ideas that stand up for themselves

**Continuing in this way is correct –
achievements are possible
It is good to have a goal**

32 line 1

——×——

Unfortunate – no progress

JUDGEMENT It is always wrong to make decisions before the evidence has been weighed.
INNOCENCE Making a move without adequate experience is always wrong.
AWARENESS It is wrong to claim higher awareness prematurely.
EMOTION Rushing into an emotional commitment is always wrong.
CREATIVITY It is never right to express an idea without adequate thought.
COMMUNICATION It is always wrong to come to an agreement prematurely.
AMBITION it is always wrong to aim for a goal without enough planning.
SERVICE It is never right to attempt a task without enough preparation.
NURTURE It is never right to expect too much.
ECONOMY It is never right to speculate without a solid financial base.
NEUTRALITY Creating permanence too quickly.
REASON Trying to come to a conclusion too quickly is always wrong.

32 line 2

——□——

Avoiding future guilt

JUDGEMENT Acting within the limits of power.
INNOCENCE Acting within the limits of experience.
AWARENESS Avoiding any moral superiority.
EMOTION Seeing feelings for what they really are.
CREATIVITY Not going beyond the limits of what is acceptable.
COMMUNICATION Not saying too much.
AMBITION Not pushing too hard.
SERVICE Not taking on responsibilities that are beyond capabilities.
NURTURE Not expecting too much.
ECONOMY Not going beyond financial limits.

NEUTRALITY Not going beyond the limits of resources.
REASON Not going beyond the limits of understanding.

32 line 3

——□——

Continuing in this way leads to regret

JUDGEMENT Weighing evidence inconsistently leads inevitably to wrong decisions.
INNOCENCE Not always acting within the bounds of experience leads to inevitable insecurity.
AWARENESS Inconsistent moral behaviour leads to an inevitable loss of awareness.
EMOTION Not always being honest about feelings leads to persistent unhappiness and disappointment.
CREATIVITY Not remaining true to original ideas leads to persistent artistic failure.
COMMUNICATION Occasional lies lead to inevitable disagreements.
AMBITION Not always acting within the limits of abilities leads to inevitable frustration.
SERVICE Occasional unreliability leads to being considered untrustworthy.
NURTURE Inconsistent care leads to inevitable problems.
ECONOMY Not always being prudent leads to inevitable loss.
NEUTRALITY Lack of consistency.
REASON Not being consistent in method leads to inevitable mistakes.

32 line 4

——□——

JUDGEMENT It is impossible to make a decision.
INNOCENCE There is nothing to be learned here.
AWARENESS There is no higher value in this situation.
EMOTION There is no love to be found
CREATIVITY This is not a valid idea.
COMMUNICATION There can be no agreement.
AMBITION There is no goal to be pursued.
SERVICE There is no worthwhile task to be performed.

NURTURE   This is not a situation where growth can occur.
ECONOMY   There is no profit to be made.
NEUTRALITY   Nothing to be gained.
REASON   No solution is to be found in this way.

32 line 5

───×───

Luck in small ways – unfortunate for important matters

JUDGEMENT   Following dogma in simple decisions is acceptable, but in the case of difficult decisions it is wrong.
INNOCENCE   It is all right to trust others where there has been previous experience, but it is wrong where there has been none.
AWARENESS   Relying on faith is good, but there are times when that faith must be challenged.
EMOTION   Emotional stability is good in a relationship but can be seen as coldness by others.
CREATIVITY   It is good to follow accepted methods of expression but bad not to be original.
COMMUNICATION   Speaking predictably is good in order to get along with others but bad when seeking real agreement.
AMBITION   Predictability is good when there are no ambitions, but it is not a virtue when chasing new goals.
SERVICE   Normal methods are good in the case of simple duties but bad in the case of those that are more difficult.
NURTURE   Simple discipline is good in order to deal with normal problems but bad in sensitive areas.
ECONOMY   Avoiding risk is to be applauded in normal times, but it is not a virtue when real opportunities come along.
NEUTRALITY   Predictability being good in normal times but bad in exceptional times.
REASON   It is good to follow accepted methods in simple problems, but inadvisable in the case of those that are more difficult.

32 line 6

───×───

Unfortunate

JUDGEMENT   Constant changes of mind lead to a loss of control.
INNOCENCE   Getting bored easily leads to insecurity.
AWARENESS   Constantly changing beliefs leads to a loss of awareness.
EMOTION   The need constantly to satisfy feelings leads to unhappiness.
CREATIVITY   Flitting from idea to idea is not creative.
COMMUNICATION   Talking for its own sake does not bring agreement.
AMBITION   Not being able to decide on a goal leads to failure.
SERVICE   A tendency to change loyalties leads to being considered untrustworthy.
NURTURE   Erratic care de-stabilizes a relationship.
ECONOMY   Constantly looking for new speculation leads to loss.
NEUTRALITY   Restlessness.
REASON   Not being able to concentrate on one problem means solutions cannot be found.

33
·RETREAT·

REASON — It is best not to look for logical explanations at this time.

JUDGEMENT — It is best not to make big decisions at this time.

INNOCENCE — It is best to take no chances at this time.

NEUTRALITY — A tactical withdrawal.

AWARENESS — It is best to remain passive at this time.

ECONOMY — It is best to make no financial commitments at this time.

EMOTION — It is best not to act on a feeling at this time.

NURTURE — It is best not to interfere at this time.

CREATIVITY — It is best to put an idea to one side until it can be expressed properly.

SERVICE — It is best not to act on initiative at this time.

AMBITION — It is best to make a tactical withdrawal in order to preserve strength.

COMMUNICATION — It is best to say nothing in order to avoid an unwinnable argument.

Minor achievements are possible with perseverance

33 line 1

———×———

Danger – do not act

JUDGEMENT It is very late to change a decision. It is best to do nothing.
INNOCENCE It is very late to use ignorance as an excuse. It is best to face the consequences.
AWARENESS It is very late to repair the influence that the ego may have had on a matter. It is best to let things take their own course.
EMOTION Feelings are growing too strong too change. If there is pain, it is best simply to endure it.
CREATIVITY It is very late to want to change an idea. If there is criticism, it is best to accept it.
COMMUNICATION It is very late to withdraw what has been said. It is best simply to face any rebuke.
AMBITION The time for withdrawal has been left very late. It is best to accept what happens.
SERVICE It is very late to admit to inadequacy. It is best to take the consequences.
NURTURE It is very late to have a change of heart. It is best to face the heartache.
ECONOMY It is very late to withdraw from a commitment. It is best to face the consequences.
NEUTRALITY A very late change of mind.
REASON It is very late to admit a mistake. It is best to face the consequences.

33 line 2

———×———

JUDGEMENT If a decision is fair enough, no one can argue with it.
INNOCENCE If character is pure enough, nothing can corrupt it.
AWARENESS If faith is strong enough, nothing can shake it.
EMOTION If a feeling is strong enough, nothing can change it.
CREATIVITY If an idea is strong enough, nothing can destroy it.
COMMUNICATION If the truth is strong enough, no one can stop it coming out.
AMBITION If conviction is strong enough, nothing can break it.

SERVICE If loyalty is strong enough, nothing can shake it.
NURTURE If a bond is deep enough, nothing can break it.
ECONOMY If prudence is a strong enough virtue, nothing can hurt financially.
NEUTRALITY Too strong to break.
REASON If reasoning is totally logical, no one can disprove it.

33 line 3

———□———

Lucky

JUDGEMENT It is difficult to go back on a decision. It is best done gradually to avoid a loss of respect.
INNOCENCE It is hard to admit ignorance. It is best done in a way that avoids embarrassment.
AWARENESS It is hard to let go of the ego. It is best done gradually.
EMOTION It is difficult to apologize. It is best done subtly to avoid embarrassment.
CREATIVITY It is hard to let go of an unworthy idea. It is best done in a way that minimizes criticism.
COMMUNICATION It is difficult to withdraw from an argument. It is better to do it gradually to avoid offence.
AMBITION It is hard to withdraw from competition. It is best to do it subtly to avoid loss of respect.
SERVICE It is hard to admit inadequacy in a task. It is best done in a way that minimizes lost respect.
NURTURE It is painful to have a change of heart. It is best to give way gradually.
ECONOMY It is difficult to change course. It is best done gradually to minimize risk.
NEUTRALITY Gradual retreat in dangerous circumstances.
REASON It is difficult to admit a mistake. It is best done subtly to avoid loss of respect.

TWELVE CHANNELS OF THE I CHING

33 line 4

---□---

Lucky in the long term

JUDGEMENT Admitting an error of judgement causes a loss of pride but gains the respect of those who are honest.

INNOCENCE Admitting ignorance causes lost pride but engenders protectiveness in others.

AWARENESS Withdrawal damages the ego but encourages a growth in awareness.

EMOTION An apology causes embarrassment but deepens real feeling.

CREATIVITY Admitting that an idea is not good means lost pride but a genuine artist.

COMMUNICATION Withdrawal from an argument leads to derision but increases the chances of being believed in the future.

AMBITION A withdrawal from competition hurts pride but increases real strength.

SERVICE An admission of inadequacy hurts personal pride but shows trust worthiness.

NURTURE A change of heart hurts pride but deepens a bond.

ECONOMY Withdrawal from a financial commitment raises eyebrows but improves long-term security.

NEUTRALITY Retreat causing short-term loss but long-term gain.

REASON Admitting an error means lost pride but a rational mind.

33 line 5

---□---

Perseverance brings luck

JUDGEMENT Finding the right opportunity for a change of mind and sticking to it.

INNOCENCE Finding the right opportunity to confess ignorance and meaning it.

AWARENESS Happily rejecting ego-led behaviour and sticking to it.

EMOTION Apologizing at the right time and not bringing the argument up again.

CREATIVITY Rejecting an unworthy idea at the right time and resisting the temptation to use it again.

COMMUNICATION Finding the most opportune time to withdraw from an argument and saying no more.

AMBITION Finding the right time to withdraw and not being tempted back into competition.

SERVICE Finding the right time to admit inadequacy and accepting the fact.

NURTURE Finding the right time for a change of heart and having no doubts.

ECONOMY Finding the right opportunity to make an economy and sticking to it.

NEUTRALITY Finding the right opportunity to retreat.

REASON Finding the right time to admit a mistake and accepting the consequences.

33 line 6

---□---

Progress

JUDGEMENT A change of mind at the right time makes correct decisions possible.

INNOCENCE An admission of ignorance at the right time makes real learning possible.

AWARENESS Rejecting the ego at the right opportunity allows a growth in awareness.

EMOTION An apology at the right time clears the way for mutual feeling.

CREATIVITY Rejecting an unworthy idea clears the way for real creativity.

COMMUNICATION Withdrawal from an argument at the right opportunity clears the way for meaningful dialogue.

AMBITION Tactical withdrawal makes eventual success possible.

SERVICE Admitting inadequacies hastens the arrival of more suitable duties.

NURTURE A change of heart at the right time is beneficial.

ECONOMY Making economies at the right time stimulates financial growth.

NEUTRALITY Correctly timed withdrawal.

REASON Admitting an error at the right time makes logical conclusions possible.

34

·POWER·

REASON
Great understanding; remain open-minded.

JUDGEMENT
Great wisdom; remain free of prejudice.

NEUTRALITY
Great power.

INNOCENCE
A great capacity for learning; avoid temptation.

ECONOMY
Financial power; remain prudent.

AWARENESS
Power through awareness; avoid ego-led behaviour.

NURTURE
The ability to stimulate real growth; remain understanding.

EMOTION
Powerful emotion; remain sympathetic.

Of great use to a cause; avoid self-importance.

CREATIVITY
Great creative power; avoid pretentiousness.

SERVICE

AMBITION
Great power; avoid ambition for its own sake.

COMMUNICATION
Powerful words; always be ready to listen.

Perseverance brings progress

TWELVE CHANNELS OF THE I CHING

34 line 1

———□———

Action is unlucky

JUDGEMENT Making a decision on a small amount of evidence is inevitably wrong.
INNOCENCE Acting in an area of little experience leads to insecurity.
AWARENESS Insufficient faith leading to a loss of awareness.
EMOTION Insincerity; continuing in this way leads to unhappiness.
CREATIVITY An incomplete idea; its expression would mean artistic failure.
COMMUNICATION Powerful words that do not really mean anything.
AMBITION Over-ambition; continuing leads to failure.
SERVICE Too much responsibility; continuing leads to failure in a task.
NURTURE Expecting too much; continuing in this way builds a barrier.
ECONOMY Speculation without sufficient resources leading to loss.
NEUTRALITY Acting without sufficient resources.
REASON Continuing with an incomplete understanding leads to incorrect conclusions.

34 line 2

———□———

Continuing in this way brings luck

JUDGEMENT Wisdom allowing correct decisions.
INNOCENCE Genuine innocence permitting pleasure.
AWARENESS Powerful faith bringing higher awareness.
EMOTION Genuine feelings finding expression.
CREATIVITY Powerful ideas finding expression.
COMMUNICATION Honest words bringing understanding.
AMBITION Great ability bringing progress.
SERVICE Devotion to duty being of real worth.
NURTURE Real care being of value.
ECONOMY Continued prudence bringing financial benefit.

NEUTRALITY The continued use of power.
REASON Continued open-mindedness bringing understanding.

34 line 3

———□———

Continuing in this way is dangerous

JUDGEMENT Forcing a decision is wrong. It is better to wait for it to become obvious.
INNOCENCE Indulgence is wrong. It is better to wait until an opportunity for genuine pleasure presents itself.
AWARENESS Forcing awareness is dangerous. It is better to wait until it happens naturally.
EMOTION Exaggerated feelings are dangerous. It is better to wait for the real thing.
CREATIVITY Pushing ahead with unworthy ideas is wrong. It is better to wait for real inspiration.
COMMUNICATION Forcing a point is wrong. It is better to wait until it will be properly understood.
AMBITION Forcing progress is dangerous. It is better to wait for the right opportunity.
SERVICE Exaggerated self-importance is dangerous. It is better to wait for a task suitable for abilities.
NURTURE Expecting too much is dangerous. It is better to wait for the right time.
ECONOMY Looking for quick profit is risky. It is better to wait for the right opportunity.
NEUTRALITY Danger in forcing progress.
REASON Forcing a solution is wrong. It is better to wait until there is a more complete understanding.

34 line 4

———□———

Continuing in this way brings luck and avoids guilt

JUDGEMENT A fundamental sense of fairness evens out discrepancies and allows correct decisions.
INNOCENCE A pure heart puts up with difficulties and allows genuine pleasure.

AWARENESS A solid faith allows the ego to be ignored, permitting greater awareness.

EMOTION An honest emotion conquers difficulty and leads to happiness.

CREATIVITY An original idea overcomes the difficulties of expression.

COMMUNICATION Honest words overcome disagreement and find a sympathetic hearing.

AMBITION Genuine ability removes obstacles and leads to progress.

SERVICE Devotion to duty allows difficulties to be overcome and means orders can be carried out.

NURTURE Genuine care smooths over problems and stimulates growth.

ECONOMY Prudence solves difficulties and permits a financial upturn.

NEUTRALITY Fundamental values overcoming obstacles.

REASON Fundamental understanding solves problems and points the way to greater knowledge.

34 line 5

——×——

No need for guilt

JUDGEMENT Decisions are more obvious than was thought.

INNOCENCE Security is easily found.

AWARENESS Higher awareness is more real than was expected.

EMOTION It is easier than was expected to express a feeling.

CREATIVITY Ideas come easily.

COMMUNICATION The right words come without trying.

AMBITION Progress is easier than was anticipated.

SERVICE Orders are simpler to carry out than was expected.

NURTURE Natural care comes more easily than was anticipated.

ECONOMY Financial growth is easier than was expected.

NEUTRALITY Easy progress.

REASON Understanding comes more easily than was expected.

34 line 6

——×——

No progress – lucky in the long term

JUDGEMENT Obstinacy leading to an impossible decision; it is well to learn from this.

INNOCENCE Over-confidence leading to an impossible situation; this should be a lesson.

AWARENESS Allowing the ego to act on higher values leads to a deadlock. This is a lesson from which to learn.

EMOTION Exaggerated feeling leading to problems; this should be a lesson.

CREATIVITY Forcing the creative process with unhappy results; it is well to learn from this.

COMMUNICATION Stubbornness leading to insoluble argument; this should be a lesson.

AMBITION Naked ambition leading to a no-win situation; it is well to learn from this.

SERVICE Self-importance making a mockery of loyalty; this should be seen as a lesson.

NURTURE Lack of understanding leading to resentment; it is well to learn from this.

ECONOMY Greed leading to financial deadlock; this is a lesson.

NEUTRALITY Obstinacy leading to deadlock.

REASON Inexorable logic leading to an insoluble problem; it is well to learn from this.

35
· PROGRESS ·

REASON

An acceptance of a theory permits a rapid growth in understanding.

Progress through the acceptance of a situation.

JUDGEMENT

An acceptance of previously laid down principles allows far-reaching decisions.

NEUTRALITY

INNOCENCE

Trust permits great learning.

ECONOMY

Economic progress through the acceptance of financial restraints.

AWARENESS

Taking certain things on faith allows a substantial growth in awareness.

NURTURE

Growth engendered by mutual trust.

EMOTION

Trust allowing feelings to grow.

Loyalty proving the ability to accept more responsibility.

Creative progress due to acceptance of standards.

SERVICE

Rapid progress due to acceptance of position.

Listening to others permits leaps in understanding.

CREATIVITY

AMBITION

COMMUNICATION

Progress

35 line 1

———×———

Correct – continuing in this way brings eventual luck

JUDGEMENT If decisions are not likely to be implemented, it is best to retain composure.

INNOCENCE If a prospect is worrying, it is best to remain calm.

AWARENESS If circumstances are likely to prevent awareness, it is best to remain unperturbed.

EMOTION If feelings are likely to be rebuffed, it is best to stay calm.

CREATIVITY If ideas are not likely to be appreciated, it is best to remain composed.

COMMUNICATION If the truth is likely to be misunderstood, it is well to remain calm.

AMBITION If progress is likely to be blocked, it is best to remain unperturbed.

SERVICE If circumstances are likely to prevent orders being carried out, it is well to remain composed.

NURTURE If caring is likely to be rejected, it is best to remain calm.

ECONOMY If circumstances threaten to cause loss, it is best to remain collected.

NEUTRALITY Progress is blocked.

REASON If progress towards understanding is likely to be blocked, it is well to remain composed.

35 line 2

———×———

Perseverance brings luck

JUDGEMENT Trying to make a decision that is not understood; its wisdom will eventually be seen.

INNOCENCE Feeling insecure in spite of acting correctly; security will eventually be found.

AWARENESS Continuing to act according to higher values but finding no reward; great awareness comes eventually.

EMOTION Strong feelings that are not reciprocated, but there is great happiness eventually.

CREATIVITY Persevering without appreciation; it is forthcoming eventually.

COMMUNICATION Being honest without being believed; the truth is eventually greatly appreciated.

AMBITION Ability bringing no progress; great goals can be achieved in the end.

SERVICE Devoted to duty without being appreciated; loyalty is eventually rewarded.

NURTURE Care that is not appreciated; its true value will be seen eventually.

ECONOMY Prudence that shows no results; financial growth is achieved eventually.

NEUTRALITY Progress without obvious direction.

REASON Tackling a problem without an answer in sight; great progress is made eventually.

35 line 3

———×———

No need for guilt

JUDGEMENT Decisions are supported.

INNOCENCE Innocence is understood.

AWARENESS Higher and lower self are in agreement.

EMOTION Feelings are shared.

CREATIVITY Ideas are appreciated.

COMMUNICATION Others agree with what is said.

AMBITION Progress is supported.

SERVICE Leaders and followers are in agreement.

NURTURE Care is needed and appreciated.

ECONOMY Basic finances support speculation.

NEUTRALITY Positive forces in agreement.

REASON Theories are accepted.

35 line 4

———▫———

Continuing in this way is dangerous

JUDGEMENT It is dangerous to seek power.

INNOCENCE Self-indulgence is hazardous.

AWARENESS Seeking moral superiority is dangerous.

EMOTION Selfish actions can endanger a relationship.
CREATIVITY Self-indulgence invites criticism.
COMMUNICATION Talking too much invites dangerous argument.
AMBITION Selfish ambition is dangerous.
SERVICE Self-importance is perilous.
NURTURE There is danger in using parental power for its own sake.
ECONOMY Greed is dangerous.
NEUTRALITY Danger in progressing selfishly.
REASON Danger in cleverness for its own sake.

35 line 5

—— × ——

Luck and progress – no need for guilt

JUDGEMENT Fairness is more important than anything. It is best not to worry about the outcome of decisions.
INNOCENCE A pure heart is everything; missing out on indulgence does not matter.
AWARENESS Living by higher values is everything. It does not matter whether it is rewarded with awareness or not.
EMOTION Just to feel is enough; reciprocation is unimportant.
CREATIVITY Appreciation is not important, creativity is a reward in itself.
COMMUNICATION It is enough to encourage constructive dialogue; the results of arguments are unimportant.
AMBITION Genuine ability is a reward in itself; winning or losing does not matter.
SERVICE Loyalty is enough; rewards do not matter.
NURTURE It is enough to care, whether it is appreciated or not.
ECONOMY Economic stability is everything; quick profits are unimportant.
NEUTRALITY Positive progress through not caring about results.
REASON Understanding is everything. It does not matter whether conclusions are drawn.

35 line 6

—— □ ——

Lucky – continuing selfishly leads to regret

JUDGEMENT Power should be used only in correcting wrong decisions. It is dangerous to use it in other situations.
INNOCENCE A strong will is of value only in resisting corruption. Acting in this way normally leads to humiliation.
AWARENESS Higher values should only be applied personally. It is dangerous to judge others by them.
EMOTION Forcibly exposing feelings is of value only when correcting personal selfishness. Acting in this way towards others results in humiliation.
CREATIVITY Mistakes may require ruthlessness, but it is dangerous to apply it generally.
COMMUNICATION Harsh words should be used only in self-admonishment; they should not be used against others.
AMBITION Ruthlessness is permissible only when honing abilities. It is dangerous to try to make progress in this way.
SERVICE Pride is permissible only on a personal level, otherwise it leads to humiliation.
NURTURE Harsh discipline is solely for correcting behaviour. It is self-defeating if used as a matter of course.
ECONOMY Ruthlessness has value only in correcting financial mistakes. It leads to humiliation if used generally.
NEUTRALITY Forced progress being permissible in correcting mistakes but dangerous in other situations.
REASON Hard logic should be used only in correcting mistakes. It leads to humiliation if deep understanding is the goal.

36
·NEGATIVITY·

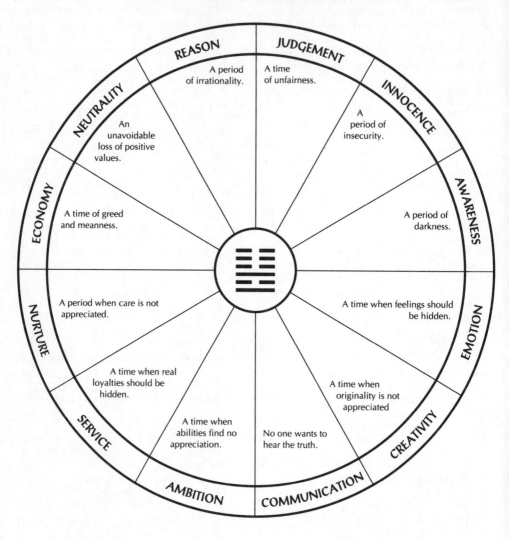

REASON — A period of irrationality.

JUDGEMENT — A time of unfairness.

NEUTRALITY — An unavoidable loss of positive values.

INNOCENCE — A period of insecurity.

ECONOMY — A time of greed and meanness.

AWARENESS — A period of darkness.

NURTURE — A period when care is not appreciated.

EMOTION — A time when feelings should be hidden.

SERVICE — A time when real loyalties should be hidden.

CREATIVITY — A time when originality is not appreciated

AMBITION — A time when abilities find no appreciation.

COMMUNICATION — No one wants to hear the truth.

Persevere virtuously – prepare for difficulties

36 line 1

---□---

There may be gossip

JUDGEMENT   Sweeping decisions would prove wrong. It is better to hold on to principles, in spite of misunderstanding.

INNOCENCE   Big moves now would be wrong. It is better to cling to innocence in spite of derision.

AWARENESS   Seeking higher awareness would end in failure. In spite of derision, it is better to hold on to beliefs.

EMOTION   Expressing deeply held feelings now would be a mistake. It is better to keep them hidden, in spite of misunderstanding.

CREATIVITY   Great originality would not be appreciated. It is better to save these ideas for another time, in spite of criticism.

COMMUNICATION   At this time great honesty would find only misunderstanding. In spite of talk, it is better to remain quiet.

AMBITION   Ambitious strides would end in failure. It is better to be content with the present position, in spite of misunderstanding.

SERVICE   It would be wrong to accept responsibility. It is better to remain loyal to the original cause, in spite of misunderstanding.

NURTURE   Allowing freedom at this time would be wrong. It is better to care in an unobtrusive way, although this may not be understood.

ECONOMY   Speculation would prove a mistake. It is wiser to hold on to money, in spite of misunderstanding.

NEUTRALITY   Non-action.

REASON   Far-reaching conclusions would prove incorrect. It is better to hold on to simpler theories, in spite of criticism.

36 line 2

---×---

JUDGEMENT   Decisions find partial disagreement, but it is best to remain loyal to principles.

INNOCENCE   Derision; in spite of insecurity, it is best to hold on to innocence.

AWARENESS   Higher values are attacked, but it is still best to hold on to them.

EMOTION   It is best to remain true to feeling, in spite of emotional pain.

CREATIVITY   Originality is criticized, but it is best to hold on to artistic values.

AMBITION   Advantage is taken of a lack of competitiveness. It is still best to continue to nurture abilities.

COMMUNICATION   The truth is attacked, but it is best to remain loyal to it.

SERVICE   Devotion to duty is misunderstood; however, it is best to remain loyal.

NURTURE   A caring attitude goes unappreciated; however, it is still better to remain caring.

ECONOMY   A loss is incurred; it is best to remain prudent.

NEUTRALITY   A partial success for negative values.

REASON   Theories are partially misunderstood; it is best to remain loyal to them.

36 line 3

---□---

JUDGEMENT   The roots of injustice are uncovered, although this is not understood straight away.

INNOCENCE   A cause of corruption is exposed for what it is, although this can be accepted only slowly.

AWARENESS   Awareness uncovers a fundamental untruth, although this cannot be acted upon too quickly.

EMOTION   A cause of pain is uncovered, although it cannot be dealt with immediately.

CREATIVITY   A creative block is removed, although time is required for development.

COMMUNICATION   An argument is won, although it takes times for this to be accepted.

AMBITION   A cause of unfair competition is seen, although this cannot be acted upon too quickly.

SERVICE   Disloyalty is exposed, although it cannot be immediately believed.

NURTURE   A cause of behaviour is discovered, although it must be dealt with gently.

ECONOMY   The cause of loss is seen, although it is best not to be too hasty.

NEUTRALITY   Negative elements are exposed.

REASON   The cause of misunderstanding is discovered, although it will not be immediately obvious.

36 line 4

———×———

JUDGEMENT Fundamental injustice can be seen and can be circumvented.
INNOCENCE Corruption can be seen for what it is and can be avoided.
AWARENESS Darkness can be seen for what it is, making an escape possible.
EMOTION Dishonest feelings are exposed, permitting an escape.
CREATIVITY The root cause of a creative block is seen, allowing it to be avoided.
COMMUNICATION Dishonest words are spotted, allowing an escape from argument.
AMBITION Naked ambition is exposed, allowing it to be avoided.
SERVICE Disloyalty is seen for what it is, allowing it to be avoided.
NURTURE A root cause of behaviour is exposed, allowing it to be avoided.
ECONOMY The real reason for loss is seen, allowing it to be avoided.
NEUTRALITY The root causes of negativity are exposed.
REASON A fault in reasoning can be seen and can be avoided.

36 line 5

———×———

Persevere

JUDGEMENT When control is everything, principles should still be retained.
INNOCENCE When corruption is all around, it is still best to cling to innocence.
AWARENESS When darkness rules, higher values should still be retained.
EMOTION In a cold situation, real feelings should not be ignored.
CREATIVITY In an uninspiring situation, it is best to hang on to originality.
COMMUNICATION When dishonesty is all around, the truth should be borne in mind.
AMBITION In a wholly competitive situation, abilities should still be nurtured for their own sake.
SERVICE When disloyalty is all around, it is best to try to remain dutiful.
NURTURE When care is totally unappreciated, a caring attitude should still be retained.

ECONOMY When greed is all around, prudence should be retained.
NEUTRALITY Hanging on to positive values in the face of overwhelming negativity.
REASON When nothing will be understood, reason should still be retained.

36 line 6

———×———

JUDGEMENT Power that begins to consume itself.
INNOCENCE Complete self-indulgence that proves unsatisfying.
AWARENESS Worldly values that feed on themselves, proving unsatisfactory.
EMOTION Selfishness ultimately proving unsatisfactory.
CREATIVITY Self-indulgence that ultimately shows itself to be worthless.
COMMUNICATION Dishonesty that inevitably exposes itself.
AMBITION Naked ambition, in which all lose.
SERVICE Neglect of duty that hurts everyone.
NURTURE Bad behaviour that leads to more bad behaviour.
ECONOMY Greed that destroys itself.
NEUTRALITY Negativity beginning to consume itself.
REASON Closed-minded logic destroys its own arguments.

37
PROPER
·RELATIONSHIPS·

REASON — Facts considered on their relationship to each other.

JUDGEMENT — Acting correctly on behalf of others.

INNOCENCE — Finding security through mutual respect.

NEUTRALITY — Acting according to position.

AWARENESS — Awareness of position in the scheme of things.

ECONOMY — Prudence exercised in a stable economic situation.

EMOTION — A stable relationship based on mutual respect.

NURTURE — Proper relationships within a family; tolerance helps.

CREATIVITY — Correct proportion.

SERVICE — Acting correctly in a team according to position.

AMBITION — Compromising personal ambition for a mutual goal.

COMMUNICATION — Balanced debate in which all are allowed to speak

Persevere in small matters

37 line 1

------□------

Avoiding future guilt

JUDGEMENT Impartiality from the beginning avoids later bias.
INNOCENCE Hard discipline, the reason for which can be appreciated only later.
AWARENESS Self-examination from the outset avoids later delusions.
EMOTION Honesty at the beginning of a relationship avoids pain later.
CREATIVITY Creative discipline at the beginning avoids later flaws.
COMMUNICATION Honesty at the beginning of a dialogue avoids lies later.
AMBITION False goals rejected at the beginning means no deviation later.
SERVICE Discipline at the beginning of a task avoids problems later.
NURTURE Dealing firmly with the young avoids bad traits becoming part of character.
ECONOMY Prudence at the beginning avoids debts in the future.
NEUTRALITY Discipline at the beginning.
REASON Attention to method from the beginning avoids later miscalculations.

37 line 2

------×------

Perseverance brings luck

JUDGEMENT Not a time for big decisions; attention should be focused on small matters.
INNOCENCE Not a time for independent action; compliance with others is best.
AWARENESS Not a time for higher awareness; practical issues need attention.
EMOTION Not a time for personal feelings; the practical needs of a relationship need attention.
CREATIVITY Not a time for artistic achievement; the mundane aspects of creativity should be attended to.
COMMUNICATION Not a time for forging agreements; just getting along is enough.
AMBITION Not a time for personal ambition; mundane matters should be attended to.
SERVICE Not the time for more responsibility; ordinary duties should be attended to.
NURTURE Not the time to allow independent action; practicalities need attention.

ECONOMY Not a time for great investment; mundane economic matters should be attended to.
NEUTRALITY Practical issues needing attention.
REASON No great solutions are to be found; basic facts need attention.

37 line 3

------□------

Lucky to an extent – danger and inevitable guilt

JUDGEMENT Imposing discipline may seem petty but is preferable to the kind of freedom that erodes stability.
INNOCENCE Punishments may seem unfair, but this is preferable to a lack of discipline.
AWARENESS Self-discipline taken too far may lead to some regret, but it is more beneficial than permitting laxity.
EMOTION Emotional honesty taken too far causes pain but is preferable to hiding feelings.
CREATIVITY Creative restraint may seem to waste ideas but is preferable to artistic indiscipline.
COMMUNICATION Lost tempers cause bad feelings, but this is preferable to dishonesty.
AMBITION Self-discipline taken too far is preferable to laxity.
SERVICE Attention to detail may seem petty, but this is preferable to laxity.
NURTURE Punishments taken too far cause heartache, but this is better than ignoring the problem.
ECONOMY Prudence taken too far can be seen as meanness, but this is preferable to extravagance.
NEUTRALITY Harsh discipline being preferable to laxity.
REASON Attention to detail may seem unimportant but is preferable to a wider view which leads to mistakes.

TWELVE CHANNELS OF THE I CHING

37 line 4

——×——

Very lucky

JUDGEMENT Unselfish decision-making encourages respect.
INNOCENCE Acting correctly brings security.
AWARENESS Acting correctly inspires a growth in awareness.
EMOTION Honesty about feelings keeps a relationship healthy.
CREATIVITY Attention to technique allows creative ideas to flow.
COMMUNICATION Personal honesty inspires open dialogue.
AMBITION Constant vigilance allows openings to be seen.
SERVICE Devotion to duty allows the success of bigger projects.
NURTURE Constant nurture inspires growth.
ECONOMY Prudence in small ways encourages general economic health.
NEUTRALITY Attention to general welfare.
REASON Approaching problems methodically permits their solution.

37 line 5

——□——

Luck – no need to worry

JUDGEMENT Leading by example.
INNOCENCE Wanting to learn, therefore admitting ignorance.
AWARENESS Higher awareness in action as an example to others.
EMOTION Showing love through action.
CREATIVITY Genuine creative expression invites inspiration.
COMMUNICATION Encouraging dialogue by being attentive.
AMBITION Uncompetitive ambition inspires mutual help.
SERVICE Dutifully following orders inspires respect.
NURTURE Encouraging by example.
ECONOMY General economic sense encouraging personal prudence.
NEUTRALITY Confident action through not fearing for position.
REASON Admitting ignorance in order to find a deeper understanding.

37 line 6

——□——

Eventual luck

JUDGEMENT Honest decisions are appreciated in the end.
INNOCENCE Acting correctly in the meantime leads to future security.
AWARENESS Moral behaviour allows eventual growth.
EMOTION Honest emotion finds its expression in the end.
CREATIVITY Genuine creativity finds appreciation eventually.
COMMUNICATION The truth is believed in the end.
AMBITION Worthy goals are achieved eventually.
SERVICE Devotion to duty is appreciated in the end.
NURTURE The benefit of real care is seen in the end.
ECONOMY The benefits of prudence are seen eventually.
NEUTRALITY Eventual results of honest endeavour.
REASON A problem tackled methodically eventually yields an answer.

__38__
· OPPOSITION ·

REASON — Opposing ideas that give rise to unexpected understanding.

JUDGEMENT — Opposing arguments giving rise to unexpected decisions.

NEUTRALITY — Opposing negative influences producing random positive results.

INNOCENCE — Unpleasantness giving rise to unexpected learning.

ECONOMY — Expenses giving rise to unexpected profit.

AWARENESS — Chance situations producing unexpected insight.

NURTURE — Clashes that produce unexpected mutual feeling.

EMOTION — Chance encounters giving rise to unexpected feelings.

SERVICE — Seemingly pointless tasks producing unexpected bonuses.

AMBITION — Challenges that can throw up unexpected abilities.

COMMUNICATION — Opposing ideas that produce unexpected agreement.

CREATIVITY — Opposing influences producing unexpected creative ideas.

Luck in small ways

38 line 1

———□———

JUDGEMENT A decision that seems impossible should be delayed; it will eventually become obvious. Beware of abusing power.
INNOCENCE If a situation seems impossible, wait; a way out will show itself eventually. Beware of temptation.
AWARENESS If awareness is prevented, accept it; it will return in time. Beware of the ego.
EMOTION A seemingly insoluble clash of temperament; time can heal this. Beware of false emotion.
CREATIVITY Do not chase after inspiration; it will come in its own time. Beware of unworthy ideas.
COMMUNICATION What needs to be said should be put off for now; the right opportunity will present itself. Beware of liars.
AMBITION If progress is blocked, do not chase after it; the right opportunity will show itself. Beware of cheats.
SERVICE If a task is too demanding, leave it for now; it will be possible eventually. Beware of untrustworthy superiors.
NURTURE If children are bad, they will feel remorse in their own time. Beware of temper.
ECONOMY If expenses cannot be met, wait; a way will be found in time. Beware of thieves.
NEUTRALITY Letting go of problems.
REASON If a problem seems too difficult, let it go; an answer will present itself in time. Beware of corrupt knowledge.

38 line 2

———□———

Blameless

JUDGEMENT Simple decisions; there is nothing wrong in this.
INNOCENCE It is all right to act in a simple way.
AWARENESS There is nothing wrong with simplicity.
EMOTION Simple feelings are not wrong.
CREATIVITY There is nothing wrong in simple ideas.
COMMUNICATION Informal conversation is not wrong.
AMBITION There is nothing wrong in taking small steps.
SERVICE It is not wrong to act within capabilities.
NURTURE There is nothing wrong in simple, caring acts.
ECONOMY Simple prudence is not wrong.
NEUTRALITY Acting in simple way.
REASON There is nothing wrong with a simple line of thought.

38 line 3

———×———

Bad start, good end

JUDGEMENT A seemingly impossible decision, which becomes obvious eventually.
INNOCENCE A bad situation, which turns out well in the end.
AWARENESS A battered ego; awareness is found eventually.
EMOTION Outbursts of temper leading to reconciliation.
CREATIVITY Seemingly useless ideas, whose worth is seen eventually.
COMMUNICATION An agreement seems absolutely impossible but will come eventually.
AMBITION A seemingly irrevocable loss, leading to eventual progress.
SERVICE A task seems impossible but is carried out eventually.
NURTURE Seemingly impossible behaviour, which can be rectified eventually.
ECONOMY A seemingly impossible financial situation, which proves tenable in the end.
NEUTRALITY Seemingly irrevocable loss.
REASON A seemingly insoluble problem which is understood eventually.

38 line 4

———□———

Dangerous but not to blame

JUDGEMENT A small piece of evidence makes a difficult decision more obvious.
INNOCENCE In a difficult situation, a friend is found.
AWARENESS In difficult circumstances, guidance is found.

EMOTION Opposing feelings find a certain reconciliation through honesty.
CREATIVITY In spite of a lack of understanding, ideas find a certain appreciation.
COMMUNICATION In spite of opposition, certain words find sympathy.
AMBITION In spite of the competition, like-minded friends are found.
SERVICE In spite of difficulties, devotion to duty is appreciated.
NURTURE A clash with a child throwing up a new line of communication.
ECONOMY A very tight financial situation showing a small but unexpected return.
NEUTRALITY Support in a difficult situation.
REASON A difficult problem throws up a clue.

38 line 5

───×───

Strength is correct – no need for guilt

JUDGEMENT It is not wrong to make unpopular decisions when they are necessary.
INNOCENCE It is not wrong to trust someone.
AWARENESS It is not wrong to follow guidance when it shows itself.
EMOTION It is not wrong to respond to genuine emotion.
CREATIVITY It is not wrong to follow inspiration, no matter how obscure.
COMMUNICATION It is not wrong to agree with those who speak the truth.
AMBITION It is right to take a chance when it is offered.
SERVICE It is not wrong to accept help when it is offered.
NURTURE Children should be encouraged when they show signs of maturity.
ECONOMY It is not wrong to accept financial help when it is needed.
NEUTRALITY Accepting help when it is offered.
REASON It is right to follow a clue.

38 line 6

───▫───

Not as dangerous as expected – eventual luck

JUDGEMENT Understanding the true nature of a decision makes it more obvious.
INNOCENCE An untrusting attitude should be abandoned; security will be found eventually.
AWARENESS A lack of awareness cannot be rectified through personal effort. Guidance leads to eventual progress.
EMOTION More sympathy should be shown for other's feelings; this permits eventual happiness.
CREATIVITY Criticism should be noted, allowing greater creativity later.
COMMUNICATION Listening to others makes agreement easier.
AMBITION Abandoning competition for its own sake permits eventual progress.
SERVICE An acceptance of position facilitates the completion of tasks.
NURTURE Anger should be contained; trying to understand encourages eventual growth.
ECONOMY Meanness should be avoided; sensible generosity leads to eventual financial growth.
NEUTRALITY Influences that appear negative, turning out to be positive.
REASON Seeing a problem for what it is increases the chance of its solution.

·OBSTRUCTION·

REASON
Seemingly insoluble problems lie ahead; it is advisable to pause and seek a new approach.

JUDGEMENT
Seemingly impossible decisions lie ahead; it is best to stop and look for a new approach.

NEUTRALITY
Obstruction requiring tactical retreat.

INNOCENCE
Being prevented from doing something. it is best to wait and figure out a way round it.

ECONOMY
Problems ahead; it is best to pause and seek financial advice.

AWARENESS
Something inside blocking higher awareness; a change of attitude is required.

NURTURE
Resistance to care; it is best to make time to find a new approach.

EMOTION
Something is blocking real emotion; a selfish attitude needs to change.

SERVICE
A problem stands in the way of duty; it is best to pause and find a new approach.

AMBITION
Obstruction to progress; it is best to pause and find a less ambitious way to deal with it.

COMMUNICATION
Disagreement ahead; it is best to pause and find a diplomatic way of dealing with it.

CREATIVITY
A creative block; it is best to stop and look for a new approach.

Seek advice –
perseverance brings eventual luck

39 line 1

——×——

JUDGEMENT It is best to wait for the right time to make a decision.
INNOCENCE Acting now would be a mistake. It is best to wait for the right time.
AWARENESS Awareness is obstructed at the moment. It is best to wait for the right time.
EMOTION Now is not the right time to express a feeling. It is best to wait.
CREATIVITY It is best to wait for inspiration to appear in its own time.
COMMUNICATION It is best to wait for the right opportunity to say what has got to be said.
AMBITION It is best to wait for the right opportunity to make progress.
SERVICE It is best to wait for the right time to carry out an order.
NURTURE Now is not the time to allow freedom. It is best to wait.
ECONOMY This is not the time for speculation. It is best to wait for the right opportunity.
NEUTRALITY Forced progress.
REASON It is best to wait until a solution presents itself.

39 line 2

——×——

JUDGEMENT Inability to make a decision due to lack of evidence.
INNOCENCE Action is not possible because of others.
AWARENESS An obstruction to higher awareness is caused by physical circumstances.
EMOTION An emotional block is someone else's fault.
CREATIVITY A creative block is the result of external circumstances.
COMMUNICATION Disagreements that prevent open dialogue are the fault of others.
AMBITION Obstruction to progress caused by others.
SERVICE Problems that stand in the way of duty are the fault of others.
NURTURE Resistance to care caused by outside influences.
ECONOMY Financial problems caused by external circumstances.
NEUTRALITY Obstructions caused by external circumstances.
REASON Understanding is not possible because of a lack of information.

39 line 3

——▫——

JUDGEMENT A decision seems impossible. It is best to give up.
INNOCENCE An impossible situation; it is best to give up.
AWARENESS Forced awareness leading to problems; it is best to stop.
EMOTION Feelings would not be reciprocated. It is best not to express them.
CREATIVITY Creative ideas are not understood. It is best to shelve them.
COMMUNICATION Words will not be understood. It is best to say nothing.
AMBITION Progress that leads to problems; it is best to turn back.
SERVICE Duties that are impossible; it is best to admit it.
NURTURE Care that meets with resistance; it is best to leave it.
ECONOMY Dangerous speculation; it is best to withdraw.
NEUTRALITY Positive progress, leading to problems.
REASON A problem proves insurmountable. It is best to leave it.

39 line 4

——×——

JUDGEMENT A decision is not possible; pausing leads to a shared perspective.
INNOCENCE An impossible situation; waiting brings good friends.
AWARENESS Awareness is blocked; waiting brings shared ideals.
EMOTION Emotions would not be returned; waiting brings shared feelings.
CREATIVITY Ideas would not be understood; pausing allows comparison with similar ideas.
COMMUNICATION An agreement looks impossible; pausing brings friendly words.
AMBITION Progress leads to problems; pausing leads to mutual co-operation.

SERVICE It would be impossible to carry out duties; waiting leads to co-operation.

NURTURE Caring would be resisted; waiting brings mutual understanding.

ECONOMY Speculation would mean problems; waiting leads to the sharing of financial obligations.

NEUTRALITY Progress leading to problems; waiting leading to co-operation.

REASON Understanding is impossible; pausing brings shared knowledge.

39 line 5

---□---

JUDGEMENT When a decision seems impossible, new evidence appears.

INNOCENCE When a situation is impossible, friends come to help.

AWARENESS When higher awareness seems impossible, guidance is found.

EMOTION When feelings are rejected, new feelings spring up to compensate.

CREATIVITY In the middle of a creative block, an idea appears.

COMMUNICATION In the middle of a disagreement, friendly words are heard.

AMBITION Co-operation springs from an obstruction to progress.

SERVICE As duties seem impossible, responsibility is spread.

NURTURE When care is rejected, a new level of relationship is found.

ECONOMY As financial stability is threatened, help arrives.

NEUTRALITY Help arising in the face of an obstruction.

REASON When a solution seems impossible, helpful information comes along.

39 line 6

---×---

Seeking advice brings luck

JUDGEMENT It is best to pause and seek a broader perspective.

INNOCENCE It is best to stop and ask for help.

AWARENESS It is best to pause and seek guidance.

EMOTION It is best to stop and seek experienced advice.

CREATIVITY It is best to pause and learn from the masters.

COMMUNICATION It is best to pause and listen to the voice of experience.

AMBITION It is best to stop pushing and seek experienced advice.

SERVICE It is best to pause and ask the advice of superiors.

NURTURE It is best to stop and try to see the situation from a higher perspective.

ECONOMY It is best to abandon speculation and seek financial advice.

NEUTRALITY Retreat from an obstruction being positive when seen from a higher perspective.

REASON It is best to stop and seek broader based knowledge.

40
·RELIEF·

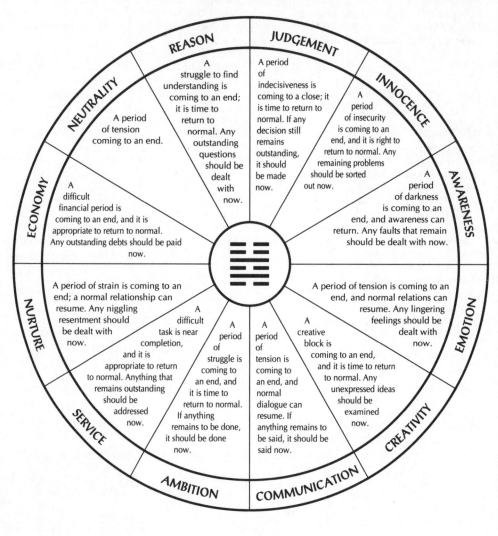

REASON — A struggle to find understanding is coming to an end; it is time to return to normal. Any outstanding questions should be dealt with now.

JUDGEMENT — A period of indecisiveness is coming to a close; it is time to return to normal. If any decision still remains outstanding, it should be made now.

INNOCENCE — A period of insecurity is coming to an end, and it is right to return to normal. Any remaining problems should be sorted out now.

NEUTRALITY — A period of tension coming to an end.

ECONOMY — A difficult financial period is coming to an end, and it is appropriate to return to normal. Any outstanding debts should be paid now.

AWARENESS — A period of darkness is coming to an end, and awareness can return. Any faults that remain should be dealt with now.

NURTURE — A period of strain is coming to an end; a normal relationship can resume. Any niggling resentment should be dealt with now.

SERVICE — A difficult task is near completion, and it is appropriate to return to normal. Anything that remains outstanding should be addressed now.

AMBITION — A period of struggle is coming to an end, and it is time to return to normal. If anything remains to be done, it should be done now.

COMMUNICATION — A period of tension is coming to an end, and normal dialogue can resume. If anything remains to be said, it should be said now.

CREATIVITY — A creative block is coming to an end, and it is time to return to normal. Any unexpressed ideas should be examined now.

EMOTION — A period of tension is coming to an end, and normal relations can resume. Any lingering feelings should be dealt with now.

Lucky

40 line 1

———×———

Blameless

JUDGEMENT   Time to take stock.
INNOCENCE   Time to enjoy.
AWARENESS   Time to contemplate.
EMOTION   Time to unwind.
CREATIVITY   Time to take stock of ideas.
COMMUNICATION   Time for small talk.
AMBITION   Time to recover.
SERVICE   Time to relax.
NURTURE   Time for mutual enjoyment.
ECONOMY   Time to take stock.
NEUTRALITY   Taking stock of the situation.
REASON   Time to contemplate.

40 line 2

———□———

Perseverance brings luck

JUDGEMENT   Fairness demands that ulterior motives be eradicated before a decision can be reached.
INNOCENCE   Innocence demands that self-indulgence be resisted before there can be real pleasure.
AWARENESS   Awareness demands that any ego-led motives be eradicated before it can return.
EMOTION   Good relationships demand that any insincerity be exposed before any mutual feeling can develop.
CREATIVITY   Creativity demands that pretentiousness be eradicated before anything worthwhile can be achieved.
COMMUNICATION   Open dialogue demands that dishonesty be exposed before an agreement can be reached.
AMBITION   Progress demands that any hidden motives be exposed before a goal can be achieved.
SERVICE   Devotion to a cause demands that any disloyalty be eradicated before responsibility can be taken.
NURTURE   Genuine care demands that any lingering resentment be eradicated.
ECONOMY   Prudence demands that any debts be settled before economic growth can begin.
NEUTRALITY   Eradicating negative motives.

REASON   Reason demands that motives of intellectual superiority be eradicated before real understanding can be found.

40 line 3

———×———

Continuing in this way leads to regret

JUDGEMENT   Using power for its own sake attracts opposition.
INNOCENCE   Self-indulgence invites trouble.
AWARENESS   Moral superiority attracts those who would expose it for what it is.
EMOTION   Over-emotional behaviour frightens others away.
CREATIVITY   Pretentiousness invites criticism.
COMMUNICATION   Monopolizing a conversation invokes loud arguments.
AMBITION   A display of strength invites those who would challenge.
SERVICE   An exaggerated sense of importance invites humiliation.
NURTURE   Stifling invites rebellion.
ECONOMY   Ostentation invites financial downfall.
NEUTRALITY   Exaggeration inviting danger.
REASON   Displaying cleverness encourages criticism.

40 line 4

———□———

JUDGEMENT   Justification is inappropriate when a decision proves to be correct.
INNOCENCE   Immature values become inappropriate as more is learned.
AWARENESS   Received morality becomes inappropriate when an awakening of awareness is realized.
EMOTION   Emotional hunger is inappropriate when a stable relationship has been established.
CREATIVITY   A temperamental attitude is inappropriate when creativity finds an outlet.
COMMUNICATION   An argumentative attitude is inappropriate when agreement has been reached.
AMBITION   Competitiveness is inappropriate when a goal has been achieved.

SERVICE   Hard discipline is inappropriate when a task has been completed.
NURTURE   Parental responsibility has to be relinquished as children grow.
ECONOMY   Greed is inappropriate when financial stability has been achieved.
NEUTRALITY   Discarding inappropriate values when a goal has been achieved.
REASON   An intellectually superior attitude is inappropriate when conclusions have been accepted.

40 line 5

——×——

Lucky

JUDGEMENT   Unwavering fairness proves wisdom to others.
INNOCENCE   Refraining from indulgence proves moral worth to others.
AWARENESS   Loyalty to higher values proves sincerity to others.
EMOTION   Emotional sincerity frightens off those who are less than sincere.
CREATIVITY   Sticking to creative ideals proves artistic worth to others.
COMMUNICATION   Holding to the truth proves sincerity to others.
AMBITION   Never flinching from a goal proves strength to others.
SERVICE   Devotion to duty proves loyalty to others.
NURTURE   Caring, no matter what, proves love in a child's eyes.
ECONOMY   Remaining prudent through economic difficulties proves trustworthiness to others.
NEUTRALITY   Sincerity proved to others through action.
REASON   Ever-searching for understanding proves intellectual worth to others.

40 line 6

——×——

Progress

JUDGEMENT   Anything that prevents a fair decision being made must be dealt with ruthlessly.
INNOCENCE   Any temptation that would corrupt has to be dealt with ruthlessly.
AWARENESS   Any fault that prevents awareness has to be eradicated ruthlessly.
EMOTION   Anything that stands in the way of honest emotion must be dealt with ruthlessly.
CREATIVITY   Any blockage that prevents creative expression must be eradicated.
COMMUNICATION   Barriers to mutual agreement must be dealt with ruthlessly.
AMBITION   Obstacles to worthwhile goals must be dealt with ruthlessly.
SERVICE   Any laxity that would prevent orders being carried out should be dealt with ruthlessly.
NURTURE   Any problem that distorts growth must be dealt with immediately.
ECONOMY   Any extravagance that prevents financial stability must be eradicated immediately.
NEUTRALITY   Dealing ruthlessly with obstacles to progress.
REASON   Anything that prevents understanding must be dealt with ruthlessly.

·EFFICIENCY·

REASON — Clever ideas need to be discarded. There is nothing wrong with simplicity if it leads to understanding.

JUDGEMENT — The time demands that unnecessary dogma be discarded. There is nothing wrong in making decisions based on simple facts.

INNOCENCE — The time demands simplicity. There is nothing wrong with this if it is sincere.

NEUTRALITY — Discarding what is superfluous.

ECONOMY — The time demands that economies be made. There is nothing wrong with a lack of ostentation.

AWARENESS — Higher awareness demands that superfluous beliefs be discarded. The way is simple and sincere.

NURTURE — A relationship needs to be brought back to basics. There is nothing wrong with natural instinct.

EMOTION — The time demands that superfluous feelings be discarded. There is nothing wrong in honest emotion.

SERVICE — A task demands that niceties be discarded. There is nothing wrong with simplicity if it gets the job done.

AMBITION — The time demands that superfluous ambitions be discarded. There is nothing wrong in streamlining if it increases strength.

COMMUNICATION — The time demands that communication be simplified. There is nothing wrong in stating the truth simply.

CREATIVITY — Ideas need to be expressed in a less pretentious way. There is nothing wrong with simplicity.

Perseverance brings good luck –
action can be taken

41 line 1

―――□―――

Correct within limits

JUDGEMENT   There is nothing wrong with a decision based on simple facts, although it is well to bear in mind that others might not understand.

INNOCENCE   There is nothing wrong in acting simply, although others may call it ignorance.

AWARENESS   There is nothing wrong with simplicity, although others may misconstrue this.

EMOTION   There is nothing wrong in stating a feeling simply, although others may be surprised.

CREATIVITY   There is nothing wrong in expressing an idea simply, although it is well to bear in mind that others might not understand.

COMMUNICATION   There is nothing wrong in stating the simple truth, although the reaction of others may not be as expected.

AMBITION   It is not wrong to progress in a simple way, although it is well to bear in mind that others might not understand.

SERVICE   There is nothing wrong in tackling a task in a simple way, although superiors may not understand.

NURTURE   There is nothing wrong in instinctive behaviour, although it is well to bear in mind that it may cause embarrassment.

ECONOMY   Necessary prudence is not wrong, although others may see it as meanness.

NEUTRALITY   Simply doing what is necessary.

REASON   There is nothing wrong in a simple explanation, although it may not be what others were expecting.

41 line 2

―――□―――

Persevere – selfish action is unfortunate

JUDGEMENT   A simple decision is valid only when it is based on an understanding of the whole situation.

INNOCENCE   Admitting ignorance is of value only where there is no loss of self-respect.

AWARENESS   Ego-less behaviour is valid only as part of a higher plan

EMOTION   A simple expression of emotion is valid only when it is sincere.

CREATIVITY   The simple expression of ideas is valid only where creativity is not lessened.

COMMUNICATION   Communicating simply is of value only when there is real understanding behind it.

AMBITION   The acceptance of occasional failure is worthwhile only where there is a larger goal to be achieved.

SERVICE   To serve properly, it is necessary not to lose self-respect.

NURTURE   Instinctive behaviour is of value only when it is unselfish.

ECONOMY   Frugality is justified only when it is part of a larger plan.

NEUTRALITY   Simplicity being of value only when based on something concrete.

REASON   A simple explanation is valid only when it is based on deep understanding.

41 line 3

―――×―――

JUDGEMENT   Dogmatic judgements mean nothing. Only decisions that are relevant to the individual situation have any real value.

INNOCENCE   Going along with the crowd achieves nothing. Only that which is learned through personal experience has any real value.

AWARENESS   Going through the motions means nothing. Only a personal awakening has any value.

EMOTION   Doing what is expected means nothing. Only sincere feeling has any real value.

CREATIVITY   Copying others means nothing. Only that which is truly original has value.

COMMUNICATION   Polite conversation means nothing. Only an honest exchange of ideas has any value.

AMBITION   Going through the motions means nothing. Only that which is achieved through personal effort has any value.

SERVICE   Simply going through the motions means nothing. Only when orders can be seen as part of a bigger plan do they have meaning.

NURTURE   Doing what is generally considered right means nothing. Only real empathy is of value.

ECONOMY Frugality for its own sake means nothing. Flexibility according to circumstances is more important.
NEUTRALITY Adopted values being meaningless; what is immediately relevant being more important.
REASON Received information means nothing. Only that which is personally understood has any real value.

41 line 4

───×───

Blameless

JUDGEMENT Relinquishing a reliance on dogma attracts the loyalty of others.
INNOCENCE Admitting innocence encourages others to protect.
AWARENESS Reducing the influence of the ego invites guidance.
EMOTION Eradicating selfish feelings encourages others to be more honest about their feelings.
CREATIVITY Eradicating pretentiousness widens the field of appreciation.
COMMUNICATION Talking less and listening more, encourages others to converse.
AMBITION Being less competitive encourages others to want to help.
SERVICE Humility encourages the confidence of superiors.
NURTURE Relaxing discipline allows children to be more natural.
ECONOMY Reducing extravagance makes a more attractive investment.
NEUTRALITY Eradicating faults.
REASON SImplification encourages others to understand.

41 line 5

───×───

Very lucky

JUDGEMENT The situation allows enlightened decisions to be made.
INNOCENCE The situation allows experience without danger.
AWARENESS The time favours a growth in awareness.
EMOTION The time is ripe for honest feeling.

CREATIVITY The situation allows inspired creativity.
COMMUNICATION The situation favours an open exchange of ideas.
AMBITION The time favours unselfish ambition.
SERVICE The time favours those who serve loyally.
NURTURE The time permits growth without heartache.
ECONOMY Financial gain is favoured.
NEUTRALITY Circumstances permitting progress.
REASON The situation allows logical conclusions to be drawn.

41 line 6

───□───

Correct – perseverance brings luck; action can be taken

JUDGEMENT Unselfish decisions benefit all.
INNOCENCE Something learned through experience can help others.
AWARENESS A growth of awareness in one, adds to the sum of total awareness. Others unconsciously realize this.
EMOTION Unselfishness brings growth to a relationship.
CREATIVITY Unpretentious creativity is appreciated by all.
COMMUNICATION Honest dialogue encourages understanding, which is of benefit to all.
AMBITION The achievement of an ambition is of benefit to all.
SERVICE The completion of a task is an essential part of a greater achievement.
NURTURE Unselfish caring deepens a mutual bond.
ECONOMY Personal gain stimulates general economic growth.
NEUTRALITY Increase is one area being of general benefit.
REASON Simple explanations benefit everybody.

42
·INCREASE·

REASON
Relinquishing logic in favour of intuition permits a leap in understanding.

JUDGEMENT
Acting on personal judgement instead of dogma allows a correct decision to be made.

NEUTRALITY
Increase through relinquishing negative behaviour in favour of positive values.

INNOCENCE
Doing what is right instead of being self-indulgent leads to unexpected pleasure.

ECONOMY
Generosity instead of meanness permits real economic growth.

AWARENESS
Relinquishing ego-led behaviour and trusting in fate permits a significant growth in awareness.

NURTURE
Relinquishing discipline in favour of empathy permits valuable care.

EMOTION
Eradicating selfishness instead of chasing emotional satisfaction permits a new depth of feeling.

Following orders instead of personal preferences permits a significant achievement.

Being receptive, instead of looking for ideas, permits real inspiration.

SERVICE
Relinquishing competitiveness in favour of improving abilities leads to significant progress.

Listening instead of talking permits a leap in mutual understanding.

CREATIVITY

AMBITION

COMMUNICATION

Progress – chances can be taken

42 line 1

———□———

Very lucky – no need for guilt

JUDGEMENT It is right to take far-reaching decisions at this time.
INNOCENCE It is right to seek new experiences at this time.
AWARENESS It is right to act on higher values at this time.
EMOTION It is right to express deeply held feelings at this time.
CREATIVITY It is right to express creative ideas at this time.
COMMUNICATION It is right to seek mutual understanding at this time.
AMBITION It is right to chase a worthwhile ambition at this time.
SERVICE It is right to take on challenging duties at this time.
NURTURE It is right to allow space for growth at this time.
ECONOMY It is right to make sensible investments at this time.
NEUTRALITY A time for positive action.
REASON It is right to seek far-reaching conclusions at this time.

42 line 2

———×———

Continuing in this way brings luck

JUDGEMENT When fairness and dogma say the same thing, far-reaching decisions are possible.
INNOCENCE When pleasure and learning unite, significant growth can occur.
AWARENESS When selflessness and higher values are united, nothing can stand in the way.
EMOTION When real emotion and honesty are united, nothing can stand in the way of mutual attraction.
CREATIVITY When inspiration and unpretentious talent are brought together, nothing can stand in the way of creativity.
COMMUNICATION When honesty and empathy come together, great understanding can be reached.
AMBITION When real strength is applied to worthwhile ambition, it is unstoppable.
SERVICE When followers and leaders share a common goal, great achievements become possible.
NURTURE When the needs of parents and children coincide, it permits healthy growth.
ECONOMY When generosity and prudence are seen to be the same thing, significant economic growth is possible.
NEUTRALITY Negative and positive united.
REASON When logic and intuition point in the same direction, it permits real understanding.

42 line 3

———×———

No need for guilt

JUDGEMENT An error of judgement can be turned to advantage if viewed from a higher perspective.
INNOCENCE Learning from mistakes can increase confidence.
AWARENESS Ego-led behaviour can exemplify a problem, which, when addressed, can rejuvenate a growth in awareness.
EMOTION An argument can open up new depths of feeling.
CREATIVITY An error can lead to new fields of creativity.
COMMUNICATION An argument can lead the way to new levels of understanding.
AMBITION Failure can show the way to a more worthwhile ambition.
SERVICE Failure in one task can lead to more suitable duties.
NURTURE Disagreements can actually instil maturity.
ECONOMY Over-generosity at the time may be reciprocated when it is needed most.
NEUTRALITY A negative situation yielding positive results.
REASON A mistake can throw light on a broader problem.

42 line 4

———×———

JUDGEMENT The ability to see both sides of an argument wins trust.
INNOCENCE Innocence combined with trustworthiness engenders protectiveness in others.

AWARENESS Higher awareness combined with moral strength wins the respect of all.
EMOTION Personalities that are both sympathetic and sensible win everybody's liking.
CREATIVITY Originality that remains accessible wins the appreciation of all.
COMMUNICATION The ability to mediate wins the respect of all.
AMBITION Strength that is tempered with modesty wins the respect of all.
SERVICE Discipline combined with flexibility wins the respect of all.
NURTURE Empathy combined with good sense wins trust.
ECONOMY Prudence combined with a willingness to speculate wins financial respect.
NEUTRALITY Neutrality that wins respect.
REASON Explanations that are both simple and logical win everyone's understanding.

42 line 5

────────── ⊟ ──────────

Very lucky

JUDGEMENT Decision-making that does not assume moral superiority will be appreciated.
INNOCENCE True innocence will find champions.
AWARENESS Selflessly raising the awareness of others will be appreciated.
EMOTION Openness will be appreciated.
CREATIVITY Creativity for its own sake will be appreciated.
COMMUNICATION Honesty will be appreciated.
AMBITION Ability that seeks no glory will be recognized.
SERVICE Service that seeks no reward will be recognized.
NURTURE Selfless caring will be appreciated.
ECONOMY Generosity that seeks no thanks will be recognized for what it is.
NEUTRALITY Positive action that seeks no reward.
REASON Understanding for its own sake will be appreciated.

42 line 6

────────── ⊟ ──────────

Unfortunate

JUDGEMENT Those who are dogmatic earn no respect.
INNOCENCE Those who are corrupt find no trust.
AWARENESS Those who merely seek moral superiority find no guidance.
EMOTION Those who are cold find no love returned.
CREATIVITY Those who are pretentious find no genuine appreciation.
COMMUNICATION Those who talk too much find no one to listen.
AMBITION Those who are merely competitive find no sympathy.
SERVICE Those who shirk duties are perceived as untrustworthy.
NURTURE Those who lack empathy find they are resented.
ECONOMY Those who are mean find no generosity in others.
NEUTRALITY Negativity engendering resentment.
REASON Those who seek to appear clever find no one is interested.

· RESOLVE ·

REASON — When logic demands action, calculations must be water-tight. There is no advantage in taking logic too far.

NEUTRALITY — Taking a risk for the sake of the truth.

JUDGEMENT — A critical decision has to be made that may not be understood. Only by commanding the trust of others can such a thing be done. It is well not to be dogmatic.

INNOCENCE — A time to be honest and ask for help. There is a risk of others taking advantage. It does not pay to be too trusting.

ECONOMY — It may be necessary to identify a cause of waste for the sake of long-term stability. It does not pay to push economies to extremes.

AWARENESS — A fault that has to be addressed honestly for further growth. There is a danger of others not understanding a radical change of attitude. It is wise not to be too obvious.

NURTURE — When the young have to be reprimanded, remain mindful of the trust they place in elders. It does not pay to go too far.

EMOTION — When feelings need to be expressed to those who do not expect it, there must be total honesty. It does not pay to be over-emotional.

SERVICE — It may be necessary to make a fault in the system known to superiors. Only one respected by all can do such a thing. It is well to remain mindful of position.

AMBITION — In striving for deserved success, be above reproach and ready for the animosity of others. It is not wise to push too hard.

COMMUNICATION — When the time comes for the truth to be told, it is necessary to be beyond reproach and to remain open to argument.

CREATIVITY — A truly creative idea may not be appreciated by others. be prepared to bear criticism in mind.

Dangerous – but action can be taken

43 line 1

------□------

Action leads to failure

JUDGEMENT Carried away by power; it leads to a mistake.
INNOCENCE Trusting too much leads to a betrayal.
AWARENESS Over-confidence in awareness lets the ego in unnoticed.
EMOTION Strong emotion turns out in time to be false.
CREATIVITY All technique and no substance means an artistic failure.
COMMUNICATION All talk and nothing to say; others will perceive this.
AMBITION Advancing confidently but without adequate preparation; a defeat is inevitable.
SERVICE Over-confidence; not being equal to a task means failure.
NURTURE Heavy-handedness leads to resentment.
ECONOMY Speculation without a solid economic base leads to inevitable loss.
NEUTRALITY Inadequate preparation.
REASON Over-confidence in the power of logic leads to an error.

43 line 2

------□------

No need to worry

JUDGEMENT An awareness of the danger of power protects from its abuse.
INNOCENCE Aware of the dangers, so there is nothing to fear from trusting others.
AWARENESS Awareness of the danger of the ego means there is nothing to fear from it.
EMOTION Prepared to be hurt and so not afraid to confront strong emotion.
CREATIVITY An awareness of the dangers of spontaneity means recognizing the difference between inspiration and impulse.
COMMUNICATION There is nothing to fear if sure of the truth.
AMBITION Being fully prepared brings confidence.
SERVICE Attention to detail assures preparedness.
NURTURE Preparing the young for the real world alleviates parental concern.
ECONOMY Prudence assures there is nothing to fear financially.

NEUTRALITY Being prepared.
REASON Correct calculations mean nothing to fear from logical argument.

43 line 3

------□------

Action now is unlucky–resolve is correct

JUDGEMENT A decision is expected, but to make it now would be wrong. Delay is necessary but not understood by others.
INNOCENCE Following seems the obvious thing to do but would be wrong. Doubts are labelled immature by others.
AWARENESS A perception appears correct but is not. It is necessary to identify the influence of the ego, although this causes self-doubt.
EMOTION To act on a feeling seems correct but would be a mistake. Something is wrong. This causes frustration.
CREATIVITY An idea seems good, but to express it now would be a mistake; it needs more thought. This means frustration.
COMMUNICATION An answer is expected, but at the moment it would be wrong. It is necessary to deflect the question, although this causes misunderstanding.
AMBITION Progress seems easy, but to claim success now would be a mistake. More preparation is needed, causing frustration.
SERVICE A task seems easy, but to call it complete would be a mistake. It needs more time, to the annoyance of superiors.
NURTURE The young say they can be trusted, but they cannot. More maturity is required, but this will not be understood.
ECONOMY A chance of profit is seen, but to take it now would be a mistake. More stability is required. The materialistic do not understand.
NEUTRALITY Action seeming necessary, but there is a hidden unpreparedness.
REASON The answer seems obvious, but to accept it would be wrong, which causes frustration.

43 line 4

------□------

Acceptance means no need for guilt

JUDGEMENT A decision seems impossible, although the answer could come through waiting. Power and dogma do not allow this.

INNOCENCE When totally lost, security could be found by trusting, but previous experience will not allow this.

AWARENESS Searching for awareness but finding none; it could be found through total acceptance, but the ego will not allow this.

EMOTION Hoping for feelings to be reciprocated but looking in the wrong place. What is searched for is very close, but cannot be seen.

CREATIVITY Searching for inspiration where there is none. Inspiration is to be found in what is simple, although pretensions will not allow this.

COMMUNICATION Continuing to talk although the argument is lost. Agreement could be found by listening, but the outspoken cannot see this.

AMBITION Pushing for a goal with no chance of success. It could be found without trying, although the ambitious would never believe it.

SERVICE It feels like a task will never be finished. Help is around the corner, but pride will not accept it.

NURTURE Reprimands fall on deaf ears. Trust could resolve the situation, but protective instincts will not allow it.

ECONOMY Resources are exhausted, but greed demands more speculation. Stability could be achieved through rejecting materialism, but greed will not allow it.

NEUTRALITY Near defeat, relief at hand.

REASON Logic is exhausted. Although the answer could be found through intuition, logic will not allow for this.

43 line 5

——————▢——————

Remaining virtuous avoids guilt

JUDGEMENT Fair decisions require firmness even though it may mean others are hurt.

INNOCENCE Pure experience requires the shedding of even the most harmless preconceptions.

AWARENESS A growth in awareness requires that the ego-led behaviour is totally eradicated.

EMOTION True emotion requires that lesser feelings, although treasured, be discarded.

CREATIVITY Creativity demands the rejection of every idea that does not contribute to the whole.

COMMUNICATION The truth requires simplicity in expression, even at the expense of popularity.

AMBITION The will to win requires ruthless self-appraisal.

SERVICE It may be necessary to clash with superiors if duties are to be carried out properly.

NURTURE True caring may mean justifiable punishments, which are painful to carry out.

ECONOMY Long-term economic stability may require short-term deprivation.

NEUTRALITY Firmness with the smallest problems.

REASON Deep understanding requires that even the smallest vestiges of cleverness should be discarded.

43 line 6

——————×——————

Unfortunate

JUDGEMENT Just as a decision is made, previously overlooked evidence appears.

INNOCENCE Just as security seems to be found, old fears return.

AWARENESS Just as awareness beckons, the ego appears from nowhere.

EMOTION When feelings are finally expressed, old doubts appear.

CREATIVITY Sudden doubts about a nearly completed idea.

COMMUNICATION Just as others are convinced, a previously unheard objection is raised.

AMBITION As a goal is nearly achieved, self-doubt appears.

SERVICE As a task nears completion, orders are changed.

NURTURE When it seems the young can be trusted, old behaviour manifests itself again.

ECONOMY As finances at last improve, forgotten debts appear.

NEUTRALITY Forgotten problems appearing almost at completion.

REASON Just as a problem is solved, a fault in reasoning is discovered.

44
·TEMPTATION·

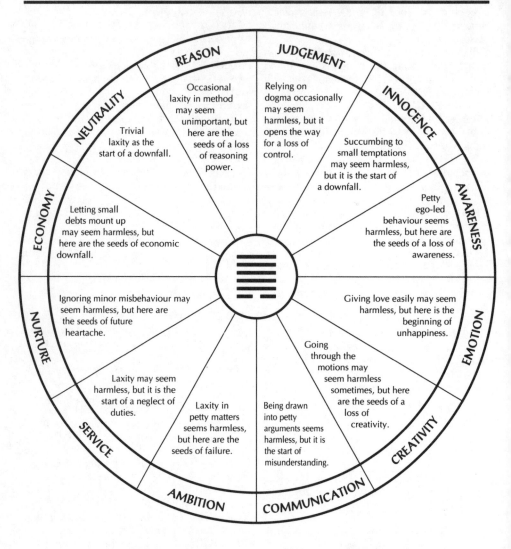

REASON

Occasional laxity in method may seem unimportant, but here are the seeds of a loss of reasoning power.

JUDGEMENT

Relying on dogma occasionally may seem harmless, but it opens the way for a loss of control.

NEUTRALITY

Trivial laxity as the start of a downfall.

INNOCENCE

Succumbing to small temptations may seem harmless, but it is the start of a downfall.

ECONOMY

Letting small debts mount up may seem harmless, but here are the seeds of economic downfall.

AWARENESS

Petty ego-led behaviour seems harmless, but here are the seeds of a loss of awareness.

NURTURE

Ignoring minor misbehaviour may seem harmless, but here are the seeds of future heartache.

EMOTION

Giving love easily may seem harmless, but here is the beginning of unhappiness.

Laxity may seem harmless, but it is the start of a neglect of duties.

Going through the motions may seem harmless sometimes, but here are the seeds of a loss of creativity.

SERVICE

Laxity in petty matters seems harmless, but here are the seeds of failure.

Being drawn into petty arguments seems harmless, but it is the start of misunderstanding.

CREATIVITY

AMBITION

COMMUNICATION

Do not give in to temptation

44 line 1

———×———

Action now is unfortunate – persevering virtuously brings luck

JUDGEMENT When dogma conditions judgements, it should be rectified immediately. Failing to do so leads to important decisions being wrong.

INNOCENCE Giving in to small temptations should be stopped immediately. Not doing so leads to major problems.

AWARENESS When petty, ego-led behaviour is noticed, it should be checked immediately. Not doing so will eventually impede awareness.

EMOTION When petty jealousy rears its head, it should be checked immediately. Not doing so leads to emotional pain.

CREATIVITY When laxity creeps into the expression of ideas, it should be eradicated immediately. Failing to do so results in artistic failure.

COMMUNICATION When petty arguments taint dialogue, they should be addressed immediately. Failing to do so results in misunderstanding.

AMBITION Small faults should be addressed immediately. Not doing so results in failure.

SERVICE Petty laxity should be dealt with immediately. Failing to do so causes serious inefficiency.

NURTURE Minor misbehaviour should be dealt with immediately. Failing to do so allows it to become a character trait.

ECONOMY Small debts should be settled immediately. Failing to do so allows them to grow out of all proportion.

NEUTRALITY Correcting small faults before they grow.

REASON When any errors in reasoning are noticed, they should be addressed immediately. Failing to do so leads inevitably to wrong conclusions.

44 line 2

———▫———

Not to blame

JUDGEMENT A difficult decision should be given only the attention it deserves. It should not be allowed to affect other areas of judgement.

INNOCENCE A weakness should be kept under control. It should not be allowed to affect other areas of life.

AWARENESS Petty, ego-led behaviour in one area should be kept under control. It should not be allowed to affect awareness.

EMOTION An emotion such as jealousy should be kept under control. It should not be allowed to affect other areas of life.

CREATIVITY An obsession with one idea should be kept under control. It should not be allowed to affect other areas of creativity.

COMMUNICATION A pet subject should be suppressed. It should not be referred to when it is not relevant.

AMBITION Failure in one area should be handled properly. It should not be allowed to affect other ambitions.

SERVICE The dislike of one aspect of a job should be kept under control. It should not be allowed to affect efficiency.

NURTURE Irritation caused by one small fault should be kept under control. It should not be allowed to affect a relationship.

ECONOMY Over-spending in one area should be kept under control. It should not be allowed to affect general finances.

NEUTRALITY Faults in one area needing to be checked in order to stop them affecting the general situation.

REASON An obsession with one problem should be kept under control. It should not be allowed to affect reasoning.

44 line 3

———▫———

Avoiding blame – danger

JUDGEMENT Circumstances prevent the postponement of a difficult decision. The reasons for this procrastination should be examined.

INNOCENCE Circumstances prevent a surrender to weakness. This is a chance to examine that very weakness.

AWARENESS Circumstances prevent ego-led behaviour. It can now be examined for what it is.

EMOTION Circumstances prevent the expression of an unworthy feeling. It should now be seen for what it is.

CREATIVITY Circumstances prevent the expression of a pet idea. This preoccupation should now be examined for what it is.

COMMUNICATION The direction of a conversation prevents the introduction of a pet topic. It should now be seen for what it is.

AMBITION Circumstances block improper progress. Motives should be examined for what they are.

SERVICE Circumstances prevent a dereliction of duty. This temptation should be seen for what it is.

NURTURE Circumstances prevent the expression of annoyance at a petty irritation. It should be seen for what it is.

ECONOMY Circumstances prevent money being wasted. This wasteful tendency should be observed for what it is.

NEUTRALITY Circumstances prevent negative behaviour.

REASON Circumstances prevent intellectual superiority. This fault should now be addressed for what it is.

44 line 4

———— ▭ ————

Unfortunate

JUDGEMENT Decisions that consolidate power alienate others.

INNOCENCE Obsessive behaviour means a loss of friends.

AWARENESS An obsession with growing awareness alienates others.

EMOTION Obsessive feelings alienate others.

CREATIVITY Artistic arrogance leads to a loss of appreciation.

COMMUNICATION Not listening to others leads to a loss of their attention.

AMBITION An obsession with winning forfeits the support of others.

SERVICE An independent attitude loses the trust of superiors.

NURTURE Selfish behaviour in elders forfeits the respect of the young.

ECONOMY Greed loses friends.

NEUTRALITY Alienating others.

REASON Mere cleverness means a loss of intellectual respect.

44 line 5

———— ▭ ————

Achievements are possible if talents are hidden

JUDGEMENT Fair decisions win the support of others.

INNOCENCE Genuine innocence wins the protection of others.

AWARENESS Genuine higher awareness engenders good feelings in others.

EMOTION Unselfish emotion is reciprocated.

CREATIVITY Unpretentious creativity gathers admirers.

COMMUNICATION Sincere words win believers.

AMBITION Unselfish determination wins support.

SERVICE Devotion to duty wins admiration.

NURTURE Genuine empathy wins the respect of children.

ECONOMY Prudence wins financial support.

NEUTRALITY Sympathy with others winning support.

REASON Simple explanations win the understanding of others.

44 line 6

———— ▭ ————

Slight regret, but not to blame

JUDGEMENT A correct decision is misinterpreted by those who do not have the full facts.

INNOCENCE Innocence is ridiculed by the corrupt.

AWARENESS Higher awareness is derided by non-believers.

EMOTION Emotional balance is perceived as coldness.

CREATIVITY A truly creative idea is ridiculed by the ignorant.

COMMUNICATION The truth is ridiculed by those who do not understand.

AMBITION An unselfish ambition is misunderstood by others.

SERVICE Devotion to duty is ridiculed by those who are disloyal.

NURTURE True caring is mistaken for a lack of love.

ECONOMY Prudence is ridiculed by the wasteful.

NEUTRALITY Correct behaviour meeting with misunderstanding.

REASON Deep understanding is ridiculed by the ignorant.

REASON — All the information is there for a conclusion to be drawn. It is worth asking questions.

JUDGEMENT — All the facts are gathered together for a decision to be made. It is worth examining precedents.

NEUTRALITY — The coming together of conditions that favour positive action.

INNOCENCE — The situation permits innocent pleasure. It is worth listening to a respected voice.

AWARENESS — All the conditions favour higher awareness. It is worth seeking guidance.

ECONOMY — The situation favours economic growth. It is worth seeking financial advice.

EMOTION — All the conditions favour emotional expression. It is worth seeking advice.

NURTURE — All the conditions are right for growth. It is worth remembering personal experience.

CREATIVITY — All the conditions to enable creativity to flourish are satisfied. It is worth studying respected masters.

SERVICE — All the conditions favour the performance of a useful service. It is worth seeking helpful advice.

AMBITION — All the conditions favour progress. It is worth seeking advice.

COMMUNICATION — Everybody is ready to talk. It is worth starting with the voice of experience.

Lucky – perseverance allows achievements
Seek advice – it is worth starting something

45 line 1

———×———

No need for regret

JUDGEMENT If all the evidence is there, one question may be all that is preventing a decision.
INNOCENCE If the conditions are right, it may be only confidence that is lacking.
AWARENESS If the situation favours higher awareness, guidance may be all that is needed.
EMOTION A hint may be all that is needed to encourage emotional expression.
CREATIVITY If the conditions favour creativity, it may be just the idea that needs to be clarified.
COMMUNICATION If open dialogue already exists, it may be just the nature of the agreement that needs to be clarified.
AMBITION If the conditions favour progress, it may be the goal that is not clear.
SERVICE If circumstances favour the fulfilment of a duty, it may be just the word of a superior that is required.
NURTURE If circumstances favour learning, the young may require only a little encouragement.
ECONOMY If economic conditions favour investment, financial advice may be all that is needed.
NEUTRALITY The conditions favouring action, but requiring a positive direction.
REASON If all the information is there, one answer may be all that is needed for a conclusion to be drawn.

45 line 2

———×———

Lucky

JUDGEMENT The evidence points to an obvious decision.
INNOCENCE The situation allows pleasurable learning.
AWARENESS Conditions encourage higher awareness.
EMOTION The conditions make emotional rapport easy.
CREATIVITY Ideas flow easily because of the circumstances.
COMMUNICATION The general mood makes agreement easy.

AMBITION Conditions encourage easy progress.
SERVICE Conditions make a task easy.
NURTURE The situation allows painless growth.
ECONOMY The general situation encourages financial growth without effort.
NEUTRALITY Conditions permitting easy progress.
REASON Following a line of reasoning leads to its own conclusion.

45 line 3

———×———

Blameless – slight embarrassment

JUDGEMENT New decisions require simple questions at first. Others may think this strange.
INNOCENCE At first, new experience requires a grasp of basics, although the more experienced may laugh.
AWARENESS New exposure to higher awareness may meet with incredulity at first.
EMOTION New feelings may at first require basic clarification, although it may appear strange.
CREATIVITY New areas of creativity at first require experimentation, although others may not understand.
COMMUNICATION At first, new dialogue requires the establishment of common ground, although this may be misinterpreted.
AMBITION New challenges at first require orientation, although this may be perceived as a lack of competence.
SERVICE At first, orders may require simple clarification, although this may annoy superiors.
NURTURE At first, new growth requires protection, although this may be perceived as fussing.
ECONOMY At first, new areas of investment require prudence, although this may be perceived as meanness.
NEUTRALITY Difficulty in establishing relations; the need to find common ground.
REASON At first, a new subject requires a grasp of what may seem simple to others.

45 line 4

—————□—————

Lucky – free of blame

JUDGEMENT Enough evidence has been gathered for a decision to be made.
INNOCENCE Enough experience has been gathered for experience to become pleasurable.
AWARENESS Life is secure enough for awareness to occur naturally.
EMOTION Feelings are clear enough to be expressed.
CREATIVITY There has been enough experimentation for real creativity to begin.
COMMUNICATION There is enough common ground for an exchange of ideas.
AMBITION Enough strength has been gathered for progress to be made.
SERVICE There is adequate experience for tasks to be successfully completed.
NURTURE Enough experience has been gathered to safely allow some independence.
ECONOMY Enough resources have been accumulated to allow the possibility of growth.
NEUTRALITY Adequate resources for action.
REASON Enough knowledge has been accumulated for conclusions to be drawn.

45 line 5

—————□—————

Correct – guilt is avoided

JUDGEMENT If, in gathering evidence, one piece has been taken for granted, it should be examined carefully.
INNOCENCE If, in seeking new experience, one piece of immature behaviour remains, it should be addressed.
AWARENESS If there are any hidden motives in seeking higher awareness, they should be carefully analysed.
EMOTION If things remain hidden when becoming emotionally involved, they should be tactfully brought out into the open.
CREATIVITY Pretentious attitudes that prevent complete creative expression should be carefully eradicated.

COMMUNICATION If, in open dialogue, there are areas of difficulty due to a lack of openness, these areas should be carefully addressed.
AMBITION If, in seeking progress, there are any inadequacies, these areas should be addressed.
SERVICE If there are any inadequacies that prevent efficiency, they should be addressed.
NURTURE If, in encouraging growth, any undesirable traits are perceived, they should be dealt with carefully.
ECONOMIC If economic stability is being established, unimportant debts should be paid.
NEUTRALITY Gathering resources. Careful checking.
REASON If, in gathering knowledge, any area has been taken for granted, it should be examined carefully.

45 line 6

—————×—————

Not to blame

JUDGEMENT Inadequate evidence prevents a decision.
INNOCENCE New experience is not possible.
AWARENESS The situation does not permit awareness.
EMOTION The situation does not merit emotional expression.
CREATIVITY Outside influences prevent creativity.
COMMUNICATION A lack of openness prevents proper dialogue.
AMBITION A lack of opportunity prevents progress.
SERVICE Failure in a task due to others.
NURTURE There is inadequate preparation for growth.
ECONOMY Loss caused by the general economic situation.
NEUTRALITY Failure due to uncontrollable events.
REASON There are not enough facts for a conclusion to be drawn.

46
·EFFORT·

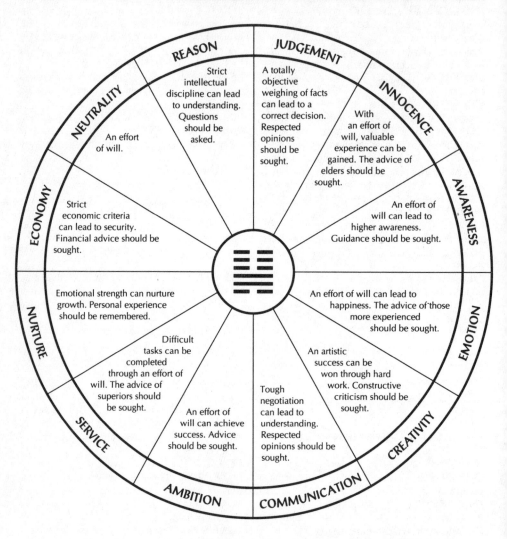

REASON — Strict intellectual discipline can lead to understanding. Questions should be asked.

JUDGEMENT — A totally objective weighing of facts can lead to a correct decision. Respected opinions should be sought.

NEUTRALITY — An effort of will.

INNOCENCE — With an effort of will, valuable experience can be gained. The advice of elders should be sought.

ECONOMY — Strict economic criteria can lead to security. Financial advice should be sought.

AWARENESS — An effort of will can lead to higher awareness. Guidance should be sought.

NURTURE — Emotional strength can nurture growth. Personal experience should be remembered.

EMOTION — An effort of will can lead to happiness. The advice of those more experienced should be sought.

SERVICE — Difficult tasks can be completed through an effort of will. The advice of superiors should be sought.

CREATIVITY — An artistic success can be won through hard work. Constructive criticism should be sought.

AMBITION — An effort of will can achieve success. Advice should be sought.

COMMUNICATION — Tough negotiation can lead to understanding. Respected opinions should be sought.

Achievements are possible – action brings luck
No need to worry

46 line 1

—————×—————

Very lucky

JUDGEMENT Basic decency makes fair decisions obvious.
INNOCENCE Natural innocence makes life a pleasure.
AWARENESS A solid moral base allows rapid growth.
EMOTION An honest feeling is readily understood.
CREATIVITY A solid idea makes its own expression easy.
COMMUNICATION Confidence in the truth encourages others to believe.
AMBITION Solid preparation gives great confidence.
SERVICE Devotion to duty makes difficult tasks seem easy.
NURTURE Natural empathy makes true caring easy.
ECONOMY A solid financial base allows economic growth.
NEUTRALITY Solid foundations.
REASON Solid basic knowledge makes new understanding easy.

46 line 2

—————□—————

Blameless

JUDGEMENT An occasional error of judgement is forgivable where there is basic decency.
INNOCENCE Occasional mistakes are forgivable in the innocent.
AWARENESS Strange behaviour is forgivable in those who truly seek higher awareness.
EMOTION Occasional misunderstanding is forgivable where there is honest feeling.
CREATIVITY Artistic failure is forgivable where there is true originality.
COMMUNICATION The odd *faux pas* is forgivable where there is sincerity
AMBITION Occasional failure is forgivable if ambitions are worthy.
SERVICE Occasional failure is forgivable where there is genuine loyalty.
NURTURE Occasional misunderstanding is forgivable where there is true caring.

ECONOMY Occasional loss is acceptable in pursuit of financial stability.
NEUTRALITY Understandable mistakes when acting in sincerity.
REASON Occasional mistakes are forgivable where there is striving for deep understanding.

46 line 3

—————□—————

JUDGEMENT Decisions are obvious for a period.
INNOCENCE A period of security.
AWARENESS A period of growth.
EMOTION A period of emotional honesty.
CREATIVITY A period of uninhibited creativity.
COMMUNICATION A period of open dialogue.
AMBITION A period of progress.
SERVICE Duties are easy for a time.
NURTURE A period of uninhibited growth.
ECONOMY A period of economic growth.
NEUTRALITY A period of easy progress.
REASON A period of rapid understanding.

46 line 4

—————×—————

Lucky – correct

JUDGEMENT Fairness becomes the norm.
INNOCENCE A new level of maturity is achieved.
AWARENESS A new level of awareness is reached.
EMOTION A mutual feeling becomes a solid foundation.
CREATIVITY A creative idea achieves permanence.
COMMUNICATION A permanent understanding is reached.
AMBITION A goal is achieved.
SERVICE Loyalty is rewarded with responsibility.
NURTURE A new level of maturity is encouraged.
ECONOMY Some financial security is achieved.
NEUTRALITY A new level of permanence.
REASON A theory is accepted.

———×———

Continuing in this way brings luck

JUDGEMENT   Big decisions should be implemented gradually.

INNOCENCE   New experience should be sought in its own time.

AWARENESS   A growth in awareness should be achieved in gradual steps.

EMOTION   Relationships should be allowed to proceed at a natural pace.

CREATIVITY   Ideas should express themselves in their own time.

COMMUNICATION   Dialogue should be allowed to develop in its own time.

AMBITION   Progress should be made in stages.

SERVICE   Tasks should be tackled step by step.

NURTURE   Maturity should be encouraged a step at a time.

ECONOMY   Financial growth should be achieved a step at a time.

NEUTRALITY   Gradual steps towards progress.

REASON   Knowledge should be assimilated gradually.

———×———

Persevere

JUDGEMENT   Unknown   quantities demand very careful examination.

INNOCENCE   New experiences demand extreme care.

AWARENESS   New areas of awareness should be explored with extreme care.

EMOTION   New feeling should be expressed only with great delicacy.

CREATIVITY   New areas of originality need to be explored extremely carefully.

COMMUNICATION   Dialogue   with unknown persons requires great tact.

AMBITION   Progressing into unknown territory requires extreme care.

SERVICE   New demands require that duties are carried out with care.

NURTURE   Careful monitoring is required when the young experience something new.

ECONOMY   New investments need to be monitored extremely carefully.

NEUTRALITY   Advancing   into   the unknown.

REASON   New understanding requires meticulous attention to detail.

47
·OPPRESSION·

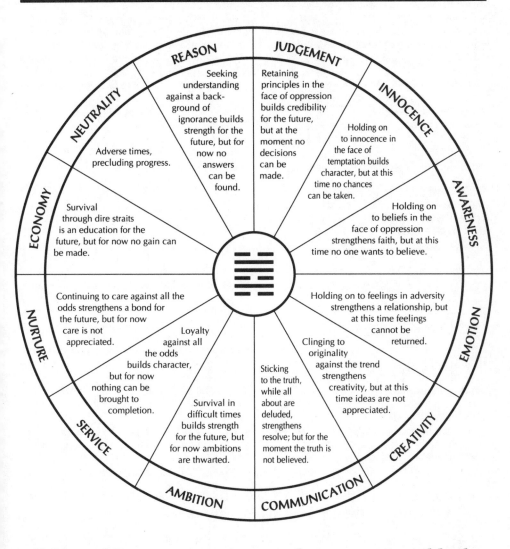

REASON
Seeking understanding against a background of ignorance builds strength for the future, but for now no answers can be found.

JUDGEMENT
Retaining principles in the face of oppression builds credibility for the future, but at the moment no decisions can be made.

NEUTRALITY
Adverse times, precluding progress.

INNOCENCE
Holding on to innocence in the face of temptation builds character, but at this time no chances can be taken.

ECONOMY
Survival through dire straits is an education for the future, but for now no gain can be made.

AWARENESS
Holding on to beliefs in the face of oppression strengthens faith, but at this time no one wants to believe.

NURTURE
Continuing to care against all the odds strengthens a bond for the future, but for now care is not appreciated.

Loyalty against all the odds builds character, but for now nothing can be brought to completion.

EMOTION
Holding on to feelings in adversity strengthens a relationship, but at this time feelings cannot be returned.

Clinging to originality against the trend strengthens creativity, but at this time ideas are not appreciated.

Sticking to the truth, while all about are deluded, strengthens resolve; but for the moment the truth is not believed.

Survival in difficult times builds strength for the future, but for now ambitions are thwarted.

SERVICE

CREATIVITY

AMBITION

COMMUNICATION

Not to blame – perseverance brings eventual luck

47 line 1

———×———

JUDGEMENT Indecision leads to more indecision.
INNOCENCE Self-indulgence leads to a need for more of the same.
AWARENESS Doubts block the way to awareness.
EMOTION Negative emotions, like jealousy, lead to greater unhappiness.
CREATIVITY Laziness encourages a creative block.
COMMUNICATION Negative talk encourages more of the same.
AMBITION Dwelling on a failure encourages more failure.
SERVICE Neglecting duties encourages more neglect.
NURTURE Bad temper encourages more bad temper.
ECONOMY Wasting money leads to more waste.
NEUTRALITY Negativity feeding on itself.
REASON Intellectual laziness leads to lost understanding.

47 line 2

———▫———

Action would be unfortunate – not to blame

JUDGEMENT Depression due to the inability to win the respect of others. It is worth being decisive in small ways, although it is wise not to take any drastic decisions.
INNOCENCE Depression caused by insecurity. It is worth asking for help, although it is wise not to become dependent.
AWARENESS Depression caused by a loss of awareness. Dealing with the ego is worthwhile, although it is best not to take this to extremes.
EMOTION Depression caused by emotional coldness. Any real feeling is better than none, although it is wise not to be impulsive.
CREATIVITY Depression caused by a creative block. Any creative activity is worth pursuing, although it is wise not to get too carried away.
COMMUNICATION Depression caused by an inability to communicate. It is worth entering into an honest dialogue, although it is wise not to delve too deep.

AMBITION Depression caused by failure. Any competitive activity is worth pursuing, although it is not wise to tackle anything too difficult.
SERVICE Depression caused by lack of pride in a job. Any effort at improvement is worthwhile, although it is wise not to be over-conscientious.
NURTURE Depression caused by resentment. Any effort at reconciliation is worth it, although it is wise not to go too far.
ECONOMY Depression due to lack of money. Any effort at recovery is worth it, although it is wise not to take too big a gamble.
NEUTRALITY Stagnation caused by inactivity.
REASON Depression caused by not being able to find an answer. Any idea is worth pursuing, although it is wise not to be too clever.

47 line 3

———×———

Unfortunate

JUDGEMENT A lack of basic understanding makes decisions much harder than they ought to be.
INNOCENCE Self-indulgence makes life much harder than it ought to be.
AWARENESS Ego-led behaviour makes higher awareness much harder to achieve than it ought to be.
EMOTION Insincerity makes emotional stability much harder to find than it ought to be.
CREATIVITY Carelessness makes the expression of ideas much harder than it should be.
AMBITION A reckless attitude makes difficulties much worse than they really are.
SERVICE Neglect of duty makes tasks harder than they should be.
NURTURE Over-reaction makes nurture much harder than it should be.
ECONOMY Extravagance make financial security much harder to achieve than it should be.
NEUTRALITY Recklessness exacerbating a situation.
REASON Lack of attention to method makes solving a problem much harder than it ought to be.

47 line 4

——☐——

Eventual luck – a little regret

JUDGEMENT Obvious decisions should be taken, although respect may be lost.
INNOCENCE Help should be sought, although self-respect may suffer.
AWARENESS Guidance should be sought, although the ego may be hurt.
EMOTION Emotional honesty is needed, although it may be embarrassing.
CREATIVITY Unworthy ideas should be discarded, although this may invite criticism.
COMMUNICATION Formality should be dropped, although it may be embarrassing.
AMBITION Aggressive attitudes should be curbed, although it may seem like weakness to others.
SERVICE Help should be sought, although pride may be lost.
NURTURE Allowances should be made, although some control may be lost.
ECONOMY Economies should be made, although appearances may suffer.
NEUTRALITY A need for simple action.
REASON A simpler approach should be adopted, although intellectual standing may suffer.

47 line 5

——☐——

Accept events

JUDGEMENT Decisions are not understood by those who should know better, but slowly they see sense.
INNOCENCE Sympathy is not forthcoming from those who should know better, but slowly they realize their mistake.
AWARENESS Higher values are not appreciated by those who should know better, but slowly they learn.
EMOTION Emotional frankness is not appreciated by those who should know better, but slowly they come to understand.
CREATIVITY Artistic sincerity is not appreciated by those who should know better. Holding on to ideals slowly gathers admirers.
COMMUNICATION Those who should know better do not want to hear, but slowly the truth is believed.

AMBITION Ability is not appreciated by those who should know better, but respect slowly grows.
SERVICE Loyalty is not appreciated by superiors, but slowly their attention is drawn to the fact.
NURTURE True caring is not appreciated by the young, but as they grow older, they learn.
ECONOMY Prudence is seen as hard, but finances improve slowly.
NEUTRALITY Higher motives going unappreciated.
REASON New ideas are not understood by those who should know better, but their understanding slowly grows.

47 line 6

——×——

Lucky

JUDGEMENT Past errors of judgement sap confidence, but firm decisions are now required.
INNOCENCE Past mistakes have meant a loss of confidence, but it is needed now.
AWARENESS Failed attempts at a growth in awareness make it seem impossible, but dealing with the ego now allows it to happen.
EMOTION Past disappointments make trust difficult, but happiness now demands emotional sincerity.
CREATIVITY A lack of appreciation in the past means confidence is low. Self-belief is necessary for artistic success.
COMMUNICATION Past difficulty in communication makes it seem hard now, but the truth demands a confident voice.
AMBITION Past failures mar confidence, but confidence is now essential for success.
SERVICE Past neglect makes duties seem difficult, but devotion to duty is essential if a task is to be completed.
NURTURE Past events make caring seem difficult, but true caring is essential now.
ECONOMY Past recklessness makes responsibility seem impossible, but responsibility is now required if finances are to improve.
NEUTRALITY Overcoming past failure.
REASON Past failures sap confidence in reasoning abilities, but to obtain answers, those abilities are essential.

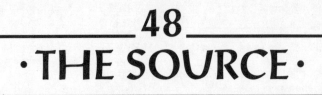

48
·THE SOURCE·

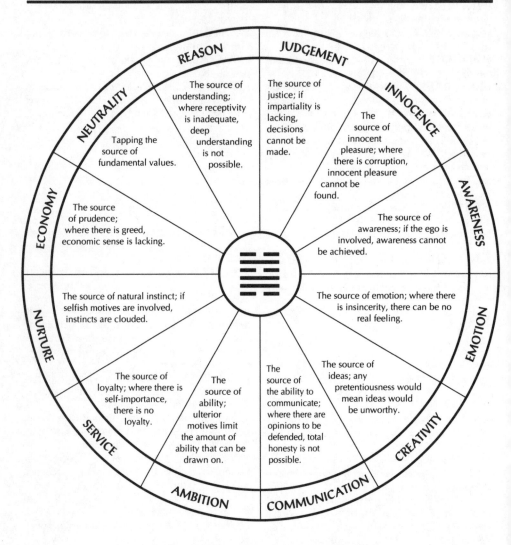

REASON — The source of understanding; where receptivity is inadequate, deep understanding is not possible.

JUDGEMENT — The source of justice; if impartiality is lacking, decisions cannot be made.

NEUTRALITY — Tapping the source of fundamental values.

INNOCENCE — The source of innocent pleasure; where there is corruption, innocent pleasure cannot be found.

ECONOMY — The source of prudence; where there is greed, economic sense is lacking.

AWARENESS — The source of awareness; if the ego is involved, awareness cannot be achieved.

NURTURE — The source of natural instinct; if selfish motives are involved, instincts are clouded.

EMOTION — The source of emotion; where there is insincerity, there can be no real feeling.

SERVICE — The source of loyalty; where there is self-importance, there is no loyalty.

AMBITION — The source of ability; ulterior motives limit the amount of ability that can be drawn on.

COMMUNICATION — The source of the ability to communicate; where there are opinions to be defended, total honesty is not possible.

CREATIVITY — The source of ideas; any pretentiousness would mean ideas would be unworthy.

Unfortunate without virtue

48 line 1

———×———

JUDGEMENT Unimportant decisions; they are irrelevant.
INNOCENCE Confused by temptation; this is not a worthwhile experience.
AWARENESS Ego-led behaviour of little value.
EMOTION Selfish feelings; these say nothing about real emotions.
CREATIVITY Inconsequential ideas of no real value.
COMMUNICATION Looking for agreement on a superficial level; this is not important.
AMBITION Petty ambition; progress cannot be made in this way.
SERVICE Superficial loyalty, of little value to a cause.
NURTURE A lack of empathy; this is not real care.
ECONOMY Pointless speculation of little value to economic growth.
NEUTRALITY Scraping the surface.
REASON Looking for superficial understanding; this is of no value.

48 line 2

———□———

JUDGEMENT Aware of principles but not applying them.
INNOCENCE Having the strength to resist temptation but not using it.
AWARENESS Having the potential for higher awareness but stifling its growth.
EMOTION Having deep feelings but being unable to face them.
CREATIVITY A wasted creative potential.
COMMUNICATION Holding something back.
AMBITION Wasting potential.
SERVICE Not giving a task the effort it deserves.
NURTURE Not trying to understand.
ECONOMY Not using economic potential to the full.
NEUTRALITY Wasted possibilities.
REASON Deep understanding is possible but not sought.

48 line 3

———□———

JUDGEMENT A potential for far-reaching decisions that is not understood.
INNOCENCE Truly innocent feelings that are not understood.
AWARENESS Higher awareness that is not understood.
EMOTION Real emotion that others find impossible to understand.
CREATIVITY Inspirational ideas, but no one is able to appreciate them.
COMMUNICATION Fundamental truth is spoken, but no one wants to listen.
AMBITION Great ability that is not appreciated.
SERVICE Fundamental loyalty that is not understood.
NURTURE Genuine care that is not understood.
ECONOMY A potential for economic growth that cannot be grasped.
NEUTRALITY Potential for positive action that is not understood.
REASON A workable theory that others find incomprehensible.

48 line 4

———×———

Correct

JUDGEMENT Assimilating wisdom for better decisions.
INNOCENCE Learning for the future.
AWARENESS Preparing the way for greater awareness.
EMOTION Learning to be emotionally mature.
CREATIVITY Acquiring the technique to express ideas.
COMMUNICATION Learning how to communicate openly.
AMBITION Working on abilities.
SERVICE Learning the value of loyalty.
NURTURE Preparing the way for future growth.
ECONOMY Learning the value of prudence.
NEUTRALITY Strengthening capabilities.
REASON Improving reasoning.

——————◻——————

JUDGEMENT   The evidence is there for far-reaching decisions to be made.
INNOCENCE   It is possible to learn from an experience.
AWARENESS   The potential for a growth in awareness is there.
EMOTION   It is possible to release deeper feelings.
CREATIVITY   Potential inspiration is there.
COMMUNICATION   Honest words are there to be spoken.
AMBITION   There is a depth of ability from which to draw.
SERVICE   It is possible to take on responsibility.
NURTURE   Growth is possible with care.
ECONOMY   There is a potential for economic growth, if it is grasped.
NEUTRALITY   Positive attributes waiting to be used.
REASON   The knowledge required for a deeper understanding is available.

——————×——————

Very lucky

JUDGEMENT   Deep-seated principles can be trusted.
INNOCENCE   Innocent pleasure can be enjoyed.
AWARENESS   Higher awareness is a fact.
EMOTION   Deep-rooted feelings are honest.
CREATIVITY   Inspiration is genuine.
COMMUNICATION   Words are true.
AMBITION   Abilities can be trusted.
SERVICE   Loyalty can be counted on.
NURTURE   Natural instincts are correct.
ECONOMY   Economic sense can be trusted.
NEUTRALITY   Trusting fundamental values.
REASON   Deep understanding can be trusted.

49
FUNDAMENTAL
·CHANGE·

REASON — Revolutionary theories can find acceptance if they can be proved.

JUDGEMENT — Far-reaching decisions, if they can be justified, will find acceptance.

INNOCENCE — New experience is possible if an innocent attitude is retained.

NEUTRALITY — A complete change.

AWARENESS — Higher awareness can be translated into action if the ego is not involved.

ECONOMY — Fundamental financial changes can be made if a sense of prudence is retained.

EMOTION — Repressed feelings, if they are sincere, can be expressed.

NURTURE — New areas of growth can be nurtured as long as there is real caring.

CREATIVITY — Highly original ideas can find acceptance if they are unpretentious.

SERVICE — It is possible to take the initiative if loyalty is genuine.

AMBITION — Great progress can be made if abilities are adequate.

COMMUNICATION — Revolutionary words, if they are honest, will be believed.

Great achievements are possible with perseverance – doubts are overcome

49 line 1

———□———

JUDGEMENT   Evidence must be weighed minutely before far-reaching decisions can be made.
INNOCENCE   New experience demands that temptations be resisted.
AWARENESS   The ego must not be involved when higher awareness is to be translated into action.
EMOTION   It is necessary to make sure that repressed feelings are totally honest before they are expressed.
CREATIVITY   Original ideas must be impeccable in expression before they can be presented.
COMMUNICATION   Arguments must be watertight before revolutionary words can be spoken.
AMBITION   Before big opportunities can be taken, abilities must be proven.
SERVICE   Capabilities must be proven before major responsibility can be taken.
NURTURE   Trust must be mutual before new freedom can be allowed.
ECONOMY   The need must be proved before fundamental financial changes can be made.
NEUTRALITY   Proving that fundamental change is necessary.
REASON   Reasoning must be watertight before new theories can be put forward.

49 line 2

———×———

Lucky – no blame

JUDGEMENT   It is right to make far-reaching decisions if the situation demands it.
INNOCENCE   If the situation demands it, it is right to explore new areas of experience.
AWARENESS   Higher values can be translated into action if the situation demands it.
EMOTION   When it becomes necessary, repressed feeling can be expressed.
CREATIVITY   Originality can be expressed when the opportunity arises.
COMMUNICATION   When the opportunity arises, revolutionary words can be spoken.
AMBITION   Chances can be taken when the opportunities open up.

SERVICE   When the situation demands it, great responsibility can be shouldered.
NURTURE   New learning can be encouraged when the opportunities present themselves.
ECONOMY   When the economic situation allows it, fundamental changes can be made.
NEUTRALITY   Fundamental change being possible at the right time.
REASON   If the problem demands it, it is right to put forward revolutionary theories.

49 line 3

———□———

Rash action would be unfortunate – long-term danger

JUDGEMENT   Far-reaching decisions can be made when the evidence has been weighed three times.
INNOCENCE   New experience can be safely explored when the opportunity presents itself for the third time.
AWARENESS   Awareness can be trusted when it is experienced for the third time.
EMOTION   Repressed feelings can be expressed when they have made themselves felt three times.
CREATIVITY   Original ideas can be expressed when they have been explored in three different ways.
COMMUNICATION   When arguments have gone round three times, revolutionary words can be spoken and will be believed.
AMBITION   Big chances can be taken when they present themselves for the third time.
SERVICE   New responsibility can be taken when the need shows itself for the third time.
NURTURE   When the need presents itself for the third time, freedom can be allowed.
ECONOMY   Fundamental financial changes can be implemented when the need has shown itself three times.
NEUTRALITY   Fundamental change being successful at the third time of asking.
REASON   When the need has been seen three times, new theories can be successfully put forward.

49 line 4

— □ —

Doubts are overcome – radical changes are lucky

JUDGEMENT Far-reaching decisions, based on impeccable principles, find acceptance.

INNOCENCE New experience, seen with innocent eyes, is rewarding.

AWARENESS Awareness, which is based on impeccable moral values, can be seen as worth following.

EMOTION Repressed feelings, expressed honestly, find sympathy.

CREATIVITY Original ideas, which have artistic worth, find appreciation.

COMMUNICATION Revolutionary words, which are honest, find agreement.

AMBITION No one begrudges progress based on proven abilities.

SERVICE Taking on new responsibility finds approval if there is proven loyalty.

NURTURE New maturity, handled with care, can strengthen mutual bonds.

ECONOMY Financial changes, based on prudent reasoning, can be seen as sensible.

NEUTRALITY Fundamental change based on positive values.

REASON Radical theories, based on fundamental understanding find acceptance.

49 line 5

— □ —

JUDGEMENT Far-reaching decisions become obvious.

INNOCENCE A pure heart is self-evident, making others want to protect it.

AWARENESS Moral worth is undeniable, making higher values acceptable.

EMOTION The need for the expression of repressed feelings is undeniable.

CREATIVITY Original ideas are immediately acceptable.

COMMUNICATION Others want to believe revolutionary words.

AMBITION Potential for great progress is obvious.

SERVICE Loyalty makes potential for responsibility self-evident.

NURTURE New maturity is self-evident and finds a natural response.

ECONOMY The need for economic change is obvious.

NEUTRALITY An obvious need for fundamental change.

REASON It is obvious that a radical theory is needed.

49 line 6

— × —

Rash action is unfortunate – perseverance brings luck

JUDGEMENT Far-reaching decisions should be implemented slowly.

INNOCENCE New experiences should be explored in their own time.

AWARENESS Higher awareness should be explored slowly.

EMOTION Fundamental feelings should be expressed only when they are sure to be understood.

CREATIVITY Original ideas should be introduced gradually.

COMMUNICATION Revolutionary words should be expressed only when they will meet with agreement.

AMBITION Chances should be taken only when the opportunities present themselves.

SERVICE New responsibility should be shouldered a step at a time.

NURTURE Growth should be encouraged in its own time.

ECONOMY Financial changes should be made as and when permissible.

NEUTRALITY Gradual change.

REASON Radical theories should be introduced patiently.

50

· CULTURE ·

REASON — The general need for deeper understanding, which sustains the development of new ideas.

JUDGEMENT — The need for justice, which makes fair decisions acceptable.

INNOCENCE — The general desire to protect the innocent, which makes uncorrupted learning possible.

NEUTRALITY — Collective values.

AWARENESS — Collective moral values, which make awareness sustainable.

ECONOMY — The need for general economic growth, which makes profit desirable.

NURTURE — The general need for growth, which makes caring necessary.

EMOTION — The general need to express feelings, which makes mutual emotion desirable.

SERVICE — The need for trusted helpers, which makes loyalty appreciated.

CREATIVITY — Cultural heritage, which makes originality desirable.

AMBITION — The need for progress, which makes abilities appreciated.

COMMUNICATION — The general longing for agreement, which stimulates the need for honest dialogue.

Very lucky – achievements are possible

50 line 1

———— × ————

Correct

JUDGEMENT The smallest decision, if it is fair, can aid progress towards an enlightened society.

INNOCENCE Even insignificant experiences can add to development if viewed from a truly innocent point of view.

AWARENESS Even a small amount of increased awareness can add to the overall growth of consciousness if it is free from the influence of the ego.

EMOTION Even insignificant feelings, if expressed honestly, can add to a relationship.

CREATIVITY Even the smallest idea, if it is truly original, can add to cultural heritage.

COMMUNICATION Even insignificant words, if they are true, can help the cause of open dialogue.

AMBITION Progress can be aided by even the smallest improvement in ability.

SERVICE Seemingly unimportant duties, if they are performed meticulously, can help a greater cause.

NURTURE The smallest amount of growth, if it is nurtured with care, is significant.

ECONOMY Even the smallest profits can help general economic growth if they are obtained honestly.

NEUTRALITY The insignificant being of value to the whole.

REASON Even a small amount of knowledge, if it is genuine, can add to overall understanding.

50 line 2

———— ▫ ————

Lucky

JUDGEMENT Far-reaching decisions are possible. This power may cause envy, but this can do no harm.

INNOCENCE New experience is possible. There may be jealousy, but this cannot hurt.

AWARENESS Higher awareness is possible. Any derision is harmless.

EMOTION Mutual feeling is a possibility. There may be envy, but this cannot do any harm.

CREATIVITY Great creativity is possible. There is criticism, but it cannot hurt.

COMMUNICATION Agreement is possible. There may be argument, but this does not harm open dialogue.

AMBITION Progress can be made. Rivals may be envious, but this cannot detract from progress.

SERVICE The acceptance of responsibility is feasible; envy cannot harm this.

NURTURE New maturity is possible. It may seem too fast to others, but this is not the case.

ECONOMY Economic growth is possible. Others may be envious, but this can do no harm.

NEUTRALITY Potential for positive progress.

REASON Greater understanding is possible. Others may not comprehend, but this does not matter.

50 line 3

———— ▫ ————

Doubts will be overcome – eventual luck

JUDGEMENT Not yet the right time for a far-reaching decision; however, the right time will present itself.

INNOCENCE Circumstances deny new experience, although the right opportunity will come eventually.

AWARENESS Higher values are not yet acceptable. The time will come eventually.

EMOTION This is not yet the right time to express a feeling; however, the opportunity will eventually present itself.

CREATIVITY Original ideas cannot yet find appreciation; however, the time will come.

COMMUNICATION Not yet the right time for honest words; however, the right opportunity will eventually come along.

AMBITION Although there is readiness, progress is not yet possible. The right opportunity will eventually present itself.

SERVICE Capabilities are not yet appreciated, although they will be eventually.

NURTURE A new level of maturity is possible, but the situation does not allow it. It will happen in time.

ECONOMY   The potential for profit is there, but the situation does not allow it. The right opportunity will come eventually.
NEUTRALITY   Stifled potential finding an outlet in time.
REASON   Deep understanding cannot yet be appreciated, but the time will come when it is.

50 line 4

———□———

Unfortunate – deserved blame

JUDGEMENT   Decisions are beyond powers.
INNOCENCE   There is not enough experience to cope with the situation.
AWARENESS   The ego is too involved to permit awareness.
EMOTION   Motives are too selfish for mutual emotion.
CREATIVITY   Talent is inadequate for the expression of creative ideas.
COMMUNICATION   Not honest enough to come to any meaningful agreement.
AMBITION   Abilities are not adequate for ambitions.
SERVICE   Capabilities are inadequate for responsibility.
NURTURE   Care is inadequate to be of value.
ECONOMY   Financial resources are too limited for investment.
NEUTRALITY   Inadequate resources for progress.
REASON   Knowledge is beyond understanding.

50 line 5

———×———

Persevere

JUDGEMENT   It is worth trying to sustain objectivity.
INNOCENCE   Innocence is worth hanging on to.
AWARENESS   It is worth trying to sustain higher awareness.
EMOTION   Genuine emotion is worth hanging on to.
CREATIVITY   It is worth trying to hang on to genuine creativity.

COMMUNICATION   Open dialogue is worth sustaining.
AMBITION   It is worth keeping abilities to a high standard.
SERVICE   It pays to remain efficient.
NURTURE   It pays to sustain genuine care.
ECONOMY   It is worth keeping up the methods that engender economic growth.
NEUTRALITY   Positive attributes, worth sustaining.
REASON   It is worth trying to sustain the state of mind that leads to deep understanding.

50 line 6

———□———

Very lucky – achievements are possible

JUDGEMENT   Far-reaching decisions, which are in accord with the time.
INNOCENCE   Genuine innocence, which is instinctively protected by others.
AWARENESS   Higher awareness, which is welcomed instinctively.
EMOTION   Genuine feelings, which find instinctive reciprocation.
CREATIVITY   Original ideas, which find acceptance easily.
COMMUNICATION   Honest words, which are accepted without question.
AMBITION   Natural abilities, which allow progress without struggle.
SERVICE   Efficiency, which allows duties to be carried out with ease.
NURTURE   Instinctive care, which nurtures growth in a natural way.
ECONOMY   Prudent investments, which sustain economic growth without need for worry.
NEUTRALITY   Adding to collective resources in a positive way.
REASON   Deep understanding, which is naturally welcomed.

51
·SHOCK·

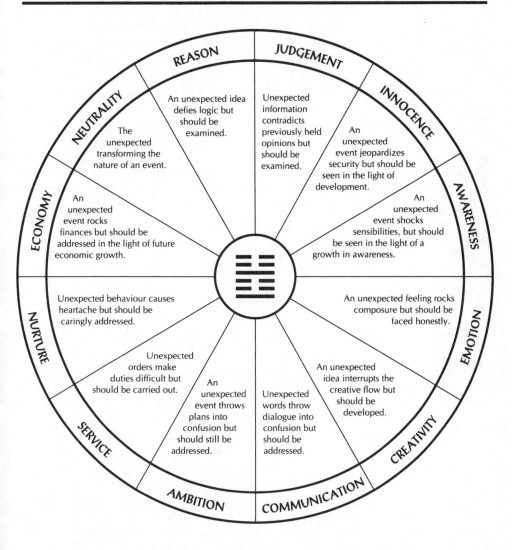

REASON

An unexpected idea defies logic but should be examined.

JUDGEMENT

Unexpected information contradicts previously held opinions but should be examined.

NEUTRALITY

The unexpected transforming the nature of an event.

INNOCENCE

An unexpected event jeopardizes security but should be seen in the light of development.

ECONOMY

An unexpected event rocks finances but should be addressed in the light of future economic growth.

AWARENESS

An unexpected event shocks sensibilities, but should be seen in the light of a growth in awareness.

NURTURE

Unexpected behaviour causes heartache but should be caringly addressed.

EMOTION

An unexpected feeling rocks composure but should be faced honestly.

Unexpected orders make duties difficult but should be carried out.

An unexpected event throws plans into confusion but should still be addressed.

Unexpected words throw dialogue into confusion but should be addressed.

An unexpected idea interrupts the creative flow but should be developed.

SERVICE

AMBITION

COMMUNICATION

CREATIVITY

Remain calm – achievements are possible

51 line 1

— □ —

Lucky

JUDGEMENT Unexpected information contradicts opinions, but throws new light on a decision.

INNOCENCE An unexpected event threatens security but is a lesson.

AWARENESS An unexpected event shocks sensibilities but is nourishment for a growth in awareness.

EMOTION An unexpected emotion throws feelings into disarray but is more honest.

CREATIVITY An unexpected idea interrupts the creative flow but turns out to be inspirational.

COMMUNICATION Unexpected words threaten to end dialogue but turn out to be constructive.

AMBITION An unexpected event threatens to impede progress but turns out to be advantageous.

SERVICE An unexpected order threatens to make duties difficult but is, in fact, of practical benefit.

NURTURE Unexpected behaviour causes heartache but is part of growth.

ECONOMY An unexpected event threatens financial security but turns out to be an advantage.

NEUTRALITY The unexpected threatening fortunes, but turning to advantage.

REASON An unexpected idea defies logic but turns out to be constructive.

51 line 2

— × —

Danger

JUDGEMENT Unexpected developments cause a temporary loss of judgement. It will return in its own time.

INNOCENCE An unexpected event causes fear, but security will return in its own time.

AWARENESS Unexpected events cause a loss of belief, but it will be rediscovered in time.

EMOTION Unexpected events cause numbness, but feelings should be allowed to return in their own time.

CREATIVITY Unexpected events cause a creative block. It will disperse in its own time.

COMMUNICATION Unexpected words cause silence, but dialogue should be allowed to restart in its own time.

AMBITION Unexpected events cause a loss of confidence. It will return in its own time.

SERVICE Unexpected events cause a temporary neglect of duty. Loyalty will return in time.

NURTURE Unexpected behaviour causes a rift that should be allowed to heal itself.

ECONOMY Unexpected events cause the abandonment of prudence. Good sense will be seen in time.

NEUTRALITY Unexpected events causing a temporary loss.

REASON An unexpected event causes the abandonment of reason, but logical thought should be allowed to return in its own time.

51 line 3

— × —

Immediate action avoids misfortune

JUDGEMENT Unexpected information requires immediate consideration.

INNOCENCE A sudden fright means growing up quickly.

AWARENESS The unexpected appearance of the ego demands immediate attention.

EMOTION Unexpected feelings need to be addressed immediately.

CREATIVITY Unexpected inspiration requires immediate expression.

COMMUNICATION Unexpected words require an immediate response.

AMBITION Unexpected failure requires immediate action.

SERVICE Unexpected orders need an immediate response.

NURTURE Unexpected behaviour needs to be addressed immediately.

ECONOMY Unexpected debts require immediate attention.

NEUTRALITY The unexpected causing confusion.

REASON Unexpected results require immediate examination.

51 line 4

JUDGEMENT Being dogmatic means the opportunity for an enlightened decision is ignored.
INNOCENCE Ignorance causes a lesson in life to be missed.
AWARENESS Insensitivity causes a chance of increased awareness to be missed.
EMOTION A self-centred attitude causes an honest feeling to be ignored.
CREATIVITY Artistic ideals cause real inspiration to be dismissed.
COMMUNICATION Verbosity causes the truth to be misheard.
AMBITION Naked ambition causes a real chance of progress to be missed.
SERVICE Inflexibility means a chance to be of real use is missed.
NURTURE Over-protectiveness leads to a chance of real growth being missed.
ECONOMY Greed causes a chance of real profit to be missed.
NEUTRALITY The unexpected being met by inflexibility.
REASON A reliance on logic means a radical idea is dismissed.

51 line 5

Danger

JUDGEMENT Remain impartial in the face of information that contradicts opinions. Judgement will be needed.
INNOCENCE Retain an innocent attitude in the face of confusing events. They contain lessons in life that need to be learned.
AWARENESS Retain inner calm in the face of unexpected events. Clarity will be needed to understand their significance.
EMOTION Remain calm in the face of repeated emotional shocks, as feelings will need to be appraised honestly.
CREATIVITY Retain artistic judgement in the midst of unexpected inspiration; it will be needed.
COMMUNICATION Remain attentive in the face of shocking revelations; they will need to be discussed.
AMBITION Remain enthusiastic in the face of unexpected setbacks; that enthusiasm will be needed.

SERVICE Remain steadfast when unexpected demands are made. Dependability will be needed to complete tasks.
NURTURE Remain caring in the face of repeated heartaches; that care will be needed.
ECONOMY Remain sensible in the face of economic chaos. Prudence will be needed to get out of it.
NEUTRALITY Standing firm in the face of unexpected events.
REASON Keep an open mind in the face of illogical events; it will be needed to find understanding.

51 line 6

Action is unfortunate; no need for guilt; gossip

JUDGEMENT Unexpected events cloud judgement. Knowing this, it is better to make no decisions, although this may not be understood.
INNOCENCE Unexpected events cause confusion all round. Seeing this, it is better not to get involved, although others may deride this.
AWARENESS Unexpected events cause a loss of awareness. Knowing this, it is better not to seek it, although the ego may not agree.
EMOTION Unexpected events cause emotional turmoil. Awareness of this engenders caution, although others may not understand.
CREATIVITY Unexpected events cause artistic judgement to be impaired. Knowing this, simplicity is best, although others may not understand.
COMMUNICATION Unexpected words cause shock. Knowing this, it is best to remain collected, although others may not understand.
AMBITION Unexpected setbacks cause a loss of enthusiasm. Knowing this, it is better to keep going, although others may not understand.
SERVICE Unexpected events lead to a dereliction of duty. Knowing this, it is better to remain steadfast, although others may not understand.

NURTURE Shocking events cause instinctive over-reaction. Knowing this, it is better not to react, although others may not understand.

ECONOMY Unexpected events affect financial judgement. Knowing this, it is better not to enter into financial commitments, although this may not be understood.

NEUTRALITY Unexpected events causing confusion.

REASON Unexpected events affect reasoning abilities. Knowing this it is better not to draw conclusions, although this may seem irrational to others.

52
·REST·

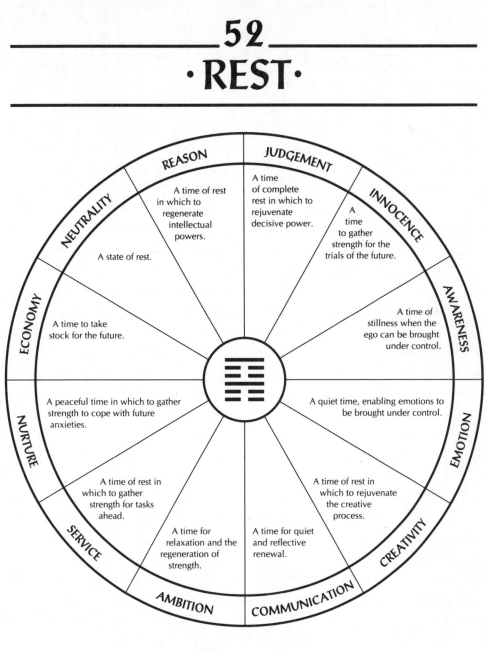

REASON — A time of rest in which to regenerate intellectual powers.

JUDGEMENT — A time of complete rest in which to rejuvenate decisive power.

INNOCENCE — A time to gather strength for the trials of the future.

NEUTRALITY — A state of rest.

ECONOMY — A time to take stock for the future.

AWARENESS — A time of stillness when the ego can be brought under control.

NURTURE — A peaceful time in which to gather strength to cope with future anxieties.

EMOTION — A quiet time, enabling emotions to be brought under control.

SERVICE — A time of rest in which to gather strength for tasks ahead.

CREATIVITY — A time of rest in which to rejuvenate the creative process.

AMBITION — A time for relaxation and the regeneration of strength.

COMMUNICATION — A time for quiet and reflective renewal.

Blameless

52 line 1

———×———

Blameless – persevere

JUDGEMENT Pause before starting any decision-making process.
INNOCENCE Stop and think before acting. In this way the safest path can be chosen.
AWARENESS Pause in order to consider the best way to achieve a growth in awareness.
EMOTION Stop and think in order to find the best way to translate a feeling into action.
CREATIVITY Stop and think in order to find the best way to express an idea.
COMMUNICATION Pause and consider the best way to communicate the truth.
AMBITION Stop and think in order to find the best way to make progress.
SERVICE Stop and decide the best way to tackle a task.
NURTURE Stop and think before pointing a child in any one direction.
ECONOMY Pause and consider the most sensible options.
NEUTRALITY Pausing before acting.
REASON Pause in order to decide the best way to approach a problem.

52 line 2

———×———

JUDGEMENT The current of the time forces distasteful decisions.
INNOCENCE Those who lead are untrustworthy; a time of insecurity.
AWARENESS Ego-orientated behaviour is forced by the time.
EMOTION The situation forces action that does not feel right.
CREATIVITY The situation demands ideas that are less than creative.
COMMUNICATION The atmosphere means things are said that are not strictly true.
AMBITION The nature of the competition forces underhand methods.
SERVICE It is difficult to follow orders that are known to be wrong.
NURTURE The situation demands action that is less than caring.
ECONOMY The economic tide forces unwise decisions.

NEUTRALITY Circumstances forcing unwise behaviour.
REASON The current of the time forces irrational action.

52 line 3

———□———

Danger

JUDGEMENT Deliberately putting off a decision is dangerous.
INNOCENCE Not acting because of fear is dangerous.
AWARENESS Forcibly stifling awareness is dangerous.
EMOTION Stifling emotion is dangerous.
CREATIVITY Deliberately stifling creativity is destructive.
COMMUNICATION Suppressing the truth is dangerous.
AMBITION Suppressing natural ambition is destructive.
SERVICE Suppressing true loyalties is dangerous.
NURTURE Stifling growth is dangerous.
ECONOMY Frugality for its own sake is not constructive.
NEUTRALITY Forced non-action.
REASON Forcibly suppressing intelligence is dangerous.

52 line 4

———×———

Blameless

JUDGEMENT There is no blame in not wanting to make a decision at this time.
INNOCENCE It is not wrong to seek security.
AWARENESS There is nothing wrong in seeking peace.
EMOTION There is nothing wrong in seeking emotional calm.
CREATIVITY There is nothing wrong in seeking solitude.
COMMUNICATION There is nothing wrong in seeking silence.
AMBITION There is no blame in wanting to rest.
SERVICE There is no blame in not wanting responsibility.

NURTURE   It is not wrong to want peace and quiet.
ECONOMY   There is no blame in being unmaterialistic.
NEUTRALITY   Seeking peace.
REASON   There is no blame in not wanting to think.

52 line 5

———×———

Regret is avoided

JUDGEMENT   Carefully weighing the evidence now means no regrets later.
INNOCENCE   Taking care not to be overconfident now means no regrets later.
AWARENESS   Dealing with the ego now avoids future regret.
EMOTION   Keeping emotions under control now saves regret in the future.
CREATIVITY   Care in developing an idea now means no regret in the future.
COMMUNICATION   Care in what is said now means no regrets later.
AMBITION   Future regret is avoided by curbing ambition for now.
SERVICE   Attention to duty now means no regrets later.
NURTURE   Caring now means no regrets later.
ECONOMY   Prudence now means no regrets in the future.
NEUTRALITY   Care taken now avoiding future problems.
REASON   Being methodical now means no regrets in the future.

52 line 6

———□———

Lucky

JUDGEMENT   Rejecting power as a goal in itself allows enlightened decisions to be made.
INNOCENCE   Admitting ignorance allows valuable lessons to be learned.
AWARENESS   Quieting the ego allows a growth in awareness.
EMOTION   Emotional balance encourages feelings in others.
CREATIVITY   Stilling the mind invites inspiration.
COMMUNICATION   Keeping quiet inspires open dialogue among others.
AMBITION   Renouncing selfish ambition allows worthwhile goals to be achieved.
SERVICE   Serving without complaint means more responsibility can be shouldered.
NURTURE   Voluntarily standing back inspires growth.
ECONOMY   Voluntary prudence encourages an upturn in finances.
NEUTRALITY   Enlightened non-action.
REASON   The rejection of cleverness for its own sake allows deep understanding.

53
·GRADUAL PROGRESS·

REASON — A gradual assimilation of knowledge is the way to understanding.

NEUTRALITY — Progressing incrementally.

JUDGEMENT — Considering one fact at a time is the way to a correct decision.

INNOCENCE — Moving a step at a time is the way to maturity.

ECONOMY — Gradual growth is the way to economic stability.

AWARENESS — A gradual shedding of the ego is the way to higher awareness.

NURTURE — Nurturing growth gradually develops a strong character.

EMOTION — Getting to know each other gradually is the way to a lasting relationship.

SERVICE — Moving a step at a time gets a job done.

CREATIVITY — Gradual development of an idea is the way to artistic success.

AMBITION — Gradual progress is the way to achieve a goal.

COMMUNICATION — Step-by-step negotiation is the way to agreement.

Lucky – persevere

53 line 1

——×——

Blameless

JUDGEMENT Indecisiveness at the beginning is both understandable and correct. There may be criticism.

INNOCENCE Nervousness at the beginning is understandable and also a safeguard. There may be talk.

AWARENESS When awareness is a new experience, doubts are understandable and necessary. There may be misunderstanding.

EMOTION At the beginning of a relationship, nervousness is both understandable and a safeguard. There may be gossip.

CREATIVITY On first being inspired, uncertainty is both understandable and necessary. There may be controversy.

COMMUNICATION At the beginning of a conversation reticence is both understandable and correct. There may be rumours.

AMBITION Nervousness at the beginning is understandable and correct. There may be rumours.

SERVICE Hesitancy in starting a task is understandable and necessary. There may be talk.

NURTURE At the beginning, concern is both understandable and necessary. There may be misunderstanding.

ECONOMY Hedging at the beginning is both understandable and prudent. There may be rumours.

NEUTRALITY Hesitancy at the beginning.

REASON Hesitancy when first tackling a problem is understandable and necessary. There may be criticism.

53 line 2

——×——

Lucky

JUDGEMENT A decision is clear. It is well to spread confidence among others.

INNOCENCE The future looks secure. It is well to share enjoyment with others.

AWARENESS Awareness clears the path ahead. It is well to share joy with others.

EMOTION The path to happiness seems clear. It is well to share this feeling with others.

CREATIVITY The direction an idea is taking can be clearly seen. It is well to share it with others.

COMMUNICATION An agreement can be confidently predicted. It is well to share this confidence with others.

AMBITION An achievement can be confidently predicted. It is well to help others.

SERVICE The completion of a task can be confidently predicted. It is well to spread this confidence.

NURTURE A secure future can be predicted with confidence. It is as well to enjoy the relationship.

ECONOMY A way to achieve financial stability can be seen. It is well to be generous.

NEUTRALITY A clear path ahead.

REASON A solution can be confidently predicted. It is good to share understanding.

53 line 3

——□——

Unfortunate

JUDGEMENT Enjoyment of power leads to a wrong decision. Beware of challengers.

INNOCENCE Arrogance leads to trouble. Beware of corrupting influences.

AWARENESS Ego-led behaviour leads to a loss of awareness. Beware of false ideals.

EMOTION Over-eagerness ends a relationship. Beware of empty words.

CREATIVITY Trying too hard spoils an idea. Beware of imitators.

COMMUNICATION Talking too much causes offence. Beware of liars.

AMBITION Over-ambition causes a goal to be missed. Beware of cheats.

SERVICE Over-zealousness causes failure in duty. Beware of disloyalty.

NURTURE Expecting too much causes resentment. Beware of bad influences.

ECONOMY Greed causes a loss. Beware of confidence-tricksters.

NEUTRALITY Overshooting a goal.

REASON Trying to be too clever leads to a mistake. Beware of inaccuracies.

53 line 4

——×——

Avoiding blame

JUDGEMENT An unusual decision requires meticulous deliberation.
INNOCENCE A new situation requires great care.
AWARENESS An unexplored area of awareness requires the exclusion of the ego.
EMOTION An inappropriate feeling needs to be examined honestly.
CREATIVITY A strange idea demands unpretentious expression.
COMMUNICATION Strange company demands tact and diplomacy.
AMBITION A strange challenge requires adaptability.
SERVICE Strange orders demand flexibility and discipline.
NURTURE New maturity demands even more understanding.
ECONOMY A risky speculation requires great prudence.
NEUTRALITY An unusual situation.
REASON A bizarre problem requires lateral thinking.

53 line 5

——□——

Lucky

JUDGEMENT Successful decision-makers become isolated, but in time others see the value in strong leadership.
INNOCENCE Inexperience is sometimes ridiculed, but in time others wish for innocent pleasure.
AWARENESS With new-found awareness comes isolation, but others eventually understand.
EMOTION When happiness is found, others may need time to understand.
CREATIVITY With originality comes misunderstanding, but appreciation comes in time.
COMMUNICATION With total honesty comes isolation, but others see the value of the truth in time.
AMBITION With success comes isolation, but others may need time to come to terms with it.

SERVICE Pride in a job alienates those who do not care, but in time they come to see the value of loyalty.
NURTURE Growing up can lead to a gulf between parent and child, but in time they grow together again.
ECONOMY Financial success alienates others, but in time they come to terms with it.
NEUTRALITY Achievements leading to isolation.
REASON Proven intelligence alienates the less able, but in time they come to value knowledge.

53 line 6

——□——

Lucky

JUDGEMENT Decisiveness tempered with fairness is an example for others.
INNOCENCE The happiness of innocence is an example to others.
AWARENESS The benign nature of higher awareness is an example to others.
EMOTION Genuine happiness is an example to others.
CREATIVITY Artistic triumphs are a model for others.
COMMUNICATION The ability to communicate openly is an example to others.
AMBITION Success achieved is an example for others.
SERVICE Devotion to duty is an example for others to follow.
NURTURE A well-balanced child is an example to others.
ECONOMY Financial success shows others what can be done.
NEUTRALITY Success as an example to others.
REASON A deep understanding of a subject sets an example for others to follow.

54
·DESIRE·

REASON — Merely seeking to appear clever achieves nothing.

JUDGEMENT — Seeking to control a situation achieves nothing substantial.

NEUTRALITY — That which is sought on the basis of desire.

INNOCENCE — Mere pleasure-seeking proves empty.

ECONOMY — Merely seeking gain does not encourage financial stability.

AWARENESS — Actively seeking higher awareness makes it more elusive.

NURTURE — Merely desiring to appear a good parent achieves nothing.

EMOTION — Chasing love achieves nothing.

SERVICE — Merely wanting to appear loyal is an empty gesture.

CREATIVITY — Merely seeking appreciation achieves nothing creative.

AMBITION — Seeking success for its own sake achieves nothing of value.

COMMUNICATION — Merely seeking attention achieves nothing constructive.

Any action is unfortunate

54 line 1

————▢————

Lucky

JUDGEMENT   Accepting restraints allows freedom to make decisions within those limits.
INNOCENCE   The acceptance of imposed restraints allows freedom within those limits.
AWARENESS   Awareness of personal limitations permits a growth of awareness within those limits.
EMOTION   Knowing someone well permits emotional expression within the limits they impose.
CREATIVITY   Understanding the restraints imposed by taste allows artistic freedom within those limits.
COMMUNICATION   Knowing how far to go permits honesty within those limits.
AMBITION   Respecting a hierarchy permits progress within the limits imposed.
SERVICE   Respecting discipline allows freedom within the limits imposed.
NURTURE   Allowing freedom within imposed limits.
ECONOMY   Awareness of a complete economic situation allows speculation within its limits.
NEUTRALITY   Respect for imposed restraints.
REASON   Setting boundaries on a problem allows conjecture within those limits.

54 line 2

————▢————

Persevere

JUDGEMENT   It is worth holding on to principles, even when those values are no longer appreciated.
INNOCENCE   It is worth hanging on to innocence, even when there seems to be nothing to lose.
AWARENESS   It is worth holding on to higher values, even when materialism is in the ascendancy.
EMOTION   It is worth holding on to a feeling, even when it is not reciprocated.
CREATIVITY   It is worth holding on to creative ideals, even when they are not appreciated.

COMMUNICATION   It is worth holding on to the truth, even when no one wants to listen.
AMBITION   It is worth keeping sight of a goal, even when all hope is lost.
SERVICE   It is worth remaining loyal, even when a cause seems lost.
NURTURE   It is worth caring for the young, even when they do not appreciate it.
ECONOMY   It is worth remaining prudent, even when there seems to be no point.
NEUTRALITY   Holding on to positive values in a negative situation.
REASON   It is worth looking for understanding, even when there seems to be no point.

54 line 3

————×————

JUDGEMENT   Wanting to control a situation so much that principles are abandoned.
INNOCENCE   Wanting pleasure so much that innocence is left behind.
AWARENESS   Wanting awareness so much that its moral basis is forgotten.
EMOTION   Wanting a relationship so much that true feelings are ignored.
CREATIVITY   Wanting appreciation so much that artistic standards are forgotten.
COMMUNICATION   Wanting attention so much that it does not matter what is said.
AMBITION   Wanting success so much that any method is used.
SERVICE   Wanting personal freedom so much that duties are ignored.
NURTURE   Wanting to appear a good parent so much that the real needs of children are ignored.
ECONOMY   Wanting more so much that prudence is abandoned.
NEUTRALITY   Wanting something so much that standards are lowered.
REASON   Wanting intellectual superiority so much that real understanding is forgotten.

54 line 4

———□———

JUDGEMENT Acting on principle is shown to be correct eventually.
INNOCENCE Holding on to innocence is an advantage in the end.
AWARENESS Loyalty to higher values means that a growth in awareness is achieved eventually.
EMOTION Holding on to a sincere feeling means it is reciprocated eventually.
CREATIVITY Loyalty to artistic ideals means that appreciation is found eventually.
COMMUNICATION Continuing to listen allows the truth to be spoken eventually.
AMBITION Continuing to nurture abilities allows goals to be achieved eventually.
SERVICE Loyalty is appreciated eventually.
NURTURE True caring shows results eventually.
ECONOMY Continued prudence is shown to be wise eventually.
NEUTRALITY Perseverance showing eventual results.
REASON A continued search for understanding brings conclusions eventually.

54 line 5

———×———

Lucky

JUDGEMENT Relinquishing power for the common good.
INNOCENCE Showing more restraint and strengthening character.
AWARENESS Eliminating ego-led behaviour for the sake of a growth in awareness.
EMOTION Eradicating selfish feelings for the sake of a better relationship.
CREATIVITY Rejecting pretensions for more genuine creativity.
COMMUNICATION Being more honest for the sake of better dialogue.
AMBITION Suppressing personal ambition for the sake of a greater goal.
SERVICE Accepting less responsibility in order to serve more efficiently.
NURTURE Loosening parental influence for the sake of a child.
ECONOMY Being less greedy for the sake of economic stability.

NEUTRALITY Accepting loss for the common good.
REASON Admitting ignorance for the sake of a greater understanding.

54 line 6

———×———

No progress

JUDGEMENT Merely being decisive to demonstrate power.
INNOCENCE Mere play-acting.
AWARENESS Merely going through the motions to prove moral superiority.
EMOTION Devoid of feeling.
CREATIVITY Uninspired and unoriginal.
COMMUNICATION Empty words.
AMBITION Merely being competitive.
SERVICE Merely being subservient
NURTURE A show of caring.
ECONOMY Ostentation.
NEUTRALITY Merely going through the motions for the sake of form.
REASON Merely seeking to demonstrate intelligence.

55
·PLENTY·

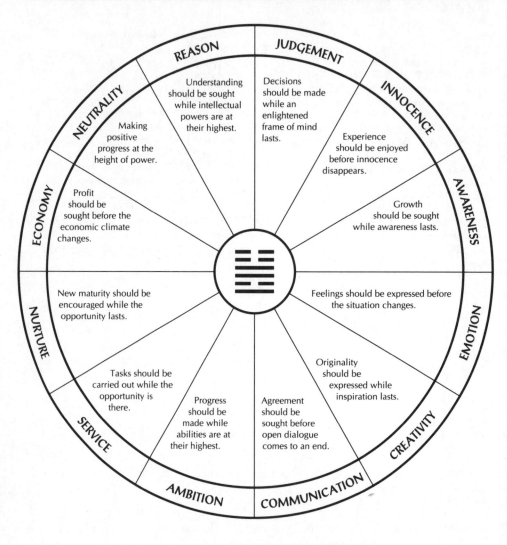

- **REASON** — Understanding should be sought while intellectual powers are at their highest.
- **JUDGEMENT** — Decisions should be made while an enlightened frame of mind lasts.
- **NEUTRALITY** — Making positive progress at the height of power.
- **INNOCENCE** — Experience should be enjoyed before innocence disappears.
- **ECONOMY** — Profit should be sought before the economic climate changes.
- **AWARENESS** — Growth should be sought while awareness lasts.
- **NURTURE** — New maturity should be encouraged while the opportunity lasts.
- **EMOTION** — Feelings should be expressed before the situation changes.
- **SERVICE** — Tasks should be carried out while the opportunity is there.
- **CREATIVITY** — Originality should be expressed while inspiration lasts.
- **AMBITION** — Progress should be made while abilities are at their highest.
- **COMMUNICATION** — Agreement should be sought before open dialogue comes to an end.

Achievements are possible now

55 line 1

———□———

Blameless – worthy of praise

JUDGEMENT It is not wrong to make decisions at the height of powers.
INNOCENCE Innocent pleasure is not wrong while it lasts.
AWARENESS Translating awareness into action is not wrong.
EMOTION It is not wrong to express a feeling while the moment lasts.
CREATIVITY While inspiration lasts, it is not wrong to express new ideas.
COMMUNICATION It is not wrong to seek agreement while the opportunity lasts.
AMBITION Progress is not wrong as long as the opportunities are there.
SERVICE It is not wrong to carry out duties if the capability is there.
NURTURE Encouraging new experience is not wrong if the opportunity is there.
ECONOMY It is not wrong to seek profit while the economic climate allows it.
NEUTRALITY A limited time when positive action is possible.
REASON It is not wrong to seek understanding if the opportunity is there.

55 line 2

———×———

Lucky

JUDGEMENT Forcing decisions meets with resentment. It is better to demonstrate fairness.
INNOCENCE Chasing new experience leads to being unpopular. An innocent enjoyment of life is better.
AWARENESS The promotion of higher values meets with mistrust. It is better to demonstrate awareness through action.
EMOTION Expressing feelings causes unease. It is better to let things happen naturally.
CREATIVITY Pushing original ideas meets with criticism. Letting others see their worth for themselves is better.
COMMUNICATION Forcing opinions causes arguments. It is better to let others come to the same conclusions for themselves.

AMBITION Forcing progress causes resentment. It is better to let abilities speak for themselves.
SERVICE Taking the lead is seen as mutiny. It is better to be an example.
NURTURE Expecting too much causes resentment. Nurturing growth naturally is better.
ECONOMY Chasing profit leads to mistrust. It is better to be an example of prudence.
NEUTRALITY Forced progress as opposed to natural progress.
REASON Pushing ideas leads to misunderstanding. It is better to demonstrate their logic.

55 line 3

———□———

Blameless

JUDGEMENT The situation does not allow far-reaching decisions to be made.
INNOCENCE Genuine innocence is not appreciated in this situation.
AWARENESS The situation does not allow higher awareness to be applied.
EMOTION The situation prevents genuine feelings being expressed.
CREATIVITY Original ideas will not be appreciated in the present situation.
COMMUNICATION Honesty will not be appreciated at the present time.
AMBITION Abilities will not be recognized at this time.
SERVICE Loyalty will find no appreciation at this time.
NURTURE Outside circumstances prevent necessary care.
ECONOMY External economic circumstances prevent profit.
NEUTRALITY Positive attributes that are not appreciated in a negative situation.
REASON The situation does not permit the introduction of deeper understanding.

55 line 4

———□———

Lucky

JUDGEMENT Decisions can be made because the situation allows it.
INNOCENCE There is an opportunity for innocent pleasure.
AWARENESS An opportunity for increased awareness presents itself.
EMOTION Feelings can be expressed, as the situation allows it.
CREATIVITY The situation permits the expression of original ideas.
COMMUNICATION Honest words can be spoken because the situation allows it.
AMBITION Circumstances allow progress to be made.
SERVICE Responsibilities can be carried out because the situation allows it.
NURTURE Growth can be encouraged because the circumstances are right.
ECONOMY Economic circumstances permit profits to be made.
NEUTRALITY A negative situation opening up to allow positive action.
REASON The situation allows a deeper understanding to be sought.

55 line 5

———×———

Lucky – in accord with the time

JUDGEMENT A willingness to accept other opinions makes decisions fairer and more acceptable.
INNOCENCE Enjoying innocence brings more pleasure.
AWARENESS Ignoring the ego makes greater awareness possible and more acceptable to others.
EMOTION Genuine feelings are encouraged.
CREATIVITY Original ideas have a power of their own.
COMMUNICATION Openness makes others want to come to an agreement.
AMBITION Genuine ability finds itself encouraged.
SERVICE Genuine loyalty has a power of its own.
NURTURE Real care meets with a positive response.

ECONOMY Economic growth inspires more of the same.
NEUTRALITY Positive values encouraging positive progress.
REASON Wanting to learn brings understanding closer.

55 line 6

———×———

Unfortunate

JUDGEMENT Seeking control, which leads to alienation.
INNOCENCE Self-indulgence leading to insecurity.
AWARENESS Isolated through seeking moral superiority.
EMOTION Selfishness leading to loneliness.
CREATIVITY Pretentiousness leading to rejection.
COMMUNICATION Because of stubbornly held opinions, no one wants to listen.
AMBITION Naked ambition causing alienation.
SERVICE A lack of respect caused through self-importance.
NURTURE Resentment caused by expecting too much.
ECONOMY Alienation caused by greed.
NEUTRALITY Isolation through the abuse of power.
REASON Intellectual superiority causing isolation.

56
·STRANGE SITUATIONS·

REASON — Unfamiliar knowledge; it is best assimilated gradually.

JUDGEMENT — Decisions in strange areas; best made tentatively.

NEUTRALITY — Strange situations.

INNOCENCE — New experience; it is best to take small steps.

ECONOMY — Unknown economic areas; speculation should be small.

AWARENESS — Strange areas of awareness, which are best explored with care.

NURTURE — Strange behaviour; care should be applied sensitively.

EMOTION — Strange new feelings; these are best explored tentatively.

SERVICE — New areas of responsibility; orders are best carried out in small ways.

CREATIVITY — Strange influences, which are best assimilated gradually.

AMBITION — Strange new challenges; progress is best made gradually.

COMMUNICATION — In a strange situation, it is best to communicate in a polite way.

Minor progress – perseverance brings luck

56 line 1

——— × ———

Unfortunate

JUDGEMENT Merely examining the trivial evidence is unwise where strange decisions are concerned.
INNOCENCE Approaching a new experience in too light a way is not good.
AWARENESS It is unfortunate if the ego is allowed to tamper in new areas of awareness.
EMOTION It is unwise not to take strange new feelings seriously.
CREATIVITY It is unfortunate if new influences are not taken seriously.
COMMUNICATION In a strange situation, it is not good to dwell on trivial matters.
AMBITION It is unfortunate if, in the face of new challenges, there is only petty ambition.
SERVICE When there are new areas of responsibility, it is unfortunate if self-importance is the only goal.
NURTURE It is not good to dwell only on the outward aspects of strange behaviour.
ECONOMY In an unknown economic area petty greed is unfortunate.
NEUTRALITY Triviality in strange situations.
REASON It is unwise to dwell on the trivial aspects of an unfamiliar subject.

56 line 2

——— × ———

JUDGEMENT Winning support in strange situations through inherent fairness.
INNOCENCE Genuine innocence wins friends in strange situations.
AWARENESS Gaining guidance in new areas of awareness through being morally correct.
EMOTION Empathy engenders some mutual feeling in a strange situation.
CREATIVITY A lack of pretension enabling new influences to be assimilated.
COMMUNICATION Modest words winning supportive agreement in a strange situation.
AMBITION Winning support through a modest demonstration of ability.
SERVICE Inherent loyalty winning respect in areas of new responsibility.

NURTURE Winning some insight into strange behaviour through being caring.
ECONOMY Prudence allows a toe-hold to be gained in new economic areas.
NEUTRALITY Correctness in a strange situation.
REASON Gaining some understanding through bringing an open mind to an unfamiliar subject.

56 line 3

——— ▫ ———

Danger

JUDGEMENT Losing the crux of a strange decision through being too opinionated.
INNOCENCE Losing friends in a strange situation through headstrong behaviour.
AWARENESS Losing new awareness by allowing the ego to push too far.
EMOTION Self-centred behaviour in a strange situation leading to emotional isolation.
CREATIVITY The misuse of strange influences being a danger to creativity.
COMMUNICATION Losing sympathy through talking about subjects that are not understood.
AMBITION Danger through being over-ambitious in an unknown area.
SERVICE Self-importance in a new area of responsibility leading to a loss of respect.
NURTURE Losing trust through dealing with strange behaviour in an uncaring way.
ECONOMY Danger of loss through greed in an unknown economic area.
NEUTRALITY Forced progress in a strange situation.
REASON Losing a grip on an unfamiliar subject by not accepting it on its own terms.

56 line 4

——— ▫ ———

Doubt

JUDGEMENT An argument is partially grasped, but there are still areas of doubt.
INNOCENCE A toe-hold has been found in a new situation, but there is still insecurity.
AWARENESS New awareness is partially achieved, but the ego still lurks.

EMOTION Getting a grip on strange new feelings, but uncertainty remains.
CREATIVITY Influences are partially assimilated, but there is no creative satisfaction.
COMMUNICATION Some common ground is found, but there is always a danger of disagreement.
AMBITION Abilities are respected, but competition is always there.
SERVICE Orders can be carried out, but there is not complete trust.
NURTURE Strange behaviour can be dealt with to a certain extent, but there is still mistrust.
ECONOMY A toe-hold is gained in a new economic area, but there is not complete confidence.
NEUTRALITY An insecure haven in an unknown situation.
REASON A small grasp of an unfamiliar subject has been obtained, but there is always a danger of misunderstanding.

56 line 5

—×—

JUDGEMENT Adaptability in assimilating evidence allows eventual decisions.
INNOCENCE Adapting to circumstances brings security in the end.
AWARENESS In unknown situations, suppressing ego-led behaviour brings eventual awareness.
EMOTION Adapting to new feelings brings satisfaction in the end.
CREATIVITY Understanding and adapting strange influences brings eventual creative results.
COMMUNICATION Assimilating the customs of others brings eventual acceptance.
AMBITION Eventual progress comes through adapting abilities.
SERVICE Being flexible in carrying out unusual orders brings eventual respect.
NURTURE Empathy engenders trust in the end.
ECONOMY Flexibility in an unknown area brings eventual economic stability.
NEUTRALITY Adaptability in unfamiliar situations.
REASON Adapting methods to suit the subject brings eventual understanding.

56 line 6

—□—

Unfortunate

JUDGEMENT Not delving deep enough into strange evidence leads to wrong decisions being made.
INNOCENCE Headstrong behaviour in a new situation leads to insecurity.
AWARENESS The ego destroys growth in a new area of awareness.
EMOTION Self-centred behaviour spoils the chance of happiness in a new situation.
CREATIVITY Pretentiousness in unfamiliar areas leads to a loss of creative power.
COMMUNICATION Over-confidence in unfamiliar circumstances leads to lost arguments.
AMBITION Over-ambition in an unknown situation, leading to failure.
SERVICE Self-importance means failure in a new area of responsibility.
NURTURE Not taking strange behaviour seriously enough leads to resentment.
ECONOMY Over-confidence in unknown economic areas leads to loss.
NEUTRALITY Over-confidence in an unfamiliar area.
REASON Making light of an unfamiliar subject leads to lost understanding.

57
·ASSIMILATION·

REASON

JUDGEMENT

NEUTRALITY

INNOCENCE

ECONOMY

AWARENESS

NURTURE

EMOTION

SERVICE

CREATIVITY

AMBITION

COMMUNICATION

Slowly assimilating knowledge that will eventually accumulate into deep understanding.

A slow assimilation of evidence leading to a decision.

Gentle influence with cumulative effect.

An unnoticed influence having great effect.

Small economic measures having eventual cumulative effect.

The imperceptible accumulation of higher awareness.

Imperceptible care that is cumulatively able to stimulate growth.

Unnoticed feelings that accumulate into something bigger.

Unnoticed devotion to duty that eventually proves invaluable.

Gentle creative influence that can have a profound effect.

Barely noticeable progress that can achieve a goal.

Imperceptible influence through a subtle choice of words.

If there is a goal, gradual progress – seek advice

57 line 1

———×———

Persevere with strength

JUDGEMENT   Indecisiveness; firm decisions are required.
INNOCENCE   Easily led astray; strength of character is necessary.
AWARENESS   Confusion; firm beliefs are required.
EMOTION   Too easily influenced; feelings need to be clearly defined.
CREATIVITY   Too many influences; more artistic discipline is required.
COMMUNICATION   Too ready to agree with anything; honest opinions need to be upheld.
AMBITION   Ambitions are confused; clearly defined goals need to be adhered to.
SERVICE   Loyalties are confused; devotion to one cause is necessitated.
NURTURE   Too easy-going; firmness is required.
ECONOMY   Interests are spread too widely; an economic target is necessary.
NEUTRALITY   That which is easily influenced.
REASON   Confusion; clearly defined methods are required.

57 line 2

———□———

Lucky – correct

JUDGEMENT   Subtle influences that affect fairness should be eradicated.
INNOCENCE   It is worthwhile to try to curb seemingly insignificant bad habits.
AWARENESS   The subtle methods of the ego should be examined and eradicated.
EMOTION   Selfish feelings that are hidden should be brought out into the open.
CREATIVITY   The influences that hamper creativity should be identified and eradicated.
COMMUNICATION   It is worth seeking out those who are secretly not in agreement.
AMBITION   It is worthwhile to seek out the subtle influences that are causing a lack of progress.
SERVICE   Pettiness that lessens efficiency should be eradicated.

NURTURE   Behaviour that has been allowed to develop through laziness should be addressed.
ECONOMY   Hidden greed should be exposed.
NEUTRALITY   Exposing hidden motives.
REASON   The subtle influences that are preventing real understanding should be eradicated.

57 line 3

———□———

Foolish

JUDGEMENT   Repeated   deliberation becomes indecisiveness.
INNOCENCE   Repeated behaviour shows a lack of maturity.
AWARENESS   Constant doubt makes a mockery of faith.
EMOTION   Not being sure of feelings leads to embarrassment.
CREATIVITY   Tampering with an idea too much shows a lack of artistic judgement.
COMMUNICATION   Going over the same arguments is foolish.
AMBITION   A lack of self-confidence leads to humiliation.
SERVICE   A lack of respect results from being unsure of loyalties.
NURTURE   Care, without the discipline to back it up, is perceived as weakness.
ECONOMY   Indecision leads to financial embarrassment.
NEUTRALITY   Uncertainty.
REASON   Having to check and re-check shows a lack of understanding.

57 line 4

———×———

Doubts are overcome

JUDGEMENT   Proper deliberation will result in a decision that satisfies all.
INNOCENCE   Pleasure and learning are experienced at the same time.
AWARENESS   Higher and lower needs are satisfied.
EMOTION   Openness about feelings leads to all-round satisfaction.

CREATIVITY Both appreciation and artistic satisfaction can be achieved.
COMMUNICATION Open dialogue leads to an agreement that satisfies all.
AMBITION Using abilities leads to more than one goal being satisfied.
SERVICE Devotion to duty leads to tasks being completed to the satisfaction of all.
NURTURE Care is rewarding to both parent and child.
ECONOMY Economic growth on a personal and general level.
NEUTRALITY More than one achievement.
REASON Seeking deep understanding will yield results that satisfy all criteria.

57 line 5

_____ロ_____

Take care; doubts are overcome; perseverance brings luck

JUDGEMENT Decisions can become more obvious by looking at the evidence in a different way.
INNOCENCE A change of attitude makes for more security.
AWARENESS A change in moral values brings awareness nearer.
EMOTION Feelings are less confusing if viewed from a different perspective.
CREATIVITY Ideas can be better expressed in a different way.
COMMUNICATION Agreement is more likely if different arguments are used.
AMBITION Progress is more likely if methods are changed.
SERVICE A different approach makes tasks easier to complete.
NURTURE A different kind of care is required if growth is to be nurtured.
ECONOMY Profit is more likely if financial changes are made.
NEUTRALITY A changed approach.
REASON The solutions to problems can be found more easily by a change of approach.

57 line 6

_____ロ_____

Continuing in this way is unfortunate

JUDGEMENT The subtle influences that prevent objective decisions cannot be eradicated.
INNOCENCE Insignificant bad habits cannot be cured.
AWARENESS The subtle methods of the ego cannot be eradicated.
EMOTION Hidden selfish feelings cannot be overcome.
CREATIVITY The influences that hamper creativity cannot be eradicated.
COMMUNICATION Those who secretly disagree cannot be persuaded.
AMBITION The trivial weaknesses that are causing a lack of progress cannot be overcome.
SERVICE Pettiness, which hampers efficiency, cannot be eradicated.
NURTURE Behaviour cannot be changed.
ECONOMY Greed cannot be overcome
NEUTRALITY Hidden influences, which cannot be eradicated.
REASON The preconceptions that prevent understanding cannot be overcome.

·PLEASURE·

REASON — Taking genuine pleasure in knowledge brings deep understanding.

JUDGEMENT — The genuine pleasure derived from enlightened decisions has a big influence on others.

NEUTRALITY — An infectious feeling derived from genuine pleasure.

INNOCENCE — Genuine, untainted pleasure derived from doing something for the first time.

ECONOMY — Genuine satisfaction gained from prudence encourages financial growth.

AWARENESS — Holding on to a feeling of joy encourages higher awareness.

NURTURE — The pleasure generated from mutual care encourages real growth.

EMOTION — The pleasure derived from honest feelings encourages others to feel the same way.

SERVICE — Genuine pride in a job is infectious and allows tasks to be completed easily.

AMBITION — The feeling generated by unselfish ambition is infectious and makes achievements possible.

COMMUNICATION — The pleasure of honest dialogue is infectious and encourages the truth.

CREATIVITY — The pleasure derived from genuine creativity encourages inspiration.

Perseverance allows achievements

58 line 1

——————□——————

Lucky

JUDGEMENT   Contentment through not wanting to take control.
INNOCENCE   Pleasure that does not constantly seek new thrills.
AWARENESS   Contentment in rejecting ego-led behaviour.
EMOTION   Contentment in emotional stability.
CREATIVITY   Content to wait for inspiration.
COMMUNICATION   Contentment in merely listening.
AMBITION   Contentment in relinquishing selfish goals.
SERVICE   Content simply to be of use.
NURTURE   Contentment in deferring personal interests for the sake of another.
ECONOMY   Contentment in not being materialistic.
NEUTRALITY   Contentment.
REASON   Contentment is seeking understanding for its own sake.

58 line 2

——————□——————

Lucky – doubts are overcome

JUDGEMENT   Being happy to reject the temptation to take control avoids regret later.
INNOCENCE   Being happy to admit ignorance means no regrets later.
AWARENESS   Happily renouncing the ego means no regrets later.
EMOTION   Being happy not to exaggerate feelings means no regrets later.
CREATIVITY   Being happy not to chase inspiration means no mistakes in retrospect.
COMMUNICATION   Being happy merely to listen means no regrets later.
AMBITION   Being happy to renounce petty ambition means no regrets later.
SERVICE   Being happy simply to be of use means no blame can be attached later.
NURTURE   Being happy not to stifle another means no resentment later.
ECONOMY   Being happy to be prudent means no regrets later.
NEUTRALITY   Removing selfish motives.
REASON   Happily rejecting cleverness for its own sake means no regrets later.

58 line 3

——————×——————

Unfortunate

JUDGEMENT   Seeking to control a situation.
INNOCENCE   Mere thrill-seeking.
AWARENESS   Merely seeking moral superiority.
EMOTION   Expressing selfish feelings.
CREATIVITY   Seeking pretentious ideas.
COMMUNICATION   Merely wanting others to listen.
AMBITION   Merely wanting to achieve selfish ambitions.
SERVICE   Merely wanting an easy time.
NURTURE   Merely not wanting to let go.
ECONOMY   Simple meanness.
NEUTRALITY   Chasing pleasure.
REASON   Merely seeking to appear clever.

58 line 4

——————□——————

JUDGEMENT   Even the thought of bias must be overcome if enlightened decisions are to be made.
INNOCENCE   Even the thought of independent action must be rejected if true security is to be found.
AWARENESS   Even the thought of ego-led behaviour must be overcome before joy can be derived from a growth in awareness.
EMOTION   Even the thought of acting in a selfish way must be overcome before happiness can be found.
CREATIVITY   Even the thought of being pretentious must be overcome before true creativity can be found.
COMMUNICATION   Even the idea of forcing an opinion must be overcome if there is to be genuine open dialogue.
AMBITION   Even the thought of selfish ambition must be overcome before worthwhile goals can be achieved.
SERVICE   Even the thought of self-importance must be overcome if a task is to be completed properly.
NURTURE   Even the thought of overprotectiveness must be overcome if care is to be of value.
ECONOMY   Even the thought of recklessness must be overcome if real economic growth is to be achieved.

NEUTRALITY   The smallest doubt being able to undermine sincerity.
REASON   It is necessary to overcome even the thought of appearing clever if real understanding is the goal.

58 line 5

———□———

Danger

JUDGEMENT   Those who merely seek to control are a danger to fairness.
INNOCENCE   Those who merely seek pleasure are a danger to the innocent.
AWARENESS   Those who seek moral superiority are a danger to the truly aware.
EMOTION   Those who harbour hidden feelings are a danger to the sincere.
CREATIVITY   Those who merely seek appreciation are a danger to the truly creative.
COMMUNICATION   Those who seek to monopolize a conversation are a danger to the truly sympathetic listener.
AMBITION   Those who harbour selfish ambitions are a danger to those with greater goals.
SERVICE   Those who harbour hidden pride are a danger to those who truly seek to serve.
NURTURE   Those who think they know best are a danger to those who really care.
ECONOMY   Those who waste resources are a danger to the prudent.
NEUTRALITY   Sincerity that is susceptible to negative influence.
REASON   Those who merely wish to appear clever are a danger to those who seek deep understanding.

58 line 6

———×———

JUDGEMENT   Surrendering to bias.
INNOCENCE   Giving in to the temptation of indulgence.
AWARENESS   Surrendering to the ego.
EMOTION   Giving in to selfish emotion.
CREATIVITY   Surrendering to commercialism.
COMMUNICATION   Giving in to the temptation to force opinions on others.
AMBITION   Allowing selfish ambitions to take over.
SERVICE   Allowing personal considerations to detract from a task.
NURTURE   Allowing faults to grow for the sake of any easy life.
ECONOMY   Wasting money for the sake of ostentation.
NEUTRALITY   Giving in to weakness.
REASON   Giving in to the allure of intellectual superiority.

59
·SOFTENING·

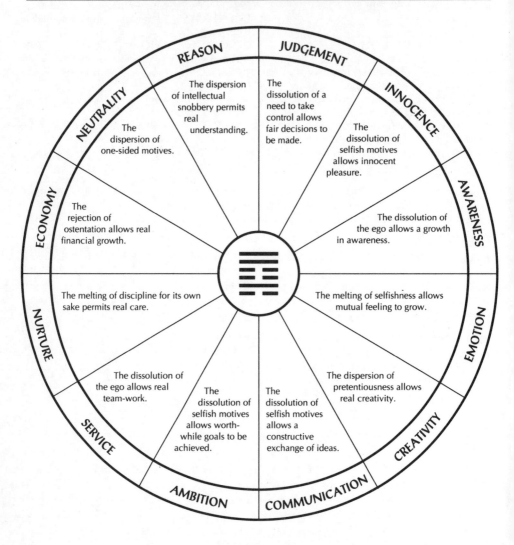

REASON

The dispersion of intellectual snobbery permits real understanding.

NEUTRALITY

The dispersion of one-sided motives.

JUDGEMENT

The dissolution of a need to take control allows fair decisions to be made.

INNOCENCE

The dissolution of selfish motives allows innocent pleasure.

ECONOMY

The rejection of ostentation allows real financial growth.

AWARENESS

The dissolution of the ego allows a growth in awareness.

NURTURE

The melting of discipline for its own sake permits real care.

EMOTION

The melting of selfishness allows mutual feeling to grow.

SERVICE

The dissolution of the ego allows real team-work.

The dissolution of selfish motives allows worth-while goals to be achieved.

The dissolution of selfish motives allows a constructive exchange of ideas.

CREATIVITY

The dispersion of pretentiousness allows real creativity.

AMBITION

COMMUNICATION

Achievements are possible – chances can be taken – persevere

59 line 1

———×———

Lucky

JUDGEMENT The urge to control a situation must be eradicated from the outset if wisdom is the goal.
INNOCENCE Selfish urges must be curbed immediately if the goal is innocent pleasure.
AWARENESS The ego must be controlled before any growth in awareness can occur.
EMOTION Selfish feelings should be eradicated at the very outset of a relationship.
CREATIVITY Pretentiousness should be eradicated from the very conception of an idea.
COMMUNICATION Selfish motives must be exposed at the very outset if there is to be constructive dialogue.
AMBITION Selfish ambitions must be eradicated from the very start if there is to be real progress.
SERVICE Egos must be dealt with immediately if there is to be real team-work.
NURTURE Discipline for its own sake is a problem that must be dealt with from the very outset.
ECONOMY Greed must be exposed immediately if there is to be shared economic growth.
NEUTRALITY Ulterior motives addressed immediately.
REASON Mere cleverness must be eradicated from the beginning if there is to be real understanding.

59 line 2

———▫———

Doubts are overcome

JUDGEMENT Errors of judgement necessitate votes of confidence.
INNOCENCE Lost innocence necessitates learning about the self.
AWARENESS Lost awareness necessitates self-examination.
EMOTION Difficulties in a relationship require the eradication of a self-centred attitude.
CREATIVITY A creative block necessitates self-criticism.

COMMUNICATION A communication breakdown necessitates listening to others.
AMBITION Failure necessitates self-examination.
SERVICE Neglect of duty requires an examination of loyalties.
NURTURE A child's problem requires that a parent's attitude be examined.
ECONOMY Broad economic problems require the examination of personal finances.
NEUTRALITY Negativity necessitating self-examination.
REASON Mistakes demand a re-evaluation of understanding.

59 line 3

———×———

No regrets

JUDGEMENT It is not wrong to be selfless in making decisions.
INNOCENCE It is not wrong to become lost in innocent pleasure.
AWARENESS It is not wrong to lose a sense of self in a state of heightened awareness.
EMOTION It is not wrong to be overwhelmed by a feeling.
CREATIVITY It is not wrong to become lost in a current of creativity.
COMMUNICATION It is not wrong to become lost in an exchange of ideas.
AMBITION It is not wrong to forget selfish motives in a struggle.
SERVICE It is not wrong to forget selfish motives for the sake of a greater goal.
NURTURE It is not wrong for parents to forget themselves for the sake of children.
ECONOMY It is not wrong to forgo personal gain.
NEUTRALITY Forgoing selfish motives.
REASON It is not wrong to become engrossed in a search for understanding.

59 line 4

———×———

Very lucky

JUDGEMENT A higher perspective permits fairer decisions.
INNOCENCE Curbing self-indulgence permits purer pleasure.

AWARENESS Overcoming ego-led behaviour engenders higher awareness.
EMOTION Overcoming selfishness permits a happier relationship.
CREATIVITY Dispensing with fashion bring bigger ideas.
COMMUNICATION Dispensing with factionalism permits a broader understanding.
AMBITION Renouncing competitiveness permits broader success.
SERVICE Aligning personal motives with those of a movement engenders greater success.
NURTURE A loosening of protectiveness permits broader based caring.
ECONOMY Renouncing greed means more chance of economic growth.
NEUTRALITY Dispensing with smaller motives to achieve multi-faceted goals.
REASON A broader perspective permits greater understanding.

59 line 5

———□———

Blameless

JUDGEMENT A decision that engenders unity.
INNOCENCE Good sense that even the inexperienced can appreciate.
AWARENESS A situation that unites awareness with practical considerations.
EMOTION Drawing attention to a mutual feeling.
CREATIVITY Original ideas that start new trends.
COMMUNICATION Words that unite opinion.
AMBITION Finding a common goal that unites those who would compete.
SERVICE Loyalty inspired by common interest.
NURTURE An event that exemplifies the bond between parent and child.
ECONOMY Economic sense that can be seen to be in the common interest.
NEUTRALITY That which focuses what is in common.
REASON An explanation that is universally understood.

59 line 6

———□———

Correct

JUDGEMENT Genuine idealism avoids bias.
INNOCENCE Refraining from indulgence avoids the corruption of innocence.
AWARENESS Unselfish behaviour avoids dangers to awareness.
EMOTION Genuine openness allows insincerity to be perceived and avoided.
CREATIVITY Genuine creativity allows pretentiousness to be avoided.
COMMUNICATION Unbiased listening allows ulterior motives to be seen.
AMBITION Renouncing ambition allows danger to be avoided.
SERVICE Devotion to duty allows a danger to the greater cause to be averted.
NURTURE Selfless caring avoids unnecessary problems in growing up.
ECONOMY Prudence avoids unnecessary financial problems.
NEUTRALITY Conscientiousness allowing danger to be avoided.
REASON A genuine thirst for knowledge allows the dangers of mere cleverness to be avoided.

60
·LIMITATION·

REASON — The solution of a problem is dependent on defining terms of reference.

JUDGEMENT — Correct decisions require that only the relevant evidence is weighed.

INNOCENCE — Personal security requires setting limits on behaviour.

NEUTRALITY — Necessary limitation.

AWARENESS — Awareness demands that limits are put on the ego.

ECONOMY — Financial growth is dependent on setting limits.

EMOTION — Emotional balance means setting limits on impulsiveness.

NURTURE — Healthy growth is dependent on the limits that are imposed.

CREATIVITY — The very expression of an idea means putting limits on inspiration.

SERVICE — An efficient worker is aware of limitations.

AMBITION — Knowing personal limitations allows peak performance within those limits.

COMMUNICATION — Knowing how far to go without offence permits the maximum possible exchange of ideas.

Conditional progress – unrealistic limits are unwise

60 line 1

— ▫ —

Blameless

JUDGEMENT It is not wrong to make a decision based on simple facts.
INNOCENCE It is not wrong not to want to take a chance.
AWARENESS It is correct not to force a growth in awareness.
EMOTION It is not wrong to express ideas in a simple way.
COMMUNICATION It is not wrong to say only as much as necessary.
AMBITION It is not wrong to act only within personal limitations.
SERVICE Doing no more than is ordered is not wrong.
NURTURE It is not wrong to put limits on behaviour.
ECONOMY It is not wrong to live within means.
NEUTRALITY Action within modest limits.
REASON It is not wrong to look for a simple answer.

60 line 2

— ▫ —

Unfortunate

JUDGEMENT A decision based on simple facts is incorrect.
INNOCENCE Not acting because of fear has unfortunate consequences.
AWARENESS Not taking the initiative means a loss of awareness.
EMOTION Unexpressed emotion causes unfortunate consequences.
CREATIVITY An idea expressed too simply is an artistic failure.
COMMUNICATION Not saying enough has unfortunate consequences.
AMBITION Underestimating personal limitations is unfortunate.
SERVICE Doing no more than is demanded has unfortunate consequences.
NURTURE Underestimating a child leads to resentment.
ECONOMY Over-cautiousness means a lost opportunity.
NEUTRALITY Underestimation of limits.
REASON An answer that is too simple has unfortunate consequences.

60 line 3

— × —

JUDGEMENT Unfairness leads to regret later.
INNOCENCE Over-indulgence leads to regret later.
AWARENESS Undisciplined awareness means regret later.
EMOTION Impulsiveness leads to regret later.
CREATIVITY Undisciplined inspiration means wasted ideas in retrospect.
COMMUNICATION Loose talk leads to regret later.
AMBITION Over-estimation of ability is regretted later.
SERVICE Over-estimating capabilities leads to regret later.
NURTURE Over-protectiveness leads to resentment later.
ECONOMY Extravagance leads to regret later.
NEUTRALITY Unlimited action.
REASON Over-estimation of reasoning ability leads to regret later.

60 line 4

— × —

Modest achievements are possible

JUDGEMENT Happy to make decisions within the limits of power.
INNOCENCE Innocent pleasure.
AWARENESS Content with the growth in awareness achieved so far.
EMOTION Contentment found in emotional balance.
CREATIVITY Happy to express ideas to the best of abilities.
COMMUNICATION Happy to converse honestly.
AMBITION Happy with a position that reflects abilities.
SERVICE Happy to carry out duties within abilities.
NURTURE Content to care naturally.
ECONOMY Happy with enough to get by.
NEUTRALITY Acting efficiently within set limits.
REASON Happy with challenges that are equal to intelligence.

60 line 5

—————☐—————

Lucky – worthy of praise

JUDGEMENT   Being happy to make decisions within the limits of power engenders respect.
INNOCENCE   The enjoyment of innocent pleasure wins the approval of others.
AWARENESS   The contentment derived from higher awareness is inspiring.
EMOTION   The contentment found through emotional balance is very attractive.
CREATIVITY   Being happy to express ideas to the best of abilities wins admirers.
COMMUNICATION   Being happy to converse honestly inspires openness in others.
AMBITION   Being happy with a position that reflects abilities inspires confidence.
SERVICE   Being happy to carry out duties to the best of abilities wins respect.
NURTURE   Being happy to care naturally engenders love.
ECONOMY   Respect is gained by being happy to live within means.
NEUTRALITY   Efficiency within set limits.
REASON   Being happy with challenges that are equal to intelligence wins respect.

60 line 6

—————×—————

Perseverance leads to misfortune but avoids guilt

JUDGEMENT   Setting unrealistic limits on decisions is not good but is better than uninhibited power.
INNOCENCE   Inhibited behaviour is not good but is preferable to unimpeded self-indulgence.
AWARENESS   Self-denial for its own sake is not good but is better than making no attempt to live by higher values.
EMOTION   Coldness is not good but is better than unimpeded impulsiveness.
CREATIVITY   Expressing an idea too simply is not good but is better than being pretentious.
COMMUNICATION   Not saying enough is not good but is better than saying too much.
AMBITION   Underestimating limits is not good but is better than over-confidence.

SERVICE   Doing as little as possible is not good but is preferable to exceeding orders.
NURTURE   Unrealistic limits on behaviour are not good but are better than nothing.
ECONOMY   Meanness is not good but is better than unimpeded extravagance.
NEUTRALITY   Extreme limitation.
REASON   Underestimation of intelligence is not good but is better than over-confidence.

61
·CONVICTION·

REASON — A deep understanding can be perceived by others.

JUDGEMENT — Implicit fairness can be perceived by others.

NEUTRALITY — Acting from conviction.

INNOCENCE — A pure heart can be perceived by others.

ECONOMY — Honesty can be perceived by others.

AWARENESS — Inner truth can permeate others.

NURTURE — True caring can be perceived unconsciously by the young.

EMOTION — Emotional sincerity can be perceived by others.

SERVICE — Devotion to duty engenders trust.

CREATIVITY — Sincerely felt ideas can find expression.

AMBITION — Real commitment can lead to progress.

COMMUNICATION — Speaking from conviction can have real influence.

Luck in simplicity – persevere

61 line 1

---◻---

Lucky

JUDGEMENT Genuine fairness leads to correct decisions, while ulterior motives create indecision.

INNOCENCE Innocence allows simple pleasure to be appreciated, but indulgence leads to insecurity.

AWARENESS Sincerely held beliefs permit awareness, but other motives only engender confusion.

EMOTION Emotional sincerity finds appreciation, but selfishness leads to unhappiness.

CREATIVITY Sincere originality wins admirers, but pretentiousness encourages criticism.

COMMUNICATION Total openness wins friends, but reticence engenders suspicion.

AMBITION True strength wins respect, but underhand motives engender suspicion.

SERVICE Devotion to duty encourages trust, but merely going through the motions leads to suspicion.

NURTURE True care permits safe growth, while merely going through the motions invites danger.

ECONOMY Genuine prudence encourages financial growth, but greed invites the worry of loss.

NEUTRALITY Preparedness.

REASON A genuine love of knowledge allows understanding, while mere cleverness leads to confusion.

61 line 2

---◻---

JUDGEMENT Genuine fairness is appreciated by others who share the same values.

INNOCENCE Genuine innocence is valued by those who know its importance.

AWARENESS Awareness is valued by those who share the same beliefs.

EMOTION Those who are sincere find emotional honesty attractive.

CREATIVITY Artistic integrity wins the respect of peers.

COMMUNICATION Openness attracts those who are honest.

AMBITION Genuine ability engenders respect in those of similar ability.

SERVICE Loyalty to a cause encourages comradeship.

NURTURE Love is reciprocated by the young.

ECONOMY Prudence is understood by those with financial experience.

NEUTRALITY Sincere positive action.

REASON Genuine understanding attracts others of like mind.

61 line 3

---×---

JUDGEMENT Dependence on dogma means that decisions are not consistently correct.

INNOCENCE Following others makes security inconsistent.

AWARENESS Following a dogma allows only a sporadic growth in awareness.

EMOTION Dependence on another for emotional stability means sporadic happiness.

CREATIVITY Dependence on others for ideas makes for sporadic creativity.

COMMUNICATION A need to seek approval makes open dialogue possible only sometimes.

AMBITION Relying on others makes for sporadic progress.

SERVICE Subservience makes for inconsistent loyalty.

NURTURE Outside influences can either encourage growth or cause heartache.

ECONOMY Dependence on one source of income makes financial growth inconsistent.

NEUTRALITY Dependence causing inconsistency.

REASON A total reliance on logic means sometimes a conclusion can be drawn, sometimes not.

61 line 4

——×——

Blameless

JUDGEMENT Fairness taken too far, requiring simple re-examination of the evidence.
INNOCENCE Inexperience in a difficult situation requiring help.
AWARENESS Pushing too hard for awareness. An examination of basic ideals is needed.
EMOTION Being over-emotional. It is necessary to take a cold, hard look at feelings.
CREATIVITY Originality taken too far means having to go back to the original idea.
COMMUNICATION Dialogue that has developed too far needing to be brought back to the original point.
AMBITION Pushing too hard necessitates the re-assessment of goals.
SERVICE Devotion to duty taken too far, requiring re-appraisal of loyalties.
NURTURE Genuine care taken too far, requiring that the purpose of nurture be re-examined.
ECONOMY Prudence taken too far, requiring the re-examination of financial goals.
NEUTRALITY Positive action taken too far.
REASON Logic taken too far, requiring re-examination of the original question.

61 line 5

——□——

Correct

JUDGEMENT A decision that makes sense of things.
INNOCENCE Innocence that unites others in protectiveness.
AWARENESS Higher truth that finds common understanding.
EMOTION The common ground of an emotional tie.
CREATIVITY Originality that strikes a chord.
COMMUNICATION Profound words with which others agree.
AMBITION The ability that others seek to emulate.

SERVICE Heart-felt loyalty that is shared by others.
NURTURE The common bond between parent and child.
ECONOMY Prudence in which others can see sense.
NEUTRALITY Conviction with which others identify.
REASON A theory that makes sense of other ideas.

61 line 6

——□——

Unfortunate

JUDGEMENT Seeking to control a situation achieves nothing.
INNOCENCE There is no ultimate satisfaction in self-indulgence.
AWARENESS Merely performing rituals means nothing.
EMOTION Words without feeling mean nothing.
CREATIVITY Creativity without originality is meaningless.
COMMUNICATION Empty words.
AMBITION Ambition without originality is meaningless.
SERVICE Servility without loyalty is of no use to a greater cause.
NURTURE Care without understanding achieves nothing.
ECONOMY Thrift without planning achieves nothing.
NEUTRALITY Going through the motions.
REASON Logic without understanding explains nothing.

62
·TRIVIAL MATTERS·

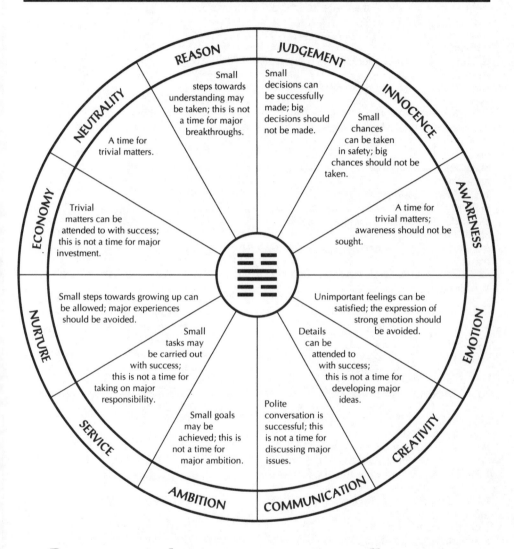

REASON — Small steps towards understanding may be taken; this is not a time for major breakthroughs.

JUDGEMENT — Small decisions can be successfully made; big decisions should not be made.

INNOCENCE — Small chances can be taken in safety; big chances should not be taken.

NEUTRALITY — A time for trivial matters.

ECONOMY — Trivial matters can be attended to with success; this is not a time for major investment.

AWARENESS — A time for trivial matters; awareness should not be sought.

NURTURE — Small steps towards growing up can be allowed; major experiences should be avoided.

EMOTION — Unimportant feelings can be satisfied; the expression of strong emotion should be avoided.

SERVICE — Small tasks may be carried out with success; this is not a time for taking on major responsibility.

CREATIVITY — Details can be attended to with success; this is not a time for developing major ideas.

AMBITION — Small goals may be achieved; this is not a time for major ambition.

COMMUNICATION — Polite conversation is successful; this is not a time for discussing major issues.

Perseverance brings progress in small matters – lucky

62 line 1

———×———

Unfortunate

JUDGEMENT Taking too big a decision leads to a mistake.
INNOCENCE Problems arise through taking too big a chance.
AWARENESS Ego-led behaviour leads to lost awareness.
EMOTION Losing another's love through being over-emotional.
CREATIVITY Trying to develop too big an idea leads to artistic failure.
COMMUNICATION Trying to say too much leads to misunderstanding.
AMBITION Over-ambition leads to failure.
SERVICE Taking on a task that is beyond capabilities leads to failure.
NURTURE Being strict for its own sake leads to rebellion.
ECONOMY Making a loss through being financially over-stretched.
NEUTRALITY Taking steps that are too big.
REASON Making a mistake through trying to be too clever.

62 line 2

———×———

Correct

JUDGEMENT Modestly making correct decisions, though misunderstood by others.
INNOCENCE Doing what feels right but not knowing why.
AWARENESS Modestly suppressing the ego for the sake of awareness.
EMOTION Suppressing emotion for someone who is unaware of the sacrifice.
CREATIVITY Unappreciated but carrying on because of artistic integrity.
COMMUNICATION Modestly sticking to the truth, though misunderstood by others.
AMBITION Resisting the temptation to push ahead for the sake of a greater goal.
SERVICE Conscientiously dutiful, although unappreciated.
NURTURE Doing what is best for a child but being unappreciated.
ECONOMY Resisting ostentation for the sake of prudence.

NEUTRALITY Acting in a correct way that is misunderstood.
REASON A correct deduction is misunderstood by others.

62 line 3

———□———

Unfortunate

JUDGEMENT Seemingly insignificant facts could destroy the validity of an important decision.
INNOCENCE What seems totally unimportant could prove to be very serious.
AWARENESS Seemingly insignificant faults could destroy higher awareness.
EMOTION Small, unvoiced doubts could destroy a meaningful relationship.
CREATIVITY Small, unnoticed faults could spoil a worthy idea.
COMMUNICATION Seemingly insignificant words could destroy a valid argument.
AMBITION Seemingly insignificant rivalry could destroy a push for success.
SERVICE Unrealized inadequacies could spoil the chance of completing an important task.
NURTURE Trivial arguments could destroy a much deeper trust.
ECONOMY Insignificant debts could destroy financial security.
NEUTRALITY Insignificant events that have the capability to destroy something worthwhile.
REASON Insignificant lapses in method could disprove an otherwise logical theory.

62 line 4

———□———

Do not act – take care – blameless

JUDGEMENT A decision seems obvious but at the present time would be wrong. It is best to do nothing while remaining conscious of the original facts.
INNOCENCE What to do seems obvious, but would prove to be wrong. It is best to do nothing and hold on to innocence.
AWARENESS It seems obvious what to do, but it would be a mistake. It is better to do nothing without losing faith.

EMOTION It looks safe to translate a feeling into action, but it would lead to pain. It is best to do nothing while not letting go of the feeling.

CREATIVITY The way to express an idea seems obvious, but would be an artistic failure. It is best to do nothing while not forgetting the original idea.

COMMUNICATION What must be said seems obvious, but would in fact be misunderstood. It is necessary to stay quiet, while not losing sight of the truth.

AMBITION The way ahead seems clear, but is in fact dangerous. It is necessary to stop, but without losing sight of the original goal.

SERVICE A task looks easy, but this is not the case. It is best to do nothing, while remaining aware of responsibilities.

NURTURE A child seems capable of new maturity, but this is not the case. It is best to do nothing while continuing to care.

ECONOMY An opportunity seems irresistible, but would prove to be a mistake. It is best to remain prudent.

NEUTRALITY The obvious way ahead hiding dangers. ·

REASON A conclusion seems obvious, but would prove to be wrong. It is best to do nothing while not forgetting the original idea.

62 line 5

——×——

Seek help modestly

JUDGEMENT A decision is near to being made, but the advice of others is needed.

INNOCENCE It is possible to achieve something, but the voice of experience is needed.

AWARENESS Awareness is possible but requires an act of faith.

EMOTION A strong emotion needs to be shared but requires others to listen.

CREATIVITY An original idea is near to completion but requires an opinion.

COMMUNICATION The truth needs to be told, but will not be believed without the word of others.

AMBITION A goal is in sight but cannot be attained without help.

SERVICE A task is near to completion but cannot be finished without the help of superiors.

NURTURE New maturity is possible but requires an outside influence.

ECONOMY A chance of gain presents itself but requires financial help.

NEUTRALITY The achievement of a goal requiring assistance.

REASON A logical conclusion is near to being drawn but requires the input of others.

62 line 6

——×——

Unfortunate

JUDGEMENT Being carried away by power means a wrong decision is made.

INNOCENCE Over-confidence means a simple lesson in life is missed.

AWARENESS Awareness is impaired by aiming too high.

EMOTION Asking too much means honest feeling disappears.

CREATIVITY A simple idea fails due to over-elaboration.

COMMUNICATION A simple agreement is not reached because too much is said.

AMBITION A simple goal is missed through trying too hard.

SERVICE A simple task ends in failure through being too keen.

NURTURE Growth is distorted because too much is expected.

ECONOMY Greed leads to a missed opportunity.

NEUTRALITY Over-shooting a goal.

REASON Mistakes are made through being too clever.

63
· AFTER COMPLETION ·

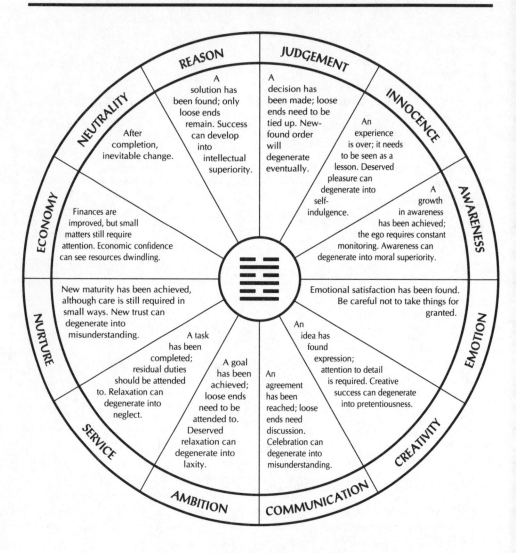

REASON
A solution has been found; only loose ends remain. Success can develop into intellectual superiority.

JUDGEMENT
A decision has been made; loose ends need to be tied up. New-found order will degenerate eventually.

NEUTRALITY
After completion, inevitable change.

INNOCENCE
An experience is over; it needs to be seen as a lesson. Deserved pleasure can degenerate into self-indulgence.

ECONOMY
Finances are improved, but small matters still require attention. Economic confidence can see resources dwindling.

AWARENESS
A growth in awareness has been achieved; the ego requires constant monitoring. Awareness can degenerate into moral superiority.

NURTURE
New maturity has been achieved, although care is still required in small ways. New trust can degenerate into misunderstanding.

EMOTION
Emotional satisfaction has been found. Be careful not to take things for granted.

SERVICE
A task has been completed; residual duties should be attended to. Relaxation can degenerate into neglect.

AMBITION
A goal has been achieved; loose ends need to be attended to. Deserved relaxation can degenerate into laxity.

COMMUNICATION
An agreement has been reached; loose ends need discussion. Celebration can degenerate into misunderstanding.

CREATIVITY
An idea has found expression; attention to detail is required. Creative success can degenerate into pretentiousness.

A lucky start, an unfortunate end – persevere: small achievements are possible

63 line 1

———□———

Blameless

JUDGEMENT Remaining objective after a decision has been made avoids major mistakes.

INNOCENCE Holding on to innocence after a major experience prevents feelings of insecurity.

AWARENESS Humility after a growth in awareness avoids great emptiness.

EMOTION Staying calm after an emotional experience avoids being very hurt.

CREATIVITY Clinging to originality after an artistic success avoids pretentiousness.

COMMUNICATION Remaining calm after an agreement avoids major misunderstanding.

AMBITION Taking stock after a success avoids major mistakes.

SERVICE Remaining dutiful after a task has been completed avoids serious failure.

NURTURE Continuing to care after a new maturity has been achieved avoids major heartache.

ECONOMY Remaining prudent after a financial gain prevents major difficulties.

NEUTRALITY Pausing after a success.

REASON Remaining hungry for knowledge after finding understanding prevents major errors.

63 line 2

———×———

JUDGEMENT Objective decisions may be misunderstood at this time, but will eventually be seen as necessary.

INNOCENCE Innocence may seem unimportant at this time, but its value will eventually be seen.

AWARENESS Higher values may be ignored at this time, but their importance will be understood eventually.

EMOTION Personal feelings may be ignored at this time but find sympathy eventually.

CREATIVITY Originality may go unappreciated at this time but will find its niche eventually.

COMMUNICATION Important words may be ignored at this time but will be believed eventually.

AMBITION Ambitions may be thwarted at this time but abilities will eventually be rewarded.

SERVICE Loyalty to a cause may go unappreciated at this time but will gain attention eventually.

NURTURE Caring may go unappreciated at this time but will be needed eventually.

ECONOMY Prudence may be seen as meanness at this time but will eventually be seen as good sense.

NEUTRALITY Positive attributes being ignored.

REASON Understanding may be ignored at this time, but its value will be seen eventually.

63 line 3

———□———

JUDGEMENT Great care must be taken if successful decisions are to be consolidated.

INNOCENCE It takes time for new experience to be seen as a lesson.

AWARENESS Great care must be taken and time allowed, if a growth in awareness is to be consolidated.

EMOTION Great care must be taken and time allowed, if a commitment is to be made on the basis of mutual feeling.

CREATIVITY Consolidation after an artistic success takes time.

COMMUNICATION Great care must be taken if the scope of an agreement is to be extended.

AMBITION If a success is to be built on, great care must be taken.

SERVICE If more responsibility is wanted, great care should be taken.

NURTURE Great care must be taken as new maturity expresses itself.

ECONOMY Great care must be taken if a financial success is to be the basis of future speculation.

NEUTRALITY Consolidating a success.

REASON The further development of a successful idea must be undertaken with great care.

63 line 4

——×——

Be vigilant

JUDGEMENT Small errors of judgement are symptomatic of a decline in standards.
INNOCENCE Small indulgences are symptomatic of future behaviour.
AWARENESS Insignificant ego-led behaviour is symptomatic of a loss of awareness.
EMOTION Seemingly unimportant selfishness is a sign of future problems.
CREATIVITY Insignificant lapses of care are a sign of declining artistic standards.
COMMUNICATION Petty lies are symptomatic of future dishonesty.
AMBITION Small failings are a sign of declining standards.
SERVICE Slight laxity in duty is symptomatic of a decline in standards.
NURTURE Insignificant lapses are symptoms of future behaviour.
ECONOMY Petty debts are a sign of economic decline.
NEUTRALITY Insignificant errors.
REASON Small errors are symptomatic of a decline in intellectual standards.

63 line 5

——□——

JUDGEMENT A display of a power can never win as much respect as one fair decision.
INNOCENCE More happiness can be derived from innocent pleasure than any amount of self-indulgence.
AWARENESS An experience of higher awareness will always mean more than any amount of doctrine.
EMOTION Displays of emotion can never mean as much as simple, sincere actions.
CREATIVITY Pretentiousness, however grand, can never be as significant as an original idea, no matter how simple.
COMMUNICATION Rhetoric can never mean as much as the simple truth.
AMBITION Naked ambition can never mean as much as simple ability.
SERVICE Displays of servility can never mean as much as simple loyalty.
NURTURE Giving a child everything it wants can never mean as much as simply caring.

ECONOMY Proportionate generosity means more than ostentatious charitability.
NEUTRALITY The small and genuine meaning more than the ostentatious.
REASON Simple understanding means more than any display of intellectual power.

63 line 6

——×——

JUDGEMENT Simply wanting to control a situation.
INNOCENCE Showing off.
AWARENESS Enjoying moral superiority.
EMOTION Looking for sympathy.
CREATIVITY Looking for appreciation.
COMMUNICATION Boasting.
AMBITION Wallowing in success.
SERVICE Enjoying self-importance.
NURTURE Seeking recognition for what should be given freely.
ECONOMY Being unnecessarily ostentatious.
NEUTRALITY Self-glorification.
REASON Wallowing in intellectual superiority.

64
·BEFORE COMPLETION·

REASON — The solution to a problem is nearly at hand, but even at this stage inattention to method could lead to a wrong conclusion.

JUDGEMENT — A difficult decision is nearly made, but even at this stage a lack of deliberation can mean a mistake.

INNOCENCE — Security seems possible, but even at this stage rash action could destroy it.

NEUTRALITY — Near to completion.

AWARENESS — A step towards higher awareness is possible, but even at this stage petty egotism could spoil it.

ECONOMY — Economic stability now seems feasible, but even at this stage a lack of prudence could lead to loss.

EMOTION — A complete relationship seems possible, but even at this stage petty feelings could spoil everything.

NURTURE — A stage of growing up is almost complete, but even at this stage a lack of care could spoil it.

CREATIVITY — A great idea is near to finding expression, but even now carelessness could mean artistic failure.

SERVICE — A task is near completion, but even at this stage inattention to duty could mean failure.

AMBITION — A goal is nearly achieved, but even at this stage a lack of caution could lead to failure.

COMMUNICATION — Agreement becomes a possibility, but even at this stage a careless word could prevent it.

Achievements are possible with care

64 line 1

———×———

Cause for guilt

JUDGEMENT A decision taken without due deliberation leads to a loss of respect.
INNOCENCE Acting in ignorance brings humiliation.
AWARENESS Striving without clarity brings confusion.
EMOTION A feeling expressed without thinking leads to embarrassment.
CREATIVITY An idea expressed without adequate thought leads to a loss of credibility.
COMMUNICATION Words spoken without thought lead to embarrassment.
AMBITION Striving for a goal without adequate preparation leads to humiliation.
SERVICE Not waiting for orders leads to embarrassment.
NURTURE Acting without consideration causes resentment.
ECONOMY Thoughtless spending brings financial embarrassment.
NEUTRALITY Premature effort.
REASON A conclusion drawn with inadequate understanding leads to embarrassment.

64 line 2

———□———

Perseverance brings luck

JUDGEMENT A little more deliberation is required, even though a decision is made.
INNOCENCE More experience is needed, in spite of having learned the ropes.
AWARENESS More self-examination is required, in spite of having the potential for higher awareness.
EMOTION More thought is required, even though feelings can be safely expressed.
CREATIVITY More thought is required, even though an idea is capable of expression.
COMMUNICATION Patience is required before speaking, even though others are ready to listen.
AMBITION Patience is required, in spite of having the ability to succeed.
SERVICE More care is required, in spite of having the capability to complete a task.
NURTURE More care is required, even though the potential for growth is apparent.

ECONOMY Prudence is required, even though there are adequate resources.
NEUTRALITY Patience being necessary, in spite of potential.
REASON A little more thought is required, even though there is adequate understanding.

64 line 3

———×———

Action now would be unfortunate – something needs to be done

JUDGEMENT There is not enough evidence to make a decision; further deliberation is needed.
INNOCENCE A situation is not really understood; help is needed.
AWARENESS Not quite ready for awareness; new self-examination is required.
EMOTION Feelings are not clear enough; communication is needed.
CREATIVITY An idea is too obscure to be accepted; sympathetic criticism is needed.
COMMUNICATION Others are not receptive enough to appreciate the truth; friends must be found.
AMBITION The requisite strength for success is lacking; help should be sought.
SERVICE The ability needed to complete a task is lacking; help should be sought.
NURTURE Note quite mature enough; mutual trust should be sought.
ECONOMY Finances will not quite stretch; financial help is needed.
NEUTRALITY A goal demanding that help is found.
REASON There is not enough information to come to a conclusion; a deeper understanding should be sought.

64 line 4

———□———

Perseverance brings luck – doubts are overcome – rewards

JUDGEMENT Difficult decisions can be made without misgivings.
INNOCENCE Great learning is possible, in spite of insecurity.
AWARENESS A growth in awareness is possible, in spite of practical hardships.

EMOTION Feelings can be expressed, even though others may be surprised.
CREATIVITY Obscure ideas can be expressed, in spite of criticism.
COMMUNICATION The truth can be told, and criticism can be ignored.
AMBITION Disciplined effort brings reward, even against the wishes of others.
SERVICE Orders can be carried out, in spite of criticism from superiors.
NURTURE New maturity can be encouraged, in spite of heartache.
ECONOMY Long-term profits can be made, in spite of hardship in the meantime.
NEUTRALITY A successful move allowing doubts to be ignored.
REASON Conclusions can be drawn, even though others do not understand.

64 line 5

———×———

Lucky – continuing in this way means no need for guilt

JUDGEMENT Enlightened decisions are now appreciated.
INNOCENCE A lot has been learned, and new confidence is found.
AWARENESS A growth in awareness has been achieved; its light can shine bright.
EMOTION True feelings can be expressed and are reciprocated.
CREATIVITY Creative ideas are now appreciated.
COMMUNICATION The truth is out and open dialogue is now possible.
AMBITION Ambitions are realized, bringing new strength.
SERVICE Devotion to duty is justified and rewarded.
NURTURE Caring is rewarded and appreciated.
ECONOMY Prudence is rewarded and investment is now possible.
NEUTRALITY Success bringing a new order.
REASON A logical explanation is found, shedding light on other areas.

64 line 6

———▫———

Blameless – take care or luck could be forfeited

JUDGEMENT Congratulations are justified, but new power should not be taken too far.
INNOCENCE Celebrations are justified, but new-found confidence should not be taken too far.
AWARENESS Self-satisfaction is justified but should not be taken too far.
EMOTION Celebration is justified, but emotion should not be allowed to take over.
CREATIVITY Satisfaction is justified, but new creative freedom should not be taken too far.
COMMUNICATION Excited words are justified, but care should still be taken.
AMBITION Celebrations are justified, but over-confidence should be avoided.
SERVICE Celebrations are justified, but new respect should not be abused.
NURTURE New maturity can be celebrated, but care is still necessary.
ECONOMY Celebrating financial success is justified, but prudence should still be practised as a matter of course.
NEUTRALITY Justifiable celebrations.
REASON It is justifiable to wallow in new understanding, but new intellectual confidence should not be taken too far.

FURTHER READING

THE I CHING ITSELF

I Ching or Book of Changes, the Richard Wilhelm translation, rendered into English by Cary F. Baynes with a foreword by C.G. Jung, Arkana

I Ching, The Book of Change, John Blofeld, Mandala

I Ching, Book of Changes, translated by James Legge, Citadel Press

THE TWELVE CHANNELS

The Purpose of Love, compiled and presented by Richard Gardner, Rigel Press

RELATED TOPICS

A Guide to the I Ching, Carol K. Anthony, Anthony Publishing Company

The Astrology of I Ching, translated by W.K. Chu, edited by W.A. Chu, edited by W.A. Sherrill, Routledge & Kegan Paul

An Anthology of I Ching, W.A. Sherrill and W.K. Chu, Arkana

The I Ching Workbook, R.L. Wing, Aquarian

The I Ching and its Associations, Diana ffarrington Hook, Arkana

I Ching and the Genetic Code: The Hidden Key to Life, Schonberger, Aurora Press

BACKGROUND TO THE I CHING

The Taoist Inner View of the Universe and the Immortal Realm, Ni, Hua-Ching, the Shrine of the Eternal Breath of Tao, College of Tao and Traditional Chinese Healing

Taoism: The Way of the Mystic, J.C. Cooper, Crucible

The Tao Te Ching: A New Translation with Commentary, Ellen M. Chen, Paragon House

HOW DOES THE I CHING WORK?

Synchronicity, An Acausal Connecting Principle, C.G. Jung, Arkana

The Tao of Physics, Fritjof Capra, Flamingo

Rhythms of Vision, The Changing Pattern of Belief, Lawrence Blair, Paladin

KEY

Upper / Lower	Chi'en	Chen	K'an	Ken	K'un	Sun	Li	Tui
Chi'en	1	34	5	26	11	9	14	43
Chen	25	51	3	27	24	42	21	17
K'an	6	40	29	4	7	59	64	57
Ken	33	62	39	52	15	53	56	31
K'un	12	16	8	23	2	20	35	45
Sun	44	32	48	18	46	57	50	28
Li	13	55	63	22	36	37	30	49
Tui	10	54	60	41	19	61	38	58

INDEX

Personal Consultations

Personal Consultations

Personal Consultations

Personal Consultations

Personal Consultations

Personal Consultations